EXUBERANT
SKEPTICISM

EXUBERANT SKEPTICISM

PAUL KURTZ

Edited by
JOHN R. SHOOK

59 John Glenn Drive
Amherst, New York 14228–2119

Published 2010 by Prometheus Books

Inquiries should be addressed to
Prometheus Books
59 John Glenn Drive
Amherst, New York 14228–2119
VOICE: 716–691–0133
FAX: 716–691–0137
WWW.PROMETHEUSBOOKS.COM

14 13 12 11 10   5 4 3 2 1

Library of Congress Cataloging-in-Publication Data

Paul Kurtz, 1925–
    Exuberant skepticism / Paul Kurtz ; edited by John R. Shook.
        p. cm.
    Includes bibliographical references.
    ISBN 978–1–59102–778–2 (pbk. : alk. paper)
    1. Skepticism. I. Shook, John R. II. Title.

B837.K86 2010
149'.73—dc22

2009039253

Printed in the United States of America on acid-free paper

CONTENTS

SECTION THREE SKEPTICISM IN THE HUMAN WORLD

SECTION FOUR THE SKEPTICAL MOVEMENT, PAST AND FUTURE

PREFACE

John R. Shook

For the first time, Paul Kurtz's most important and influential essays advancing reason and skepticism have been collected together in one convenient volume. Kurtz has long been the world's leading philosophical skeptic, but he is much more than just a skeptic. Extending insights from the philosophies of American pragmatism and scientific naturalism, Kurtz has constructed a comprehensive philosophical system. This volume's concentration on skepticism does not obscure, but rather illuminates, Kurtz's overall commitments to secular humanism and the ethical and exuberant life. For that reason, the chosen title of this volume, *Exuberant Skepticism*, is quite accurate and timely.

Kurtz raises skepticism to new heights of achievement as a philosophical position. Kurtz's positive skepticism, based on sound common sense, reason, and scientific method, builds an affirmative case for what can be known. And so much can be known, from the natural world around us to the moral responsibilities among us. These essays trace the history and varieties of skepticism, skeptically inquire into paranormal and religious claims, transform moral and political thought, and describe the trajectory of the skepticism movement into the future. These essays proclaim Kurtz's affirmative message of placing our confidence in reason and inquiry for the benefit of humanity. Only an exuberant skepticism, an optimistic confidence in the application of reason, can guide us toward joyful and creative lives.

Spanning three decades of his pioneering leadership of the skepticism movement and the Committee for the Scientific Investigation of Claims of the Paranormal (now the Committee for Skeptical Inquiry, CSI), these essays have transformed the way the world thinks about skepticism. Long categorized as merely a negative and nay-saying stance of refusal and rejection, skepticism emerges reborn as a potently positive philosophy ready to change the world. While skeptics must occasionally say "No" to unreasonable and dangerous notions, skeptics now understand why they can say "Yes!" to the methods of reason and science. And Kurtz's philosophy does say "Yes!" to the confirmed knowledge of nature and humanity provided by the sciences.

In such essays as "Scientific Method and Rational Skepticism," "Skepticism and the New Enlightenment," and "The Growth of Antiscience," Kurtz explains why the methods of inquiry used by the sciences deserve respect. Without science's light of practical knowledge, humanity would still be lost in the darkness of myth and the evils of ignorance. Kurtz's essays "Skepticism, Science, and the Paranormal," "Skepticism and Religion," and "Are Science and Religion Compatible?" demonstrate how to apply the sound skeptical method.

But there is far more to positive skepticism, in Kurtz's vision, than just knowledge of facts. The skeptic's demand for reasonable evidence and inquiry has been the real engine behind civilization's capacity to elevate humanity to more productive and empowered lives. Realizing the essential connections between scientific knowledge, technological power, and social progress, Kurtz has understood, as few other philosophers ever have, how the methods of intelligence can be applied to all areas of human endeavor. The social world, no less than the natural world, is amenable to enlightenment and improvement through critical inquiry. The essays "Skepticism and Political Inquiry," "Skepticism and Ethical Inquiry," and "Skepticism and Eupraxsophy" outline a radical new way to intelligently analyze and improve our moral and political systems.

This volume also includes Kurtz's authoritative reflections on the skeptical movement he founded and has led. "The New Skepticism: A Worldwide Movement," "Skeptical Inquiry: My Personal Involvement,"

"Science and the Public: Summing Up Thirty Years of the *Skeptical Inquirer*," and "The New Skepticism: A Statement of Principles" together yield rare treasures of insight from Kurtz's unique perspective.

As Kurtz never tires of explaining, the forces of blind faith and stubborn unreason still fight for control of the mind, so the skeptic can never rest. If there is a brighter future for humanity, a future in which every person enjoys a realistic opportunity for the pursuit of excellence, Kurtz's exuberant skepticism can show us the way.

Section One

REASONS TO BE SKEPTICAL

Chapter 1

WHAT IS SKEPTICISM?

S kepticism has historic roots in the classical philosophical tradition. The term derives from the Greek word *skeptikos*, which means "to consider, examine." It is akin to the Greek *skepsis*, which means "inquiry" and "doubt." Succinctly stated, a skeptic is one who is willing to question any claim to truth, asking for clarity in definition, consistency in logic, and adequacy of evidence. The use of skepticism is thus an essential part of objective scientific inquiry and the search for reliable knowledge.

Skepticism provides powerful tools of criticism in science, philosophy, religion, morality, politics, and society. It is thought to be exceedingly difficult to apply it to ordinary life or to live consistently with its principles, for human beings seek certitudes to guide them, and the skeptical mode is often viewed with alarm by those who hunger for faith and conviction. Skepticism is the intractable foe of pretentious belief systems. When people demand definite answers to their queries, skepticism always seems to give them further questions to ponder. Yet in a profound sense, skepticism is an essential ingredient of all reflective conduct and an enduring characteristic of the educated mind. Still, skeptics are considered dan-

["The New Skepticism," *Skeptical Inquirer* 18, no. 2 (Winter 1993/94): 134–41]

gerous because they question the reigning orthodoxies, the shibboleths and hosannas of any age. Although the skeptical attitude is an indelible part of reflective inquiry, can a person get beyond the skeptical orientation to develop positive directions and commitments in belief and behavior, and will skepticism enable one to do so?

Skeptics are viewed as dissenters, heretics, radicals, subversive rogues, or worse, and they are bitterly castigated by the entrenched establishments who fear them. Revolutionary reformers are also wont to turn their wrath on skeptical doubters who question their passionate commitment to ill-conceived programs of social reconstruction. Skeptics wish to examine all sides of a question, and for every argument in favor of a thesis, they usually can find one or more arguments opposed to it. Extreme skepticism cannot consistently serve our practical interests, for insofar as it sires doubt, it inhibits actions. All parties to a controversy may revile skeptics because they usually resist being swept away by the dominant fervor of the day.

Nevertheless, skepticism is *essential* to the quest for knowledge, for it is in the seedbed of puzzlement that genuine inquiry takes root. Without skepticism, we may remain mired in unexamined belief systems that are accepted as sacrosanct yet have no factual basis in reality. With it, we allow for some free play for the generation of new ideas and the growth of knowledge. Although the skeptical outlook may not be sufficient unto itself for any philosophy of the practical life, it provides a necessary condition for the reflective approach to life. Must skepticism leave us floundering in a quagmire of indecision? Or does it permit us to go further, and to discover some probabilities by which we can live? Will it allow us to achieve reliable knowledge? Or must all new discoveries in turn give way to the probing criticisms of the skeptic's scalpel? The answer to these questions depends in part on what one means by skepticism, for there are various kinds that can be distinguished.

NIHILISTIC SKEPTICISM

The first kind of skepticism may be identified as *nihilism*. Its most extreme form is total negative skepticism. Here I am referring to skepticism as a complete rejection of all claims to truth or value. This kind of skepticism is mired in unlimited doubt, from which it never emerges. Knowledge is not possible, total skeptics aver. There is no certainty, no reliable basis for convictions, no truth at all.

Nihilistic skepticism has also been used in ethics, with devastating results. Here the total skeptic is a complete relativist, subjectivist, and emotivist. What is "good" or "bad," "right" or "wrong," varies among individuals and societies. There are no discernible normative standards other than taste and feeling, and there is no basis for objective moral judgment. We cannot discern principles that are universal or obligatory for morality. Complete cultural relativity is the only option for this kind of skepticism. Principles of justice are simply related to power or the social contract; there are no normative standards common to all extreme doubters; all standards are equally untenable. They may thus become conservative traditionalists. If there are no reliable guides to moral conduct, then the only recourse is to follow custom. Ours is not to reason why, ours is but to do or die, for there are no reasons. Or total skeptics may become cynical amoralists for whom "anything goes." Who is to say that one thing is better or worse than anything else? they ask, for if there are no standards of justice discoverable in the nature of things, political morality in the last analysis is a question of force, custom, or passion, not of reason or of evidence.

This kind of total skepticism is self-contradictory, for in affirming that no knowledge is possible, these skeptics have already made an assertion. In denying that we can know reality, they often presuppose a phenomenalistic or subjectivistic metaphysics in which sense impressions or ideas are the constitutive blocks out of which our knowledge of the world, however fragmented, is constructed. In asserting that there are no normative standards of ethics and politics, total skeptics sometimes advise us either to be tolerant of individual idiosyncrasies and respect cultural relativity or to be courageous and follow our own quest to satisfy ambition or appetite. But this imperceptibly masks underlying value judgments that skeptics cherish. This kind of skepticism may be labeled "dogmatism"; for in resolutely rejecting the very possibility of knowledge or value, such skeptics are themselves introducing their own questionable assertions.

Neutral Skepticism

One form of nihilistic skepticism that seeks to avoid dogmatism does so by assuming a completely neutral stance. Here skeptics will neither affirm nor deny anything. They are unwilling to utter any pronouncements, such as that sense perception or formal reasoning is unreliable. They reject any type of skepticism that masks a theory of knowledge or reality in epistemology, metaphysics, ethics, and politics. Neutralists claim to have no such theory. They simply make personal statements and do not ask anyone to accept or reject them or be convinced or persuaded by their arguments. These are merely their own private expressions, and they are not generalizable to others. For every argument in favor of a thesis, they can discover a counterargument. The only option for neutral skeptics is thus to suspend judgment entirely. Here agnosticism rules the roost. They are unable in epistemology to discover any criteria of knowledge; in metaphysics, a theory of reality; in religion, a basis for belief or disbelief in God; in ethics and politics, any standards of virtue, value, or social justice.

The ancient pre-Socratic Greek philosopher Cratylus (fifth–fourth century BCE) was overwhelmed by the fact that everything is changing, including our own phenomenological worlds of experience, and he therefore concluded that it is impossible to communicate knowledge or to fully understand anyone. According to legend, Cratylus refused to discuss anything with anyone and, since it was pointless to reply, only wiggled his finger when asked a question. The neutral state of suspension of belief, now known as *Pyrrhonism*, was defended by Pyrrho of Elis and had a great impact on the subsequent development of skepticism. It applied primarily to philosophical and metaphysical questions, where one is uncertain about what is ultimately true about reality, but it put aside questions of ordinary life, where convention and custom prevail. This form of skepticism also degenerates into nihilism, for in denying in any form of knowledge it can lead to despair.

MITIGATED SKEPTICISM

There is fundamental difficulty with the forms of skepticism outlined above, for they are contrary to the demands of life. We need to function in the world—whatever its ultimate reality—and we need to develop some beliefs by which we may live and act. Perhaps our beliefs rest ultimately upon probabilities; nevertheless, we need to develop knowledge as a pragmatic requirement of living and acting in the world. A modified form of skepticism was called *mitigated skepticism* by David Hume, the great eighteenth-century Scottish philosopher. It is a position that was also defended by the Greek philosopher Carneades of the second century BCE. Mitigated skeptics have confronted the black hole of nothingness and are skeptical about the ultimate reliability of knowledge claims. They are convinced that the foundations of knowledge and value are ephemeral and that it is impossible to establish ultimate truths about reality with any certainty. Nonetheless, we are forced by the exigencies of practical life to develop viable generalizations and to make choices, even though we can give no ultimate justification for them. One cannot find any secure basis for causal inferences about nature, other than the fact that there are regularities encountered with experience, on the basis of which we make predictions that the future will be like the past. But we have no ultimate foundation for this postulate of induction. Similarly, one cannot deduce what *ought* to be the case from what *is*. Morality is contingent on the sentiments of men and women who agree to abide by social convention in order to satisfy their multifarious desires as best they can.

Mitigated skepticism is not total, but only partial and limited, forced upon us by the exigencies of living. It would be total if we were to follow philosophy to the end of the trail, to irremediable indecision and doubt. Fortunately, we take detours in life, and thus we live and act *as if* we had knowledge. Our generalizations are based upon experience and practice, and the inferences that we make on the basis of habit and custom serve as our guide.

UNBELIEF

The term *skepticism* has sometimes been used as synonymous with *unbelief* or *disbelief* in any domain of knowledge. There are actually two aspects to this—one is the reflective conviction that certain claims are unfounded or untrue, and hence not believable, and this seems a reasonable posture to take; the other is the negative a priori rejection of the belief without a careful examination of the grounds for that belief. Critics call this latter form of skepticism *dogmatism*. The word *unbelief* in both of these senses is usually taken to apply to religion, theology, the paranormal, and the occult.

In religion the unbeliever is usually an atheist—not simply a neutral agnostic—for this kind of skepticism rejects the claims of theists. The atheist denies the basic premises of theism: that God exists, that there is some ultimate purpose to the universe, that men and women have immortal souls, and that they can be saved by divine grace.

Reflective unbelievers find the language of transcendence basically unintelligible, even meaningless, and that is why they say they are skeptics. Or, more pointedly, if they have examined the arguments adduced historically to prove the existence of God, they find them invalid, hence unconvincing. They find the so-called appeals to experience unwarranted: neither mysticism nor the appeal to miracles or revelation establishes the existence of transcendental realities. Moreover, they maintain that morality is possible without a belief in superstition. Indeed, they consider the God hypothesis to be without merit, a fanciful creation of human imagination that does not deserve careful examination by emancipated men and women. Many classical atheists (Baron d'Holbach, Diderot, Marx, Engels) fit into this category, for they were materialists first, and their religious skepticism and unbelief followed from their materialistic metaphysics. Such skeptics are dogmatic only if their unbelief is a form of doctrinaire faith and not based on rational grounds.

In the paranormal field, unbelievers similarly deny the reality of psi phenomena. They maintain that ESP, clairvoyance, precognition, psychokinesis, and the existence of discarnate souls are without sufficient evidence and contrary to our knowledge of how the material universe operates. Some skeptics deny paranormal phenomena on a priori grounds, that is, they are to be rejected because they violate well-established physical laws. They can be considered dogmatists only if they refuse to examine the evidence brought by the proponents of the paranormal, or if they consider the level of science that has been reached on any one day to be its final formulation. Insofar as this kind of unbelief masks a closed mind, it is an illegitimate form of skepticism. If those who say that they are skeptics simply mean they deny the existence of the paranormal realm, they are aparanormalists. The question to be asked of them always is, Why? For much as the believers can be judged to hold certain convictions on the basis of inadequate evidence or faith, so the dogmatic unbelievers may reject such new claims because these violate their own preconceptions about the universe. This latter kind of skepticism has many faults and is in my judgment illegitimate. These skeptics are no longer open-minded inquirers, but debunkers. They are convinced that they have the Non-Truth, which they affirm resolutely, and in doing so they may slam shut the door to further discoveries.

SKEPTICAL INQUIRY

There is yet another kind of skepticism, which has emerged on the contemporary scene and which differs from the kinds of skepticism encountered above. Indeed, this form of skepticism strongly criticizes nihilism, total and neutral; mitigated skepticism; and dogmatic unbelief—although it has learned something from each of them. This kind of skepticism I label "skeptical inquiry," with inquiry rather than doubt as the motivation. I call it *new skepticism*, although it has emerged in the contemporary world as an outgrowth of pragmatism. A key difference between this and earlier forms of skepticism is that it is positive and constructive. It involves the transformation of the negative critical analysis of claims to knowledge into a positive contribution to the growth and development of skeptical inquiry. It is basically a form of methodological skepticism, for here skepticism is an essential phase of the process of inquiry; but it does not and need not lead to unbelief, despair, or hopelessness. This skepticism is not total, but is limited to the context under inquiry. Hence we may call it *selective* or *contextual* skepticism, for one need not doubt everything at the same time, but only certain questions in the limited context of investigation. It is not neutral, because it believes that we do develop knowledge about the world. Accordingly, not only is human knowledge possible, but it can be found to be reliable, and we can in the normative realm act on the best evidence and reasons available. Knowledge is not simply limited to the descriptive or the formal sciences, but is discoverable in the normative fields of ethics and politics. Although this is a modified form of skepticism, it goes far beyond the mitigated skepticism of Hume, for it does not face an abyss or ultimate uncertainty, but is impressed by the ability of the human mind to understand and control nature.

The new skepticism is not dogmatic, for it holds that we should never by a priori rejection close the door to any kind of responsible investigation. Thus it is skeptical of dogmatic or narrow-minded atheism and aparanormalism. Nonetheless, it is willing to assert reflective *unbelief* about some claims that it finds lack adequate justification. It is willing to assert that some claims are unproved, improbable, or false.

Skepticism, as a method of doubt that demands evidence and reasons for hypotheses, is essential to the process of scientific research, philosophical dialogue, and critical intelligence. It is also vital in ordinary life, where the demands of common sense are always a challenge to us to develop and act upon the most reliable hypotheses and beliefs available. It is the foe of the absolute certainty and dogmatic finality. It appreciates the snares and pitfalls of all kinds of human knowledge and the importance of the principles of fallibilism and probabilism in regard to the degrees of certainty of our knowledge. This differs sharply from the skepticisms of old, and it can contribute substantially to the advancement of human knowledge and the moral progress of humankind. It has important implications for our knowledge of the universe and our moral and social life. Skepticism in this sense provides a positive and constructive *eupraxsophy* (see chapter 13) that can assist us in interpreting the cosmos in which we live and in achieving some wisdom in conduct.

The new skepticism is more in tune with the demands of everyday knowledge than with speculative philosophy. Traditional skepticism has had all too little to say about the evident achievements of constructive skeptical inquiry. And derisive skeptical jabs hurled from the wings of the theater of life are not always appreciated, especially if they inhibit life from proceeding without interruption.

Skeptical inquiry is essential in any quest for knowledge or deliberative valuational judgment. But it is limited and focused, selective, and positive, and it is part and parcel of a genuine process of inquiry. This form of modified skepticism is formulated in the light of the following considerations.

There has already been an impressive advance in the sciences, both theoretically and technologically. This applies to the natural, biological, social, and behavioral sciences. The forms of classical skepticism of the ancient world that reemerged in the early modern period were unaware of the tremendous potential of scientific research. Pyrrhonistic skepticism is today invalidated, because there now exists a considerable body of reliable knowledge. Accordingly, it is meaningless to cast all claims to truth into a state of utter doubt. The same considerations apply to postmodernist subjectivism and Richard Rorty's pragmatic skepticism, which I believe are likewise mistaken.

Contrary to traditional skeptical doubts, there are methodological criteria by which we are able to test claims to knowledge: empirical tests based upon observation, logical standards of coherence and consistency, and experimental tests in which ideas are judged by their consequences. All of this is related to the proposition that it is possible to develop and use objective methods of inquiry in order to achieve reliable knowledge.

Doubt plays a vital role in the context of ongoing inquiry. It should, however, be selective, not unlimited, and contextual, not universal. The principle of fallibilism is relevant. We should not make absolute assertions, but be willing to admit that we may be mistaken. Our knowledge is based upon probabilities, which are reliable, not ultimate certainties or finalities.

Finally, skeptical inquirers should always be open-minded about new possibilities and unexpected departures in thought. They should always be willing to question or overturn even the most well-established principles in the light of further inquiry. The key principle of skeptical inquiry is to seek, when feasible, adequate evidence and reasonable grounds for any claim to truth in any context.

Chapter 2

SKEPTICISM AS SELECTIVE DOUBT

Knowledge is a property of human action in a world of objects, but it is not an absolute picture of reality. It is *we* who claim that something is understood and appreciated as true. It is this form of knowledge that we believe in and are prepared to act upon. If what we believe is true, then it can have important consequences for our goals and purposes. That tuberculosis is caused by a bacillus and that certain antibiotics can arrest its development is not only known but acted upon. That the moons of Jupiter encircle the planet in predictable orbits is knowledge that has pragmatic significance as a spacecraft is programmed to pass through Jupiter's gravitational field. We cannot say that *all* knowledge is instrumental, as the pragmatists thought. Although the pragmatic theory of knowledge depicts how we think in ordinary life and in the applied sciences, it does not do as well in accounting for research in the theoretical sciences, except in a general, analogous way. It is thus not necessarily a comprehensive theory of knowledge, and any account must allow for the pluralistic dimensions of inquiry.

Nevertheless, the pragmatic theory does vividly illustrate the fact that belief is often formulated in response to a state of doubt. In his famous

[*The Transcendental Temptation* (1991), pp. 34–40]

essay "The Fixation of Belief," Charles Peirce denied the actuality of Descartes' generalized state of doubt.[1] Doubt is specific, said Pierce, not universal. It grows out of a concrete context in which genuine puzzlement is present. This doubt is not feigned, but is real and living. Dewey sought to relate doubt to the purposes of the investigation. For the pragmatist it is directly related to an existential problematic situation in which our behavior is blocked and our habits thrown into question. It is in this context that inquiry is initiated; we seek a hypothesis that will resolve the problem and enable action to continue. If successful, our hypotheses are incorporated into the body of belief, published in encyclopedias and textbooks, and accepted as true knowledge.

Dewey thought that even theoretical scientists and mathematicians faced problems and that their theories were introduced to settle their doubt, enabling them to make predictions and draw inferences. This theory no doubt claims too much. But it does at least make it clear that ambiguity and uncertainty play a vital role in the course of inquiry in initiating and resolving problems. It is not subjective doubt that the pragmatists focus upon; they are concerned with how we go about fixing reliable belief in the community. And here the methods of science and critical intelligence are the most effective methods to be employed. For we use objectively related criteria, tested over the years by their demonstrated effectiveness in the course of inquiry.

Skepticism is thus an essential component of inquiry and a necessary aspect of critical intelligence. Without it, science and the development of human knowledge would not be possible. It is both positive and creative.

One is always tempted to raise the question, What is real? Such terminology unfortunately does not have a clearly identifiable meaning. One meaning that may be ascribed to it is this: (1) *the real* is a term that describes concrete objects and events encountered in a situation of interaction; (2) it refers to their objective properties and characteristics; and (3) it refers to the uniform regularities that objects and events display independently of our own wishes, fancies, or desires. To know what the objective properties, characteristics, and regularities of objects and events are in any specific case depends upon the context of the investigation. Objects and events can manifest a multiplicity of properties and regularities, depending upon the level of interaction and the focus of observation.

For example, suppose we are in a baseball stadium observing a game.

Many modes of description may no doubt apply if we are to understand it. There are individual players, who demonstrate skills and excellences. There are material components present besides the players: bats, balls, uniforms, and bases. There is a stadium filled with loudly cheering fans, including us. To understand the game of baseball, we need to compute the batting averages and errors of the players for the past seasons. This is published in the program. The game of baseball needs also to be understood analytically in terms of the rules agreed upon by the ball clubs and the interpretations of the umpires. Baseball may also be understood as a socio-cultural phenomenon with a relatively recent history and an important role in some societies. Each player may be depicted psychologically in terms of his personality traits and dispositions, and these may be compared with those of his fellow players. Baseball also may be interpreted economically. Each player has a contract; an economic index in terms of his drawing power with the fans and the demand of him by other teams can be made. The players may be described purely biologically and physically in terms of height, weight, bone structure, and physical strength. Moreover, there is a physiochemical structure to their behavior that can be understood. Which of these properties refers to the *real* game? In a sense all of these characteristics are pertinent to our description of the players, the team, and the game: physical, chemical, biological, psychological, analytic, economic, and sociological. We must thus resist any simple reductive analysis that attempts to break up the observable to a set of entities or principles on a lower level, to its material components or its ideal structures. Rather, we need to provide a pluralistic, contextual account of what is observed: both the concrete events and their explanations in terms of general principles.

Any number of hypotheses can usefully describe, characterize, and explain behavior, depending upon the context of analysis and the purpose of the inquiry. I have elsewhere labeled this the *principle of coduction*, as a methodological device employed to coduce a number of explanations on different levels to account for an object or event.[2] In the preceding illustration, we don't doubt that there are a game, players, and a stadium. The ball may be hit right into the stands and strike you or someone close by you! If this is the first time you have ever been to a game, you may be puzzled by the events about you and try to decipher what is going on. Why did the umpire call a batter out? There were three strikes. Why did he walk him? There were four balls. Even if you are a veteran fan, the game is full of indeterminacy and suspense. Will the outfielder catch the high fly and get it to the third baseman on time? Will the next player strike out? Who will win the game? Or you may ask, Was Reggie Jackson safe as he slid into second base? The umpire and the fans can dispute that. What was Pete Rose's batting average? We can look it up. What were the terms of Joe DiMaggio's contract? They may not have been disclosed. Who was the best ballplayer of all time? All of these points may be arguable. In this case, doubt is always specific. For we can always question what we are observing. And we can raise questions about how to interpret what has happened.

Unlimited doubt, as I have said, is self-defeating, contradictory, nonsensical—we cannot doubt everything, all of the time, but only some things, some of the time. There are, however, forms of doubt that are meaningful. And I wish to distinguish three kinds. First, there are the principles of fallibilism (proposed by Charles Peirce) and probabilism; second, the burden-of-proof argument; and third, the essential role of doubt as a component of the process of inquiry.

Peirce argued that we can never say that something was absolutely certain, had reached its final formulation, or was ultimately unknowable. There is always the possibility that we may be in error. Our observations may need to be corrected. We may have misinterpreted the data. We may be mistaken. No one is infallible. And we must always leave open the possibility that what we today affirm strongly may in time need to be revised. The history of thought is full of such developments. Knowledge needs to be revised continually; at least we should not foreclose inquiry. Even the most firmly held postulates and theories have at some time been questioned by later investigations, and even the most revered truths of mankind—whether in religion, ethics, politics, philosophy, or science—have often been replaced. Only a fool will refuse to see the possibility that he may be in error, or a fanatic; that his first principles and final conclusions are beyond criticism. The pope may claim infallibility, but surely no one besides certain Catholics are so presumptuous as to think that the pope has a special monopoly on truth.

There is another reason why fallibilism should be an intrinsic element in human knowledge: The sample on the basis of which we may make a generalization or infer a theory may be limited or partial. New data may be uncovered. These may be bizarre, anomalous, and unexpected. The old theories thus may have to give way to new, more comprehensive explana-tions. Here *probabilism* is a better term than *fallibilism*, for it points to the fact that a sample is never complete or final. Although on the basis of our observations thus far we may rather confidently assert that all crows are black, we may find a white mutant, however unlikely that may be.

Nor should we be purists and thereby conclude that no knowledge is possible. Because we can never be absolutely certain that we have not made a mistake, that new facts will not be uncovered, or that our present generalizations and theories will not be modified at some time in the future, can we conclude that no knowledge is reliable? There *is* a well-established body of knowledge: science, history, medicine, and the prac-tical arts all belie this form of skepticism. Some measure of doubt, how-ever, is a therapeutic element in the quest for knowledge, whether in the sciences or in ordinary life.

And there are degrees of doubt and probability. If no inference can be said to be absolutely or finally certain and if we reserve the right to concede that we may be wrong, this does not mean that we do not have relatively strong degrees of reliability in many cases. Where? First, in mathematics and logic. If one's axioms and postulates are assumed, we can deduce conclusions and theorems with deductive necessity. That two and three are five, that a straight line is the shortest distance between two points, or that a triangle is a three-sided figure cannot be doubted, if I understand the nature of numbers, arithmetic, and the principles of Euclidean geometry. Of course, we may question their foundations—as has been done in the history of thought. And given different postulate sys-tems (non-Euclidean geometries, for example), one may deduce different conclusions. Still, analytic tautological truths are necessary and certain, if we presuppose certain assumptions.

And there are other hypotheses and beliefs that I can assert without much hesitation: that I see my hand that I hold up before me, that it is raining outside at the present moment, or that the river has crested and is flooding its banks. Given the testimony of the senses, under normal condi-tions, I need not doubt that what I observe is as I describe it. Of course, I may be mistaken. I may be sleepy or color-blind or drunk, and misper-ceiving. It may be a mirage or a dream, or I may be hallucinating. The tes-timony of the senses is often confused and distorted. Thus, we cannot assert with absolute certainty that what is observed is always true—only probable. Two men are standing at a bar drinking heavily. One says to the other: "You better stop drinking; your face is getting bleary!" Where is the bleariness—in the perceiver or the perceived? This does not deny that for all practical purposes we may assert that some observed facts are true.

To say that I have observed something to be the case is one thing; however, to interpret it or to explain it is, of course, another. Similar considerations apply to more complex scientific hypotheses and theories. Often even the most well-established principles have been overthrown by later experiments and theories. Ptolemaic cosmological explanations gave way to Newtonian physics, and this was modified and supplemented by modern Einsteinian physics, which may still be brought into question. Thus no scientist can affirm with complete certainty that his or her theories have reached their final formulation, that they are perfect, eternal, and beyond question. Only theologians reserve the right to maintain their infallibility. The better part of prudence thus is to adopt the principles of fallibilism and probabilism.

Another consideration in support of selective skepticism is the burden-of-proof argument. We are constantly bombarded on all sides by the claims of those who insist they have the truth. Whether it is belief in religion, politics, ideology, philosophy, science, the paranormal, ethics, or ordinary life, the question may be asked: Is what they claim true? Was there an eclipse in 322 BCE? Did Christ rise from the dead? Will vitamin C prevent colds? Have space astronauts been visiting the planet Earth from another galaxy? Is there life on Mars? Is reincarnation true? May people be possessed by the devil? What is the temperature at the center of the earth? Was Tchaikovsky a homosexual? Did he commit suicide? Will the stock market advance? What is the age of the universe?

For many of these questions, we may not have answers. We may be unable to ascertain the facts. Some of our knowledge is based upon our own direct perceptions, and we may be rather certain of its accuracy. Some of it is based on the testimony of the senses of other people, second- or thirdhand; if we think they are competent observers, we may be willing to accept it. In other cases, the questions at issue are so complex that only the authorities in the field can resolve the matter. Who are the experts? Does every field have them? What do we do when they dispute about the relevant facts and the appropriate theories?

It is clear that where we think the observation or testimony of others or the judgment of experts is reliable, we may defer to them. But in other cases, when someone makes a claim, the burden of proof is upon that person to provide the supporting evidence and proofs. If someone maintains that mermaids exist, the burden of proof is not upon me to show that they do not, but upon the claimant to show that they do. Old seafaring men reputedly claim to have seen them, especially after weeks and months at sea. The proponents of this claim often ask, "Can you disprove what we have said?" For example, can you prove that God or angels do not exist, or that Sasquatch does not exist, or that UFOs are not manned by extraterrestrial beings from afar? If you cannot, then we have the right to believe, they insist.

Now I suppose anyone has the right to believe anything that he or she wishes. The questions are whether what they wish to accept is actually true and whether they can distinguish their wishes from objective reality. Here, doubt becomes an essential component of rationality. I don't have to prove to my five-year-old granddaughter that Santa Claus does not exist. One may never be able to do that satisfactorily to the inquisitive mind. For if I take the child to the North Pole, she may wonder whether Santa Claus is at the South Pole, or whether he has dematerialized. All beliefs should be considered to be hypotheses; whether they are true depends upon the range of evidence and the kinds of reasons that are adduced to support them. If there is insufficient evidence, then the best option may be to suspend judgment pending further inquiry. I am not denying that we can falsify some claims as ridiculous or patently false. Whether tar water can cure the hives or whether the moon is made of green cheese can presumably be tested and confirmed or disconfirmed rather conclusively.

Therefore, some questions can be solved by reference to a range of evidence; some can be disconfirmed in the same way. Some questions may, however, be beyond present confirmation or proof. And for those, if they are meaningful options, the best course is to suspend judgment, to assume the posture of the skeptic and not postulate a conclusion until the relevant facts are in.

In some cases, of course, we may have some evidence, but this may not be sufficient. We may suspect that something is the case, yet not be able to say that it is so. Here we can frame a hypothesis and say that it is supported to such-and-such a degree, that it is probable or improbable, without being willing to say so conclusively either way.

This is the method that is used in the sciences. And one must grant that it is the sciences that have been the most effective in developing knowledge. Science presupposes some skepticism, but it also contributes to the positive achievement of knowledge.

NOTES

1. Charles Hartshorne and Paul Weiss, eds., *Collected Papers of Charles Sanders Peirce* (Cambridge, MA: Harvard University Press, 1934), vol. 5, pp. 223–47.
2. Paul Kurtz, *Decision and the Condition of Man* (Seattle: University of Washington Press, 1965), chap. 5.

Chapter 3

SCIENTIFIC METHOD AND RATIONAL SKEPTICISM

WHAT IS SCIENCE?

S ince science presupposes some degree of skepticism in its method, we may ask, "Is there such a thing as *the* scientific method?" Some have denied it. If there is such a method, how does it operate? Scientific methodology is surely not an esoteric road to knowledge available only to a limited sophisticated elite. Rather, it grows out of the interests and purposes of ordinary life, and it is continuous with the use of critical intelligence elsewhere.

Some have interpreted science solely in terms of its findings, that is, as a coherent body of abstract knowledge systematically organized. As such, science is divisible into fields of specialization. Some of these overlap and share common principles. The natural sciences, for example, draw on the principles of physics and chemistry; theories of astronomy reinforce those of geology. Similarly, the life sciences use the principles of genetic and molecular biology. The behavioral and social sciences also interact in sharing in some instances common concepts, hypotheses, and theories.

[*The Transcendental Temptation* (1991), pp. 41–59]

But science, in a deeper sense, is a form of human behavior, a way of inquiring into nature. Science, in this sense, refers to an active process of investigation, a procedure for testing hypotheses and laws. The organized body of scientific knowledge accordingly is simply the product of its process or methods of inquiry.

The purposes of science are no doubt multifarious. The aim of basic theoretical research is understanding. Here the task of scientific inquiry is (1) to observe and describe data; (2) to date, record, and classify accurately the subject matter observed; (3) to formulate general hypotheses and laws concerning regularities; (4) to explain and account for what is observed by reference to antecedent conditions and causes; (5) to verify its hypotheses and laws by means of predictions and experiments; and (6) to relate and connect these by means of more comprehensive general theories.

The preceding is a general model, but there are wide deviations from it. And there are developing or protosciences that do not appear to fulfill all of these conditions. Some sciences, particularly the social sciences, have been able thus far to develop only a limited number of lower- or middle-range statistical correlations and tested hypotheses. Some sciences have not achieved the kinds of tested general explanations or high-level theories such as are discovered in physics and the natural sciences.

Scientific inquiry grows out of the practical interests of everyday life. Theoretical research is often stimulated by such concerns. Social, political, and economic needs encourage scientists to find solutions to social problems. The science of mechanics, for example, was engendered in part by the desire of ballistics experts to plot the paths of projectiles fired from the newly invented cannons that were used to batter down fortifications. Atomic-energy research was accelerated by the competitive race for nuclear weapons during World War II and thereafter. Cancer research was encouraged by an increase in the incidence of the dreaded disease, by the widespread public desire to find a cure for it, and by the expenditure of large sums of money by governmental and private agencies. Here intelligence is pragmatic and utilitarian: The goal is to solve problems, discover remedies, overcome obstacles, and find applications.

Some scientific research, however, is largely theoretical, though the quest for explanations fulfills a pervasive human curiosity. The basic question that has been raised is: "Is there a standard methodology of science, a set of procedures that scientists follow in achieving their goals?" Many philosophers of science have attempted to depict what they thought was the process of inquiry and discovery. Thus, empiricists attempted to trace knowledge to its origin in perceptions and sensations, maintaining that the mind is blank tablet, written upon by experience. Rationalists related general theories to the deductive processes of intuition and inference. Pragmatists connected all hypotheses to problem-solving processes.

Regretfully, these efforts are misdirected. There is no simple logic of discovery that everyone follows. Knowledge may originate in a variety of ways. Penicillin was discovered through an accidental observation by Sir Alexander Fleming. Claude Bernard, wrestling with a problem concerning the cause of sugar in the blood of animals, said he arrived at his explanation by mulling over the experimental data. Einstein developed his relativity theories by questioning the postulates of Newton. The processes of creative discovery are thus complex and diverse. We need to be immersed in data, to know the empirical facts, and to be able to make inferences to solve problems encountered in the process of research.

What is central from the standpoint of science is not so much the genesis of an idea or hypothesis as its validation and verification. Thus it is the criteria of validating or verifying knowledge, how we establish or warrant belief, that should concern us. This does not meant that the scientific inquirer might not possess certain qualities of mind that are essential in the course of his research. He must be a keen observer of the facts. His mind must be passive, as it were. He should listen to what nature tells him without allowing his preconceived biases to intrude. He will formulate predictions and draw inferences, if his hypotheses are true, and observe the results meticulously and carefully. The experimental method thus depends directly on the data given.

But merely to look at the facts is never enough. The scientist must ask questions of nature. Her inquiry may be stimulated by a puzzle or doubt, and her hypothesis, which may be initiated by creative insight or contrived conjecture, is a solution to the problem. Thus the mind of the scientist is both receptive and passive, active and manipulative. The data are not simply given, but are taken, interpreted, generalized, and related to other forms of data. Some abstractive ability is thus involved. Connecting relationships and theories are developed; the coherence of a set of explanations and how they fit together is elaborated. For example, evolutionary principles have theoretical relevance not only in biology, anthropology, and genetics but also in astronomy, geology, and the other natural sciences. Similarly, the term *theory of disease* has a wide range of application. Successful scientific theories tend to be comprehensive in the scope of their explanations.

Critical intelligence—reflective, probing, interpretive, analytic, perceptive—operates throughout the process of discovery and validation of scientific hypotheses. But the question I again raise is this: What are the standards of validation? This is particularly pertinent when we ask how to distinguish veridical beliefs from false ones, science from pseudoscience.

SUBJECTIVISTIC METHODOLOGY

Some philosophers of science have denied that there are any standards of validation of scientific hypotheses and theories. Paul Feyerabend is perhaps the most extreme exponent of this radical skeptical view. He argues:

> The idea of a method that contains firm, unchanging, and absolutely binding principles for conducting the business of science meets considerable difficulty when confronted with the results of historical research. We find, then, that there is not a single rule, however plausible, and however firmly grounded in epistemology, that is not violated at some time or other.... There is only *one* principle that can be defended under all circumstances and in *all* stages of human development. It is the principle *anything* goes.[1]

He maintains, for example, that the Copernican revolution and the emergence of the wave theory of light occurred because some scientists did not feel bound by the methodological rules and broke them. "When Copernicus introduced a new view of the universe," according to Feyerabend, "he did not consult *scientific* predecessors, he consulted a crazy Pythagorean, such as Philolaos. He adopted his ideas and he maintained them in the face of all sound rules of scientific method."[2]

Now Feyerabend is obviously correct that there are no firm and unchanging, absolutely binding principles involved in scientific inquiry. The history of science clearly shows that the establishment of scientific principles is often a rather loose affair and that a whole number of irrelevant considerations enter. Scientists, like everyone else, are human beings, and subjective fancies and predilections may intrude on their work. Many scientists do indeed violate the rules of inference and experimentation. Yet their results remain, and eventually they may be accepted by other scientists and incorporated into the body of scientific principles. The fact that one aspect of a scientist's research may be warranted does not mean that other parts of his worldview may not be flawed. Newton, for example, believed firmly in the Bible and astrology. The point is: scientists do not follow neatly laid out rules of validation in all of their inquiries.

May we then infer that there are *no* rules or criteria for establishing scientific knowledge? Is the only dependable theory epistemological anarchy? Feyerabend believes that although science was liberating during the Enlightenment, it now has become a religion and an ideology and that it is often the enemy of freedom of thought. As a result, he defends astrology and even the teaching of creationism along with the theory of evolution in the public schools. For Feyerabend the theories of science today are no closer to the truth than fairy tales or other myths, and if taxpayers believe in Chinese herbal medicine and acupuncture, voodoo, faith healing, or the Hopi ceremonial rain dance and cosmology, then it should be taught in the schools along with established science, which he compares to a state church.

This extreme, subjectivistic theory has puzzling consequences. For if there are no objective standards, then is *any* belief as true as the next? If there are no rigorous standards for testing claims, then is not anything as true as anything else? But surely there is a difference, for example, between a scientific procedure that can isolate and locate the viruses that cause polio and develop a vaccine against them and one that attributes the disease to the devil. What is meaningful is that there is a relevant range of evidence that decides the question. If we grant that it is difficult to identify firm and fixed rules, this does not mean that there are none. The choice between hypotheses and theories is not arbitrary.

Surely, one of the tests of a scientific claim is its *results*, in technology and practice. However, Feyerabend disputes this point, claiming that other ideologies also have results. Religions build cathedrals and save souls, and revolutionary doctrines overthrow established societies. But the kinds of experimental consequences of scientific inquiry are independent, in one sense, of our own wishes imposed upon the world. When asked why he takes airplanes rather than brooms, Feyerabend replies flippantly, "I know how to use planes but don't know how to use brooms, and can't be bothered to learn." If Feyerabend doesn't believe in objective standards of truth, why doesn't he jump out the window of a fifty-story building?[3] The answer is clear: There are obdurate realities that impose upon, block, or fulfill our desires. Feyerabend's theory is self-defeating, for he can give no objective reasons why we should accept his theory other than taste or caprice. There *are* principles that govern air travel, and one jump out of a high window should lay to rest his views that there are no differentiating standards of inquiry.

According to Feyerabend, science is a social phenomenon, deeply embedded in an entire cultural milieu. It may be related to a religious worldview (as during the days of Aquinas) or stand in opposition to it (during the modern period). It has strong affinities to the state and the economy, which benefit from its findings and applications and either encourage (by support) or impede (by restrictions) its worldview. Lysenko was aided by the Stalinist state because his theory of biological evolution supported the reigning ideology, and nuclear research was massively supported during and after World War II because of its military potential. All of that is granted. But is the conclusion to be drawn that scientific objectivity is a complete myth and all that remains is a form of social relativism?

Thomas S. Kuhn, in a famous book, *The Structure of Scientific Revolutions*, points to the fact that in some historical epochs an entire conceptual framework or paradigm may give way to another.[4] In such revolutionary periods, diverse social and cultural factors may contribute to such a shift. Kuhn describes "the transfer of allegiance" from one paradigm to another as a kind of "conversion experience." At first there may be strong opposition to a competing theoretical framework, but eventually it may give way and virtually the whole scientific community may adopt it. Often the contributing factors are extrascientific, and the choice of a theory does not resemble a proof in formal logic or mathematics.

Are we likewise to infer from Kuhn's account of what has often happened in the history of science that there are no objective standards of scientific validity? Some have suggested that new paradigms triumphed because of some "mystical aesthetic." Some defenders of paranormal worldviews today quote Kuhn approvingly to support and sanctify their untested theories. Kuhn himself denies these implications; he thinks the continued resistance to the new theories (as in the case of Joseph Priestley, for example) may be illogical or unscientific. The man who continues to resist and oppose the new view after the entire profession has been converted to it has ceased to be a scientist. Although Kuhn believes that extralogical forms of persuasion intervene, this does not mean that "there are not many good reasons for suggesting one theory rather than another." He maintains that these are "reasons of exactly the kind standard in 'the' philosophy of science."[5]

TESTING TRUTH CLAIMS IN SCIENCE

The questions that we need to raise are: What constitutes good reasons for the choice of a hypothesis or theory? and What constitutes good grounds for acceptance? Here the focus should be on the *criteria* for testing a claim, not the procedure or method by which it is arrived at.

Here again, I do not think there are easily formulatable criteria or rules one can lay down beforehand. We need to extend our skepticism, to some extent, to science itself and refute any myth that science or the scientific method is unerring and infallible.

Scientists have all the frailties of other human beings, and science, where institutionalized, carries all the weight and drawbacks of tradition and prejudices. Scientists may be as dogmatic and hostile to new departures in thought as others. Encrusted habits are not the exclusive possession of religion, economic class, or ethnicity but affect all human endeavors.

Still, there are some standards for testing claims. These may be ideal, and there may be wide deviations from them in actual practice. There are at a minimum three important criteria: (1) the need for evidence, (2) logical consistency, and (3) technological and experimental consequences.

EVIDENCE

The Principle of Corroboration

The logical positivists attempted to introduce rigorous criteria that they thought would enable us to determine the adequacy of scientific hypotheses. These criteria have since come under heavy criticism—particularly the principle of verifiability, which was recommended as a theory of meaning and which was supposed to help us distinguish genuine statements from pseudostatements. An empirical or synthetic statement, said the positivists, is meaningful if and only if there are conditions under which its truth claim can be tested. Critics have pointed out that this criterion was much too stringent. Many statements in the sciences are theoretical and have no easily confirmable content. Moreover, one cannot always determine a priori what is testable.

Broadly conceived, the intent of the principle of verifiability was worthwhile: to help us disentangle patently meaningless nonsense in metaphysics, theology, and the pseudosciences from meaningful hypotheses. Unfortunately, the criteria imposed are too narrow, a straitjacket on scientific inquiry; it is an oversimplification to say that one can determine merely by analysis antecedent to inquiry which sentences are genuine and which are nonsensical. Often one is circumscribed by one's preexisting paradigm, which enables one to reject something out of hand.

The principle of *verification*, as distinct from verifiability, is a variation on the empiricist criterion. It is an essential component of scientific methodology. The principle of verification has both a positive and a negative aspect. First, a hypothesis is *true* (as distinct from *meaningful*) if it has been verified, directly or indirectly, and if there is a range of evidence that can be brought to bear to support it. As Hume pointed out, however, we can never say with certainty that our inductions based upon observation and experiment are complete. Hence, no hypothesis is definitively confirmed, only probable. Nor can we confirm the principle of induction itself.

Karl Popper has sought to modify this criterion by a negative principle: nonfalsifiability. He argued that the actual procedure in the sciences is to introduce conjectures or hypotheses, often based on creative and intuitive guesswork. This is not necessarily always supported by painstaking data gathering or experiment. However, the decisive issue is whether conjectured hypothesis is warranted, and here there are tests that can be brought to bear. At the very least we need to be able to falsify the theory by seeing whether it can be refuted or sustained by the empirical evidence. A theory is meaningless if there are no conditions under which it can be disconfirmed.

I agree with both the positive and negative verification criteria. A more adequate terminology that better conveys what is going on would be the *principle of corroboration*. We first try to establish a claim by reference to clearly established observations and experiments. However, in many cases we do not have sufficient data; some complicated hypotheses can only be established either by a single test (e.g., the Michelson-Morley experiment was thought to confirm Einstein's theory of relativity concerning the speed of light) or by a disconfirming test of alternative explanations. If a theory stands up to the most severe tests that can be formulated, it is corroborated and accepted—though it may, of course, give way when newer explanations and new data are uncovered.

Intersubjective Corroboration

The principle of corroboration refers to *public* evidence. That is, mere, private reports of introspection or subjective observations that are seen by only one person are never sufficient. In principle, they must be capable of independent corroboration by other impartial observers. Mystics and seers claim to have some inner road to truth. They refer to a kind of apprehension or illumination that they alone possess. To try to translate this into observable reports, they say, loses its essence, since it is "ineffable." But science cannot accept subjective claims to truth; it needs to replicate the experience or experiment. This means that any scientist in any laboratory under standard conditions could achieve the same chemical reactions or observe the same phenomena with his or her instruments.

One of the problems of the pseudosciences is the fact that claims so often made by devoted believers resist corroboration by independent or neutral inquirers. One of the basic problems in parapsychological research today is the difficulty independent researchers have in replicating the results of others. The researchers include not only skeptics, who almost never get results, but also other parapsychologists in other laboratories who find that the alleged data are elusive and that it is difficult to specify or determine the conditions under which the effect is supposed to occur. A similar problem applies to so-called revelatory knowledge basic to the major religions. How do we know that the experiences of those who allegedly received revelations were "authentic" unless they could be corroborated by others? There must be at least some reliable eyewitness testimony, particularly about the claims that deviate from our normal expectations about the world. I am not talking about hearsay evidence, which is notoriously unreliable, but rather the direct testimony of more than one person.

One should raise a serious word of caution even here about some so-called testimony. Although sense perception is the bedrock of any empiricist-experimentalist criterion of evidence, without which science cannot proceed, it may be a snare. In the first case, the untrained or undisciplined observer can often misjudge the "facts" before him. The blind men who used different shapes to describe the same elephant illustrate the difficulty. Many people may witness a crime, as was the case in the film *Rashomon*, and each will give a different version of what happened; this is based on one's vantage point. I have personally met people who swear they were taken aboard a UFO into outer space or have been visited by the spirit of a deceased relative. Rarely is something perceived without interpretation in terms of a preconceived idea, hypothesis, or theory, particularly when we are seeking causes. Here a *critical* eye is an essential component of observation. To see something, we must know what to look for. Percepts without interpretive concepts may be unintelligible. We need the creative use of inference and logic to interpret the data—however, not inference that distorts the facts or colors them to fit a preconceived theory, but inference conditioned by what is actually there. What is necessary is that there be trained observers who can check the veracity of an observation and then give it some intersubjective corroboration. We need to ask not only *what* is happening, but *why* or *how*; and only active investigations can answer this by posing questions and unraveling possible responses.

A question often raised is: What constitutes sufficient evidence for a claim to be accepted? There are no simple answers. If one is predisposed toward a theory, then only a few instances may be taken as sufficient to establish its credibility. In some cases, a single decisive experiment may be sufficient. In other cases, however, we may need to test and retest the data before we are satisfied that our hypothesis is warranted.

Probability, Fallibility, Skepticism

Here we come back to our earlier point, namely, that no theory is *ultimately* confirmed decisively, since we may be mistaken and new data may be uncovered. A theory is only as good as the evidence adduced in its support, and this is often only comparative. All other explanations may either seem less likely or fail entirely, though the theory we have may not be airtight. Here constructive doubt again emerges as the basic ingredient of ongoing inquiry. Hypotheses are working ideas or tentative formulations until they are corroborated. Many such hypotheses become well established by repeated collaboration. Given the history of science, however, we must be prepared to allow the possibility that they may be in need of revision at some later date.

The question concerning the *degree* of certainty of one's theories is especially relevant to Hume's famous interpretation of miracles; we are more likely to accept a claim if it is not discordant with our own experience or what we already know to be true. The hypothesis may be new, but it need not contradict the body of evidence that has already been amassed. Where a claim promises to overturn a whole body of data and hypotheses that we now accept on the basis of strong grounds, then before we accept it we must have even stronger grounds to do so. Extraordinary claims thus require extra degrees of evidence. Thus, before we can invoke miraculous or occult explanations that overturn well-established laws and regularities of experience and nature, we would need very strong evidence.

We can see the relevance of Hume's argument in parapsychology, astrology, and the paranormal fields. Often a claim is made that, if true, would supplant well-established principles of both science and ordinary life. C. D. Broad has pointed out a number of principles parapsychologists apparently wish to overthrow: (1) that future events cannot affect the present *before* they happen (backward causation); (2) that a person's mind cannot effect a change in the material world: there has to be intervention of some physical energy or force; (3) that a person cannot know the content of another person's mind except by the use of inferences based on experience and drawn from observations of speech or behavior; (4) that we cannot directly know what happens at distant points in space without some sensory perception or energy transmitted to us; and (5) that discarnate beings do not exist as persons separable from physical bodies.[6] These general principles have been built up from a mass of observations and should not be abandoned until there is an overabundant degree of evidence that would make their rejection more plausible than their acceptance. Those who use the term *paranormal* believe that they uncovered a body of empirical facts that call into question precisely those principles. Whether or not they do remains to be seen by future inquiry. These principles are not sacred and may one day need to be modified—but only if empirical evidence makes it necessary.

Now it seems to me that Hume's argument can be pushed too far. We need to be dubious of efforts by a priori reasoning to say that since hypotheses are incomprehensible to the present conceptual framework, they are therefore false. Hume's argument can be used as a club by narrow-minded skeptics to disavow all new revolutionary theories; one must guard against its possible misuses. Nonetheless, we must be prepared to radically alter our conceptual framework, but only if there is sufficient new data that cannot be explained by any other means. All theories, in the last analysis, must give way to the *evidence.* One needs strong and reliable evidence before one is prepared to overthrow well-established theories. But in the process of scientific inquiry, it has often happened, and we must always be prepared to do so.

LOGICAL COHERENCE

Analytic Clarity

The beginning test of the adequacy of belief is the precision with which it is stated. Thus before we can evaluate a statement, we need to analyze the meaning of the ideas and concepts that are involved in it. Before we can tell whether the statements that are made are warranted, we must know whether they make sense. Linguistic and logical clarification is thus a pro-legomenon to any empirical inquiry. There are many errors that people commit. Ideas may not be clearly stated; they may be vague, even inco-herent. Sometimes abstract ideas lack any referent; they may be devoid of clear meaning. It is doubtful that there is a single criterion for clarity, but there are some important guidelines.

First, we should always seek to define our terms, if possible, by the use of synonyms or by pointing to characteristics or properties to which the words refer, particularly if they are descriptive terms. Some terms lack clear connotation. (Ethical terms, for example, such as *good* or *right* are difficult to define by designating observable properties in the world. Yet they are understood.)

Second, we should seek to examine the contexts in which terms are used to see if we can understand what they mean. This means that to understand language we need to be intimately acquainted with the subject matter and how terms and concepts interact in situations.

Third, to do this we need to see how terms are employed and what role or function they perform. We should thus always seek the use of a term and see what job it does in a context in order to comprehend what it might mean.

In the sciences some precision is essential, as far as possible, especially if we are to develop hypotheses or theories that are testable. In poetry and religion, terms may have only metaphorical or symbolic uses, and they may serve to evoke feelings or moods, to arouse passion and commitment, rather than to stimulate cognitive thought or perceptual imagery. It is important that we do not confuse the meanings of terms in various usages. They may convey information, particularly when found in sentences in the form of affirmative statements or denials, but they may be imperatives (expressing commands), interrogatives (raising questions), or performatives (ceremonial) in function. Contemporary analytic philosophy has made important contributions to our understanding of language. But we are here talking about the meaning of language, not the truth of claims or beliefs. We cannot say that something is true if it is gibberish or nonsensical. But to make it clear still leaves open the question of whether it is true.

We are speaking not only of the clarification of parts of speech, words, terms, and concepts, but also of sentences or statements. These may be classified as descriptive, analytic, expressive, prescriptive, imperative, performative, interrogative, and so on, in form and function. From the standpoint of knowledge, we are concerned with (1) descriptive, theoretical, or explanatory statements, and whether and how they can be established as true; and (2) prescriptive statements, and whether or not they work and the consequences of their use.

Internal Validity

Ideas, hypotheses, beliefs, or statements are never held or uttered in isolation. If they were, they would be fragmentary bits. We need to see how they are related to other beliefs or sentences in a framework or structure. Our beliefs thus are connected by logical inference, and they have some internal symmetry. Accordingly, a necessary (but not sufficient) condition for the truth or adequacy of a hypothesis is that it be consistent with other statements that are accepted. Here the rules of deductive logic apply. Some philosophers have thought that this internal consistency was sufficient in itself.

If Rip Van Winkle returned to his home after twenty years, unaware of any of the factual claims made by people around him, he could still check the veracity of their statements by seeing whether they contradicted earlier assertions. But he could not fully account for what he encountered unless he corroborated the data empirically. Our premises and theories always need some empirical content if they are to be taken as true.

Comprehensive Coherence

Nonetheless, although we can and do judge specific syllogisms and arguments, or hypotheses and theories in a single science, by criteria internal to that inquiry or discipline, there is always the effort to reach out and generalize. We seek to relate the specific sciences to one another, and then to broader principles.

Some philosophers have thought that if they could develop a comprehensive and elegant enough system, eventually they might incorporate all possible statements and thus comprehend the truth about the universe as a whole. This is known as the *doctrine of internal relations*. The danger in this that although one can establish as valid a set of philosophical, theological, or ideological propositions and integrate them into a broader system, whether the entire framework is true is often what is precisely at issue. Thomism and Marxism illustrate such comprehensive systems. Great efforts have been expended ad hoc to account for any discrepancies found in such systems. Unfortunately, the commitment to a total system may distort one's judgment and perception. One may be so swept away by its comprehensive outlook and its totalistic answer to the root questions that factual discrepancies are denied, overlooked, or explained away. Though the arguments used to elaborate and defend the system of belief may be formally valid, they may not be truthful about the material world. Many theories are internally consistent, but since one or more of their premises are false, the system is false. The question to be asked always is: Are the premises factually true or supportable? These should not be tested simply by an appeal to "intuition" or cognition, but by the evidence. Thus, the problem with Thomism is its premise about God, which is unsubstantiated, and with Marxism, the unconfirmed dialectical laws of history.

Here we have gone beyond science to metaphysics, theology, and philosophy proper. It is one thing to seek and develop unifying statements with one science or across the sciences (the principle of evolution illustrates the latter), but it is quite another to develop a unifying theory of history or an ontological theory of ultimate reality. Here we are in the metascientific realm. A comprehensive philosophy of nature is often based upon a generalization from the sciences at one stage of the development of knowledge and upon philosophical reflections on the first principles of science, religion, and the arts. Such enterprises, however, are often perilous. Efforts to construct comprehensive philosophical systems no doubt have some merit, for they give us some perspective and seek to integrate our knowledge. But such systems cannot be tested solely by analytic and/or deductive criteria; they need empirical and consequential tests if they are to have any degree of reliability.

PRAGMATIC CONSEQUENCES

Experimental Testing

This criterion is related to empiricism and the requirement that there be corroborative evidence, but it goes one step beyond. For knowledge is not simply a description of what *is* but of what *can be*. Belief claims, in a sense, are plans or rules of action; they make predictions about what is likely to happen if we undertake certain forms of behavior.

To say that "sugar is soluble" means that if we were to put a spoonful of sugar into a glass of water, it would most likely dissolve. The statement can be interpreted in operational terms. Many or most sentences in science take a hypothetical or conditional form, such that if we were to do something, then certain consequences would ensue. Every explanatory theory has within it some implied predictions (directly or indirectly); otherwise it cannot be said to be true. By this, I do not mean that every sentence in a theory is equivalent to its operational meaning—this rigorous criterion is much too narrow—but only that a theory could be related, at least indirectly, to sentences that are operationally testable.

Experimentalism is not reducible to empiricism. The latter refers to sense-data and observational reports, passively viewed; the former refers more explicitly to conditions by which hypotheses are tested. We judge them by their verified consequences.

Problem Solving and Technological Applications

Another test that is more difficult to generalize about is the fact that our beliefs and hypotheses have a bearing upon our behavior by generating further ideas that can modify the world in which we live. Pure research in the natural sciences has been justified in startling ways in modern times because of the technological application of the principles discovered and the fact that such knowledge has been put to powerful uses.

Ideas are thus prescriptions and directives: They fulfill our purposes and goals and can thus be appraised by whether we find the end achieved worthwhile. There is thus an *evaluative* component. Here, the test is not simply whether a statement or hypothesis is descriptively true or analytically sound, but whether it is satisfactory or fitting to the situation. We judge ideas in part by their effectiveness—by what they lead to, what they breed, what they bring into existence. Newtonian physics gave us the technology of the steam engine and water pump, and contemporary physics brought us space travel and computer technology. We might not always value the technological applications, but the results of ideas are relevant in some way to their truth. It is the *power* of a belief that can be demonstrated to be true that in some sense provides a test of its adequacy.

Ideas help to assuage doubts, overcome obstacles, and solve problems. They are instruments and tools—but more, they are tools of discovery and creation. Thinking is instrumental both for the ordinary man, whose thoughts can be judged by whether they enable him to cope with life, and for the scientist, whose ideas have observable consequences in the world.

VINDICATION OF THE SCIENTIFIC METHOD

In summation, the scientific method involves three main components: (1) evidence, (2) logical validity, and (3) practicality. These criteria are continuous with the way beliefs function in everyday life where critical intelligence is at work. This is relevant to another important issue: the vindication or justification of the scientific method. Two rather fundamental considerations are pertinent. First, the commitment to scientific method is in accord with the use of critical intelligence in ordinary experience, and, second, the method has pragmatic convenience.

Many philosophical and theological critics of science have demanded the total justification of science and the scientific method. But this is inappropriate, for science is implicit in our ordinary ways of thinking and in the technological processes of reasoning already involved in practice.

Moreover, the rules governing ordinary thinking are not culturally relative or merely a predilection of Western civilization, as Zen Buddhists and others seem to argue when they claim that the conceptual and empirical scientific method is Western, whereas there is an "intuitive" and "mystical" way of knowing in Asian cultures. Rather, as far as we can tell from an analysis of anthropological data, some teleonomic means-end way of knowing applies to all cultures, even primitive ones. Claude Lévi-Strauss's theory of structuralism seems to support the notion of an underlying set of invariant conditions to human mentality.[7] That is, even if the primitive person's mind is fixated on a mystical religious tradition, this does not undermine or invalidate a commitment to technological reasoning; rather, reasoning complements it and is always present as a necessary component of living. Indeed, to deny a minimal level of objective thinking would make life in any culture impossible. Thus, again, we cannot deny the important uses of common sense and scientific method in certain areas of life, for both the primitive and the modern. To do so would be to fly in the face of the obvious. The question, however, is, How far shall we *extend* this method?

To demand a justification of the first principles already deeply embedded and functioning in the lifeworld of practice is to raise a spurious question. In regard to the justification of deduction, the justification of general rules derives as much from the particular judgments in which we reject or accept deductive inferences as from an examination of the general rules themselves. Aristotle could only formulize principles of deductive inference that were already implicit in the judgments of ordinary men and in the Sophists' skills of argumentation. Thus, rules and particular inferences alike are justified by being brought into agreement with each other. A rule is amended if it yields an inference we are unwilling to amend. Similar considerations apply to the hypothetic-deductive method of scientific inductions. Particular hypotheses are justified if they conform to the valid canons of inductive inquiry, and the canons are valid if they accurately codify accepted inductive practices.

Thus, we can stop plaguing ourselves with illegitimate questions about the justification of scientific induction and examine actual usage instead.

The definition of a general rule relates to such usages. This logical point is important. The vindication of scientific methodology is based to a large extent upon an analysis and reflection of what we already do, the rules intrinsic to usages. It is not a metarule imposed on the subject matter of our ordinary processes of inquiry.

Since the scientific method is at the same time a normative proposal, the appeal to existing usage by itself does not suffice—especially if one wishes to justify an extension of the method to other areas. Hence, additional considerations must be brought to bear on the question of justification.

There is another important logical point concerning the kinds of questions being raised. There are no "ultimate" questions, only penultimate ones, and this applies equally to the justification of what we already do, the procedures we employ, and what we ought to do. To demand the justification of first principles by deriving them from still more basic first principles would require either that we reduce them to indefinable terms or undemonstrable propositions, which are ultimate, or that we commit a *petitio principi* by assuming the very principle that we wish to prove. Hence, one does not "justify" first principles; one does, however, attempt to make them seem reasonable. Here, a philosophical vindication involves a reasoned argument, wherein we try to make a case for our general position. The procedure is not unlike that employed in a legal context, wherein one attempts to prove a case not simply by deduction from first principles, but by a drawing together, focusing, or converging of considerations, factors, and arguments that make the defense seem cogent.

There is a basic contextual consideration here. We never begin such reasoning de novo or from scratch. Discussions of vindication are forced upon the case at hand by real situations and concrete problems. In human experience there are no first beginnings and no final endings to the succession of moral principles. Rather, different levels of questions can be raised and appropriate responses given. The defense of the first principle of scientific humanism—that is, the use of scientific knowledge as the ideal—is not unlike the vindication given in everyday life for one set of procedures that we wish to adopt rather than another, whether in gardening, cobbling, or mechanics. Similar considerations apply to reasoning in the ethical domain and the vindication of other normative principles; they are always related to the situation or context before us. Thus, even for those areas in which we do not now use scientific methods and procedures, the kind of vindication we can give for gaining adoption is the kind of vindication that should appeal to the ordinary man, for it is used throughout life.

Empirical consequences constitute a central consideration: It is not by words but by deeds or fruits that we judge. It is how well a principle works out in practice over the long run that is the basis for our decision to continue to use it, to discard it, or to modify it. Thus, although the first principles of scientific naturalism are not necessarily true, they are plausible to the ordinary person when he or she inspects the results of their use; indeed, most human beings tend to judge ideas and ideals by their pragmatic consequences, irrespective of their philosophical persuasions. The consequences of the scientific mode of inquiry are such that (1) it facilitates the development of new knowledge, since its controlled use has led to steady progress; (2) its use enables us to make the knowledge we already possess more coherent; and (3) no matter what our desires, ends, or values, it enables us to fulfill them most adequately, being the most effective instrument we have for dealing with the world.

Here is the dilemma the scientific naturalist always faces when attempting to vindicate his or her position, and it is the charge that Plato raised against the Sophist Protagoras: Why accept what the ordinary person does when he takes into account the standards of consequences or effectiveness? The scientific naturalist begins with the ordinary person and returns to him and to common sense to warrant his or her position; the naturalist does not stay there, but considers his or her principle a normative *proposal.* The problem again is not simply to vindicate existing inductive procedures but to vindicate their extension—say, to religion or morality, where they are not now being used—and to make them a model for all knowledge and inquiry. How should we judge proposals? we ask. Proposals imply value judgments. Does not scientific naturalism thus presuppose a more basic value judgment that is controlling?

The only answer that can be given here is to admit—as Mill, Dewey, Hook, and a score of other thinkers have admitted—that there are no discoverable ultimate standards of value by which epistemological principles can be judged. The only argument in appraising key value judgments is a *comparative* argument—in other words, in the last analysis, a pragmatic case based upon a balanced appraisal of conflicting claims.

All other positions face a quandary similar to that hurled at the scientific humanist—though compounded. It is unfair to burden the scientific humanist with the "riddle of induction," for there is a "riddle of intuition" or a "riddle of subjectivism" or a "riddle" for any other method. The intuitionist, mystic, or subjectivist can only justify his position by assuming his method to do so, thus committing a *petitio principi*. The burden of proof rests with these alternative positions. Moreover, insofar as the intuitionist, mystic, or subjectivist attempts to justify his method and employs argument and reason to do so, he is already conceding a point to the scientific naturalist. Even to seek a justification is to presuppose objectivity as an ideal. What does the word *justification* mean? In a sense, it is equivalent to that employed in the objectivistic mode of inquiry and in ordinary life when we demand grounds for belief. To even raise the question of vindication is to suggest a solution. To say that justification is an open question is to open the arena for an objective examination of all claims to knowledge, which is a key methodological criterion of methodological naturalism. The only response of the nonobjectivist is to refuse to justify his method.

We may ask, Which rules of procedure in the long run appear better or more effective in gaining results? I deny that the scientific humanist is merely stipulating or that his proposal is an arbitrary, persuasive definition of "knowledge." If all positions involve some question begging and are on the same ground in this regard, we may ask: "Which is the least self-defeating? Which accords best with the facts, with intelligibility as ordinarily understood, or which best enables us to satisfy our diverse desires?" Scientific humanists have made it clear, for example, that they do not exclude on a priori grounds the reports of mystics, intuitionists, psychics, or even of people under the influence of LSD and other psychedelics; they do not exclude, simply by definition, reference to a transcendental realm, God, or immortality. On the contrary, we should examine such reports with care and with caution. But we do insist upon some responsibility in appraising claims made on behalf of subjectivism or transcendentalism. We need to leave the question open and not block inquiry by denying on a priori grounds, as to subjectivists, that such things cannot be known by objective methods of inquiry. On the contrary and as we have seen, all other methods at some point must presuppose the use of objective methods in addition to their own methods. In other words, some objective methods are to some extent unavoidable if we are to live and function in the world, and everyone has to assume them up to a point; the same thing cannot be said of other methods.

We should not maintain a blind faith in scientific methodology or believe that an extension of these rigorous methods to other fields of inquiry must inevitably succeed. We should not be so naive as to assume that all human problems can be solved and all quandaries settled. If, however, we examine the chief arguments that were used in the past against the scientific study of nature and human behavior, we may question such a priori negativism. One can imagine in pre-Aristotelian or pre-Galilean days someone objecting to the proposal to develop a science of ways of looking at the world. Yet I readily concede that whether the first principle of scientific humanism—that is, the use of scientific methodology—is the most reliable approach in explaining all the complexities of nature and human behavior is still an open question and can only be judged as inquiry proceeds. Again, that it must succeed is not deductively certain. But in light of fruitful gains already registered in the natural, biological, and behavioral sciences, we have good reasons to believe that scientific inquiry will continue to progress. Some skepticism, no doubt, should still be present, even about this expectation, especially if it is framed in the form of an overly confident scientism.

NOTES

1. Paul Feyerabend, *Against Method* (New York: Schocken Books, 1977). Quoted in Ernest Nagel, "Philosophical Depreciations of Scientific Method," *Humanist* 36, no. 4 (July/August 1976): 34–35.

2. Paul Feyerabend, "How to Defend Society against Science," *Radical Philosophy* 11 (1975): 3–8. Quoted in E. D. Klemke, Robert Hollinger, David Wÿss Rudge, and A. David Kline, eds., *Introductory Readings in the Philosophy of Science* (Amherst, NY: Prometheus Books, 1981).

3. See Martin Gardner, "Anti-Science: The Strange Case of Paul Feyerabend," *Free Inquiry* 3 (Winter 1982/83): 32–34.

4. Thomas Kuhn, *The Structure of Scientific Revolutions*, 2nd ed. (Chicago: University of Chicago Press, 1971).

5. Thomas Kuhn, "Theory Choice," in *Criticism and Growth of Knowledge*, ed. I. Lakatos and A. Musgrave (New York: Cambridge University Press, 1970), pp. 260–62. Quoted in Klemke et al., *Introductory Readings in the Philosophy of Science*, p. 208.

6. C. D. Broad, "The Relevance of Psychical Research to Philosophy," *Philosophy* 24 (1949): 291–309.

7. Claude Lévi-Strauss, *Structural Anthropology* (New York: BasicBooks, 1963).

Chapter 4

SKEPTICISM AND THE NEW ENLIGHTENMENT

The term *the Enlightenment* refers to a unique set of ideas and ideals that came to fruition in Europe in the seventeenth and eighteenth centuries. It began with Bacon, Descartes, Locke, and other philosophers who sought a universal method for establishing knowledge. They looked to science as the model for knowledge and debated whether reason or experience was most important (actually, both are equally important). No doubt they took impetus from the remarkable discoveries of Newton and Galileo in mathematics, physics, and astronomy. The Enlightenment culminated with the French philosophes—Voltaire, Diderot, Condorcet, and d'Holbach—who popularized its ideas in Parisian salons, pamphlets, and books, enabling those ideas to spread to a wider educated public.

The philosophes criticized the ancien régime of religious superstition and dogmatism, hidebound social traditions, and repressive morality. They wished to use science and reason to understand nature and solve social problems. They were optimistic that in this way human progress could be advanced. In politics, they developed social contract theories, defended the secular state and the rights of man, and advocated economic liberty. The

["A New Enlightenment," *Free Inquiry* 24, no. 3 (April–May 2004): 5–8]

American Revolution was influenced by their ideals (through Jefferson, Franklin, Madison, and Paine). They influenced the French Revolution also, though many of them were opposed to its excesses. They wished to reform the penal code and end cruel punishments. They were anticlerical, castigating the corruption and hypocrisy of the churches, especially Roman Catholicism ("Écrasez l'infáme," cried Voltaire). Most were deists; some were atheists. The Enlightenment defended a humanist outlook that drew its values from the Renaissance and Greco-Roman Hellenic culture, which had also extolled the role of reason.

In his influential essay "What Is Enlightenment?" (1785), Immanuel Kant, a key figure of the Enlightenment, sought to define Enlightenment as follows:

> Enlightenment is the emancipation of man from a state of self-imposed tutelage. This state is due to his incapacity to use his own intelligence without external guidance.... Dare to use your own intelligence! This is the battle-cry of the Enlightenment.[1]

According to Karl Popper, "It was this idea of self-liberation through knowledge that was central to the Enlightenment. "Dare to be free," added Kant, "and respect the freedom and autonomy of others." For Kant, the dignity of human beings lay in their freedom, and in their respect for other people's autonomous and responsible beliefs. However, it is only through the growth of knowledge that a person can be liberated "from enslavement by prejudices, idols, and avoidable errors."[2]

The Enlightenment's quest for knowledge inspired numerous scientists, philosophers, and poets, including Goethe, Bentham, Mill, Darwin, Marx, Freud, Einstein, Crick, and Watson. It has continued to inspire research on the frontiers of scientific knowledge, such as the development of chemistry and biology in the nineteenth century and the emergence of the social and behavioral sciences in the twentieth. The application of the methods of science heralded new breakthroughs in science and technology that contributed to the betterment of humankind. These included the Industrial Revolution (with the subsequent capacity to expand production); impressive gains in medicine (such as surgery, anesthesia, and antibiotics, which extended life spans); a swelling bounty of consumer goods (which can be used and enjoyed by everyone); a reduction of drudgery and labor (which has shortened the work week and has afforded more leisure time to ordinary people); vastly improved transportation and communication technologies; the green revolution (increased agricultural production); the information revolution (computers, the Internet); biogenetic engineering (we are on the threshold of new powers for humankind to reduce genetic diseases); and the space age (with its vast potential for exploration of the solar system and outer space beyond).

Scientific knowledge has extended our understanding of the universe. It has altered our interpretation of the place of the human species within nature, as the theory of evolution has replaced theories of creation. It has aroused awe and astonishment, following Hubble, at the sheer size of the expanding universe. New planetary star systems and galaxies are being discovered almost daily. Scientific naturalism has thus dislodged theological supernaturalism as the cosmological outlook of the contemporary intellectual world. The promise of further exciting discoveries in science and technology, with their consequent benefits to humankind, is truly enormous.

Unfortunately, there has been a massive retreat from Enlightenment ideals in recent years, a return to premodern mythologies. There has been a resurgence of fundamentalist religions worldwide—Hinduism, Sikhism, Islam, Roman Catholicism, and Orthodox Judaism. Added to this are occult-paranormal claims, which allegedly transcend the existing scientific paradigm.

In the United States—the preeminent scientific-technological-military superpower in the world—significant numbers of Americans have embraced primitive forms of biblical religion. These focus on salvation, the Rapture, and the Second Coming of Jesus. Evangelical Protestant Christians have made alliances with conservative Roman Catholics and neoconservative Jews, and they have captured political power—power they have used to oppose secular humanism and naturalism. Incredibly, the Bush administration has rejected therapeutic stem cell research based on the questionable theological-moral doctrine of "ensoulment": Even discarded cells that have begun to divide are held to have "souls." Part and parcel with this is "evangelical capitalism," also allied with a triumphalist imperial foreign policy convinced that "God blesses" America in military adventures embarked upon abroad. As a result, many people are were troubled by the present Bush administration now in control of this country, and they have focused closely on the upcoming national elections of 2004—as they no doubt should.

But certain irreconcilable underlying cultural conflicts are larger than even a very important election. These conflicts must not be overlooked, for we are confronted by powerful forces eager to overthrow the basic premises of the Enlightenment. I submit that we need to awaken reenchantment with the Enlightenment; there is indeed a pressing need for a New Enlightenment, not only for America but for the global community.

Regrettably, post–World War II Parisian savants spawned a vulgar postmodernist cacophony of Heideggerian-Derridian mush. Incoherent as some of their rhetoric may be, it has been influential in its rejection of the Enlightenment, the ethics of humanism, scientific objectivity, and democratic values. This literary-philosophical movement had made great inroads in the academy, especially within humanities faculties (though, fortunately, it is already being discredited in France itself). But it has taken a terrible toll, undermining confidence in any progressive agendas of emancipation. In part such thinking is an understandable response to the two grotesque twentieth-century ideologies—fascism and Stalinism—that dominated the imagination of so many supporters in Europe and betrayed human dignity on the butcher block of repression and genocide. "After Auschwitz," wrote Theodor Adorno, we cannot praise "the grandeur of man." Surely the world has recovered from that historical period of aberrant bestiality. However, many intellectuals are still disillusioned because of the failure of Marxism to deliver on the perceived promises of socialism, in which they had invested such faith. Whatever the causes of pessimism, we cannot abandon our efforts at reform or at spreading knowledge and enlightenment. We cannot give in to nihilism or self-defeating subjectivism. Although science has often been co-opted by various military-technological powers for antihumanistic purposes, it also can help fulfill ennobling humanitarian goals.

When I say that we critically need a New Enlightenment, I mean a radical reorientation of the religious-moral outlook that now pervades so much of contemporary society. This involves a cultural reformation, the restructuring of first principles, beliefs, and values. Essential for this to occur is some confidence in the capacity of human beings to advance human knowledge, to contribute to scientific discovery, and to engage in rational inquiry. Many problems may seem intractable or hopeless. But there are no viable alternatives to using the method of intelligence. It is not faith or revelation, authority or custom, mysticism or spirituality that will save us, but diligent work and some measure of goodwill. The theist believes that only God will save us, to which I respond, "No deity will save us, we must save ourselves!"[3]

What are the distinctive characteristics of the New Enlightenment? I can only sketch some of them:

First, it is incumbent upon us to extend the methods of science and reason to all areas of human interest. This form of methodological naturalism is grounded in the recognition that the methods of science serve us as powerful tools in unlocking the secrets of nature and solving human problems. Scientific principles should be considered as hypotheses, tested by their experimental effects and predictive power, integrated into theories, and validated by their comprehensive character and mathematical elegance. They are always open to change in the light of new discoveries or more powerful theories; hence, science is fallible and self-correcting, though its methods have some degree of objectivity. Since the eighteenth-century Enlightenment, science has expanded rapidly, entering into fields never before imagined possible, such as understanding consciousness, the brain, the biological world and the genome, and the micro and macro dimensions of the universe. Using powerful instruments of observation, it has probed aspects of nature thought to be beyond reach. We should be prepared in the future to extend the methods of scientific inquiry still further to all areas of human interest. How and in what sense we can do this depends on the subject matter under consideration. In many areas, the best term to describe this process is *critical thinking*, which provides a normative model for appraising claims to truth.

Second, we need to respond to the besetting existential question, What is the meaning of life? Many theists believe that without belief in a supernatural deity, life would be meaningless. People are unable to face death, they say; only belief in life beyond the grave will console them. Science has disabused us of such primitive concepts of God and immortality, though such skepticism has not always penetrated to a wider public. We can no longer accept the ancient metaphysical-theological interpretations of reality in the light of naturalistic accounts of cosmology. Moreover, scientific and scholarly criticisms of biblical and Qur'anic texts have shown the specious character of historic claims of so-called revelations from on high. They lack confirmation or corroboration by any reliable empirical evidence.

Theists are mistaken on another count: It is possible to live a full and meaningful life in a naturalistic universe, informed by scientific knowledge and devoid of supernatural illusions. Indeed, countless generations of people have experienced satisfying, creatively enriched, and morally significant lives without belief in God. A person's life in one sense is like a work of art, blending colors, tones, lines, and forms. It is what he or she chooses to do, the sum of his or her dreams and aspirations, plans and projects, ends and goals, tragedies and successes that define who and what a person is. Our ends and values are shared with others and conditioned by the societies in which we live. In open societies that respect freedom and autonomy, an individual's choices are plural and diverse and, though that person may be highly idiosyncratic, he or she is free to pursue them as long as no harm is done to others. Democratic societies afford a wider range of opportunities for free expression than do authoritarian ones. All human beings live out their lives in a universe of order and disorder, causality and contingency, regularity and chance. It is hoped that individuals can learn from experience and modify their choices in the light of consequences. They can develop common goals and values experienced with others. Thus they can find life intrinsically worthwhile and even immensely exciting—for its own sake.

Accordingly, life can be meaningful without the need of an external religious support. Ancient religious creeds were spun out of human imagination and fantasy during the infancy of the race. At a time when disease, deprivation, danger, and premature death were the norm, people were overwhelmed by fear and ignorance, and they supplicated hidden and mysterious forces that they could not comprehend. Science is able to dissipate many of these fears. It can discover the causes of natural events and fashion the best means for overcoming adversity. Such knowledge can help us to cope with challenges—it can bolster courage and help us to survive and indeed thrive. Human beings soon learn that cooperation and empathy with their fellow humans, love, and shared experiences can enhance life and help us to achieve significant lives that are bountiful, joyful, and even exuberant.

Third, and of central significance to the New Enlightenment, is the question of ethical values. Humanist ethics can provide the basis for a new morality. This is related to eupraxsophy, that is, the understanding of good wisdom and conduct drawn from scientific inquiry and philosophical rationality. Principles and values should be tested by their consequences in practice. We learn that not all means should be used to realize ends, as some exceed the parameters of decency.

Eupraxsophy focuses on two main areas. First there are excellences intrinsic to the good life of the individual where freedom and autonomy, self-determination, and the right of privacy are respected, as well as the values of creativity, aesthetic appreciation, self-respect, self-control, and rationality. The ultimate goal is human happiness and joyful exuberance. Second are the principles of virtue and responsibility as they relate to other people in communities of transaction. These include the common moral decencies of integrity, trustworthiness, benevolence, and fairness. Humanist ethical values and principles cut across cultures. They are empirical in content and are relative to human interests and needs. They have evolved over a long period of human civilization. Objective rational criteria can be applied to the comparative evaluation of moral choices. The morally developed person learns that there are duties and obligations that emerge in the contexts of social interaction and need to be respected.

The fourth and perhaps most important humanist aspect of the New Enlightenment in ethics today is the realization that it is planetary in scope and that it entails a doctrine of universal human rights. This means that all individuals on the planet enjoy similar rights that should be protected by the world community. These are related to planetary ethics; that is, they are transcultural in reference. Unlike any movement before it, the New Enlightenment considers all members of the human family to be equal in dignity and value. Planetary ethics emphasize our mutual responsibility to protect our common habitat, the planet Earth, to guard against ecological damage and pollution. It also recognizes the need to support international laws and a world court to interpret and enforce them. This would transcend national, racial, religious, gender, and ethnic divisions, and it would encourage the growth of transnational democratic institutions. These would be charged with guaranteeing collective security and peace; ensuring universal education, cultural freedom, and open media of communication; raising the standards of living; and ensuring the prosperity of all parts of the new interdependent global society.

The New Enlightenment provides important directions for the future of humankind. It can inspire commitment from all sectors of the world. It is important that naturalists and secular humanists take the lead in pointing the way forward to the new planetary civilization that is emerging.

NOTES

1. See Paul Kurtz and Tim Madigan, eds., *Challenges to the Enlightenment: In Defense of Reason and Science* (Amherst, NY: Prometheus Books, 1994), pp. 58–59.

2. Ibid., p. 59.

3. *Humanist Manifesto II*, 1973.

Chapter 5

THE GROWTH OF ANTISCIENCE

I

It is paradoxical that today, when the sciences are advancing by leaps and bounds and when the earth is being transformed by scientific discoveries and technological applications, a strong antiscience counterculture has emerged. This contrasts markedly with attitudes toward science that existed in the nineteenth and early twentieth centuries. Albert Einstein perhaps best typified the high point of the public appreciation of scientists that prevailed at that time. Paul De Kruif, in his book *The Microbe Hunters*,[1] described the dramatic results scientists could now achieve in ameliorating pain and suffering and improving the human condition. John Dewey, perhaps the most influential American philosopher in the first half of the twentieth century, pointed out the great pragmatic benefits to humankind from the application of scientific methods of thinking to all aspects of human life. But today the mood has radically changed. A recent essay in *Time* magazine begins with the following ominous note:

[*Skeptical Inquirer* 18, no. 2 (Spring 1984): 255–63]

Scientists, it seems, are becoming the new villains of Western society.... We read about them in newspapers faking and stealing data, and we see them in front of congressional committees defending billion-dollar research budgets. We hear them in sound bites trampling our sensibilities by comparing the Big Bang or some subatomic particle to God.[2]

An editorial in *Science* magazine, referring to the *Time* essay, comments:

Does this reflect a growing antiscience attitude? If so, the new movie *Jurassic Park* is not going to help. According to both the writer and producer, the movie intentionally has antiscience undertones. Press accounts say that producer Steven Spielberg believes science is "intrusive" and "dangerous." It is not only outsiders who are being critical. In recent speeches and publications, George Brown, chairman of the House Space, Science and Technology Committee, has seemed to question the very value of science. Brown has observed that despite our lead in science and technology, we still have many societal ills such as environmental degradation and unaffordable health care. Science, he says, has "promised more than it can deliver." Freeman Dyson seems to share some of this view. In a recent Princeton speech, he states, "I will not be surprised if attacks against science become more bitter and more widespread in the next few years, so long as the economic inequities in our society remain sharp and science continues to be predominantly engaged in building toys for the rich."[3]

"Are these just isolated events, or is something more going on?" asks Richard S. Nicholson in the editorial quoted above.[4]

A further sign that science has lost considerable prestige is the recent rejection of the superconducting supercollider project by the US Congress. Although the chief reason given was the need to cut the national deficit, one cannot help but feel that this decision reflects the diminishing level of public confidence in scientific research.

II

There have always been two cultures existing side by side, as Lord C. P. Snow has shown.[5] There has been a historic debate between those who wish to advance scientific culture and those who claim that there are "two truths." According to the latter, there exists, along with cognitive scientific knowledge, a mystical and spiritual realm and/or aesthetic and subjective aspects of experience. The two cultures do not live side by side in peaceful coexistence any longer; in recent decades there have been overt, radical attacks on science that threaten its position in society.

From within philosophy, dissent has come from two influential areas. First, many philosophers of science, from Kuhn to Feyerabend, have argued that there is no such thing as scientific method, that scientific knowledge is relative to sociocultural institutions, that paradigm shifts occur for extrarational causes, and that therefore the earlier confidence that there are objective methods for testing scientific claims is mistaken.

This critique is obviously greatly exaggerated. It is true that science functions in relation to the social and cultural conditions in which it emerges, and it is true that we cannot make absolute statements in science. Nonetheless, there are reliable standards for testing claims and some criteria of objectivity, and these transcend specific social and cultural contexts. How does one explain the vast body of scientific knowledge we possess? A specific claim in science cannot be said to be the same as a poetic metaphor or a religious tenet, for it is tested by its experimental consequences in the real world.

The second philosophical attack comes from the disciples of Heidegger, especially the French postmodernists such as Derrida, Foucault, Lacan, and Lyotard. They argue that science is only one mythic system or narrative among many others. They maintain that by deconstructing scientific language, we discover that there are no real standards of objectivity. Heidegger complained that science and technology were dehumanizing. Foucault pointed out that science is often dominated by power structures, bureaucracy, and the state, and that the political and economic uses of science have undermined the pretensions of scientific neutrality. Some of these criticisms are no doubt valid, but they are overstated. If the alternative to objectivity is subjectivity, and if there are no warranted claims to truth, then the views of the postmodernists cannot be said to be true either. Surely we can maintain that the principles of mechanics are reliable, that Mars is a planet that orbits the Sun, that cardiovascular diseases can be explained causally and preventive measures taken to lower the risk, that the structure of DNA is not simply a social artifact, nor insulin a cultural creation.

The postmodern critics of "modernity" are objecting to the rationalist or foundationalist interpretations of science that emerged in the sixteenth and seventeenth centuries, and perhaps rightly so. For the continuous growth and revision of scientific theories demonstrates that any "quest for certainty" or "ultimate first principles" within science is mistaken. Nonetheless, they go too far in abandoning the entire modern scientific enterprise. The scientific approach to understanding nature and human life has been vindicated by its success, and its premises, I submit, are still valid. What are some of the characteristics of this modern scientific outlook as it has evolved today?

First, science presupposes that there *are* objective methods by which reliable knowledge can be tested. Second, this means that hypotheses and theories can be formulated and that they can be warranted (a) by reference to the evidence, (b) by criteria of rational coherence, and (c) by their predicted experimental consequences. Third, modern scientists find that mathematical quantification is a powerful tool in establishing theories. Fourth, they hold that there are causal regularities and relationships in our interactions with nature that can be discovered. Fifth, although knowledge may not be universal, it is general in the sense that it goes beyond mere subjective or cultural relativity and is rooted in an intersubjective and intercultural community of inquirers. Sixth, as the progressive and fallible character of science is understood, it is seen that it is difficult to reach absolute or final statements, that science is tentative and probabilistic, and that scientific inquiry needs to be open to alternative explanations. Previous theories are therefore amenable to challenge and revision, and selective and constructive skepticism is an essential element in the scientific outlook. Seventh is the appreciation of the fact that knowledge of the probable causes of phenomena as discovered by scientific research can be applied, that powerful technological inventions can be discovered, and that these can be of enormous benefit to human beings.

III

Yet the scientific approach, which has had such powerful effectiveness in extending the frontiers of knowledge, is now under heavy attack. Of special concern has been the dramatic growth of the occult, paranormal, and pseudosciences, and particularly the promotion of the irrational and sensational in these areas by the mass media. We allegedly have been living in the New Age. Side by side with astronomy there has been a return to astrology, and concomitant with psychology there was the growth of psychical research and parapsychology. The paranormal imagination soars; science fiction has no bounds. This is the age of space travel, and it includes abductions by extraterrestrial beings and unidentified flying objects from other worlds. The emergence of a paranormal worldview competes with the scientific worldview. Instead of tested causal explanations, the pseudosciences provide alternative explanations that compete in the public mind with genuine science. The huge increase in paranormal beliefs is symptomatic of a profound antiscience attitude, which has not emerged in isolation but is part of a wider spectrum of attitudes and beliefs.

The readers of the *Skeptical Inquirer* are no doubt familiar with the singular role of CSICOP in evaluating claims made about the paranormal and by fringe sciences. Our basic aim is to contribute to the public appreciation for scientific inquiry, critical thinking, and science education. We need to be equally concerned, I submit, about the growth of antiscience in general. The most vitriolic attacks on science in recent decades have questioned its benefits to society. To a significant extent these criticisms are based on ethical considerations, for they question the value of scientific research and the scientific outlook to humankind. Here are ten categories of such objections. There are no doubt others.[6]

1. After World War II great anxiety arose about a possible nuclear holocaust. This fear is not without foundation; for there is some danger of fallout from nuclear accidents and testing in the atmosphere, and there is the threat that political or military leaders might embark, consciously or accidentally, upon a devastating nuclear war. Fortunately, for the moment the danger of a thermonuclear holocaust has abated, though it surely has not disappeared. However, such critiques generated the fear of scientific research, and even, in some quarters, the view that physicists were diabolical beings who, in tinkering with the secrets of nature, held within their grasp the power to destroy all forms of life on this planet. The fear of nuclear radiation also applies to nuclear power plants. The accident at Chernobyl magnified the apprehension of large sectors of the world's population that nuclear energy is dangerous and that nuclear power plants should be closed down. In countries like the United States, no nuclear

power plants are being built, although France and many other countries continue to construct them. The nuclear age has thus provoked an antinuclear reaction, and the beneficent symbol of the scientist of the past, Albert Einstein, has to some been transmogrified into a Dr. Strangelove. Although some of the apprehensions about nuclear radiation are no doubt warranted, to abandon nuclear fuel entirely, while the burning of fossil fuels pollutes the atmosphere, leaves few alternatives for satisfying the energy needs of the world. This does not deny the need to find renewable resources, such as solar and wind power, but will these be sufficient?

2. The fear of science can also be traced to some excesses of the environmental movement. Although the environmentalists' emphasis on ecological preservation is a valid concern, it has led at times to the fear that human technology has irreparably destroyed the ozone layer and that the greenhouse effect will lead to the degradation of the entire planet. Such fears often lead to hysteria about all technologies.

3. In large sectors of the population, there is a phobia about any kind of chemical additive. From the 1930s to the 1950s, it was widely held that "better things and better living can be achieved through chemistry" and that chemicals would improve the human condition. Today there is, on the contrary, a widespread toxic terror—of PCBs and DDT, plastics and fertilizers, indeed of *any* kind of additive—and there is a worldwide movement calling for a return to nature, to organic foods and natural methods. No doubt we need to be cautious about untested chemical additives that may poison the ecosystem, but we should not forget that the skilled use of fertilizers led to the green revolution and a dramatic increase in food production that reduced famine and poverty worldwide.

4. Suspicion of biogenetic engineering is another dimension of the growth of antiscience. From its very inception biogenetic research has met opposition. Many feared that scientists would unleash a new, virulent strain of *E. coli* bacteria into sewer pipes—and then throughout the ecosystem—that would kill large numbers of people. Jeremy Rifkin[7] and others have demanded that all forms of biogenetic engineering research be banned because of its "dehumanizing" effect. A good illustration of this can be seen in the film *Jurassic Park*, produced by Steven Spielberg. Here not only does a Dr. Frankenstein seek to bring back the dead, but we are warned that a new diabolical scientist, in cloning dinosaurs, will unleash ominous forces across the planet. Although there may be some dangers in

biogenetic engineering, it offers tremendous potential benefit for humankind—for the cure of genetic diseases as well as the creation of new products. Witness, for example, the production of synthetic insulin.

5. Another illustration of the growth of antiscience is the widespread attack on orthodox medicine. Some of these criticisms have some merit. With the advances of the scientific revolution and the growth of medical technology, we have been able to extend human life, yet many people are kept alive against their will and suffer excruciating pain; the right to die has emerged as a basic ethical concern. Medical ethicists have correctly pointed out that the rights of patients have often been ignored by the medical and legal professions. In the past, physicians were considered authoritarian figures, whose wisdom and skills were unquestioned. But to many vociferous critics today, doctors are demons rather than saviors. The widespread revolt against animal research is symptomatic of the attack on science. Granted that animals should not be abused or made to suffer unnecessary pain, but some animal rights advocates would ban all medical research on animals.

6. Another illustration of antiscience is the growing opposition to psychiatry. Thomas Szasz has no doubt played a key role here.[8] As a result of his works, large numbers of mental patients were deinstitutionalized. *One Flew Over the Cuckoo's Nest*, by Ken Kesey,[9] dramatizes the view that it is often the psychiatrist himself, rather than the patient, who is disturbed. Many, like Szasz, even deny that there are mental illnesses, though there seems to be considerable evidence that some patients do suffer behavioral disorders and exhibit symptoms that can be alleviated by antipsychotic drugs.

7. Concomitant with the undermining of public confidence in the practice of medicine and psychiatry has been the phenomenal growth in "alternative health cures," from faith healing and Christian Science to the relaxation response, iridology, homeopathy, and herbal medicines. This is paradoxical, because medical science has made heroic progress in the conquering of disease, the development of antibiotics, and the highly successful techniques of surgical intervention. These have all been a boon to human health. But now the very viability of medical science itself has been questioned.

8. Another area of concern is the impact of Asian mysticism, particularly since World War II, whereby yoga meditation, Chinese Qigong, gurus, and spiritualists have come into the Western world arguing that these ancient forms of knowledge and therapy can lead to spiritual growth

and health in a way that modern medicine does not. Unfortunately, there are very few reliable clinical tests of these so-called spiritual cures. What we have are largely anecdotal accounts, but they hardly serve as objective tests of alternative therapies.

9. Another form of antiscience is the revival of fundamentalist religion even within advanced scientific and educational societies. Fundamentalists question the very foundation of scientific culture. Indeed, in the modern world, it is religion, not science, that seems to have emerged as the hope of humankind. Far more money is being poured into religion than into scientific research and education. Especially symptomatic is the continued growth of "scientific creationism" and widespread political opposition to the teaching of evolution in the schools, particularly in the United States.

10. A final area of antiscience is the growth of multicultural and feminist critiques of science education, particularly in the universities and colleges. The multiculturist view is that science is not universal or transcultural, but relative to the culture in which it emerges. There are, we are told, non-Western and primitive cultures that are as "true" and "valid" as the scientific culture of the Western world. This movement supports the complete relativization of scientific knowledge. The radical feminist indictment of "masculine bias" in science maintains that science has been the expression of "dead, white Anglo-Saxon males"—from Newton to Faraday, from Laplace to Heisenberg. What we must do, the extremists of these movements advise, is liberate humanity from cultural, racist, and sexist expressions of knowledge, and this means scientific objectivity as well. The positive contribution of these movements, of course, is that they seek to open science to more women and minorities. The negative dimension is that multiculturalist demands on education tend to weaken an understanding of the rigorous intellectual standards essential for effective scientific inquiry. Clearly we need to appreciate the scientific contribution of many cultures and the role of women in science throughout history; on the other hand, some multicultural critics undermine the very possibility of objective science.

IV

What I have presented is a kaleidoscope illustration of many current trends that are undermining and threatening the future growth of science. They raise many questions. Why has this occurred? How shall those who believe in the value of scientific methods and the scientific outlook respond?

This is a complex problem, and I can only suggest some possible solutions. But unless the scientific community and those connected with it are willing to take the challenge to science seriously, I fear that the tide of antiscience may continue to rise. Scientific research surely will not be rejected where there are obvious technological uses to be derived from it, at least insofar as economic, political, and military institutions find these profitable. But the decline in the appreciation of the methods of science and in the scientific outlook can only have deleterious effects upon the long-term role of science in civilization.

One reason for the growth of antiscience is a basic failure to educate the public about the nature of science itself. Of crucial significance is the need for public education in the aims of science. We need to develop an appreciation of the general methods of scientific inquiry, its relationship to skepticism and critical thinking, and its demand for evidence and reason in testing claims to truth. The most difficult task we face is to develop an awareness that the methods of science should not only be used in the narrow domains of the specialized sciences but should also be generalized, as far as possible, to other fields of human interest.

We also need to develop an appreciation for the cosmic outlook of science. Using the techniques of scientific inquiry, scientists have developed theories and generalizations about the universe and the human species. These theories often conflict with theological viewpoints that for the most part go unchallenged. They also often run counter to mystical, romantic, and aesthetic attitudes. Thus it is time for more scientists and interpreters of science to come forward to explain what science tells us about the universe: For example, they should demonstrate the evidence for evolution and point out that creationism does not account for the fossil record; that the evidence points to a biological basis for the mind and that there is no evidence for reincarnation or immortality. Until the scientific community is willing to explicate openly and defend what science tells us about life and the universe, then I fear it will continue to be undermined by the vast ignorance of those who oppose it.

In this process of education, what is crucial is the development of scientific literacy in the schools and in the communications media. Recent polls have indicated that a very small percentage of the US population has any understanding of scientific principles. The figures are similar for Britain, France, and Germany, where large sectors of the population are abysmally unaware of the nature of the scientific outlook. Thus we need to educate the public about how science works and what it tells us about the world, and we should make sure this understanding is applied to all fields of human knowledge.

The growth of specialization has made this task enormously difficult. Specialization has enabled people to focus on one field, to pour their creative talents into solving specific problems, whether in biology or physics, mathematics or economics. But we need to develop generalists as well as specialists. Much of the fear and opposition to science is due to a failure to understand the nature of scientific inquiry. This understanding should include an appreciation for what we know and do *not* know. This means not only an appreciation of the body of reliable knowledge we now possess, but also an appreciation of the skeptical outlook and attitude. The interpreters of science must go beyond specialization to the general explication of what science tells us about the universe and our place in it. This is unsettling to many within society. In one sense, science is the most radical force in the modern world, because scientists need to be prepared to question everything and to demand verification or validation of any claim.

The broader public welcomes scientific innovation. Every new gadget or product and every new application in technology, where it is positive, is appreciated for its economic and social value. What is not appreciated is the nature of the scientific enterprise itself and the need to extend the critical methods of science further, especially to ethics, politics, and religion. Until those in the scientific community have sufficient courage to extend the methods of science and reason as far as they can to these other fields, I feel that the growth of antiscience will continue.

Now it is not simply the scientists who work in the laboratory who have a social responsibility to the greater society; it is also the task of philosophers, journalists, and those within the corporate and the political world who appreciate the contribution of science to humankind. For what is at stake, in a sense, is modernism itself. Unless corporate executives and those who wield political power recognize the central role science and technology have played in the past four centuries, and can continue to play in the future, and unless science is defended, I fear that the irrational growth of antiscience may undermine the viability of scientific research and the contributions of science in the future. The key is education—education within the schools, but education also within the media. We need to raise the level of appreciation, not simply among students from grammar school through the university, but among those who control the mass media—and here, alas, the scientific outlook is often overwhelmed by violence, lurid sex, the paranormal, and religious bias.

The world today is a battlefield of ideas. In this context the partisans of science need to defend courageously the authentic role science has played and can continue to play in human civilization. The growth of antiscience must be countered by a concomitant growth in advocacy of the virtues of science. Scientists are surely not infallible; they make mistakes. But the invaluable contributions of science need to be reiterated. We need public *reenchantment* with the ideals expressed by the scientific outlook.

NOTES

1. Paul De Kruif, *The Microbe Hunters* (New York: Harcourt, Brace, 1926).

2. Dennis Overbye, "Who's Afraid of the Big Bad Bang?" *Time*, April 26, 1993.

3. Richard S. Nicholson, "Postmodernism," *Science* 261, no. 5118 (1993). Dyson's comments have been published in his essay in the Fall 1993 *American Scholar*.

4. For a useful overview, see Gerald Holton, *Science and Anti-Science* (Cambridge, MA: Harvard University Press, 1993).

5. C. P. Snow, *The Two Cultures and the Scientific Revolution* (New York: Cambridge University Press, 1959).

6. For an extreme case of antiscience paranoia, see David Ehrenfeld's *The Arrogance of Humanism* (New York: Oxford University Press, 1975), where the author virtually equates humanism with science and modernism.

7. Jeremy Rifkin, *Biosphere Politics: A New Consciousness for a New Century* (New York: Crown, 1991); Jeremy Rifkin, ed., *The Green Lifestyle Handbook* (New York: Henry Holt, 1990); Ted Howard and Jeremy Rifkin, *Who Should Play God? The Artificial Creation of Life and What It Means for the Future of the Human Race* (New York: Delacorte Press, 1977).

8. Thomas Szasz, *The Theology of Medicine* (New York: Harper and Row, 1977); *The Myth of Mental Illness*, rev. ed. (New York: Harper and Row, 1984).

9. Ken Kesey, *One Flew Over the Cuckoo's Nest* (New York: New American Library, 1962).

Section Two

SKEPTICISM AND THE NONNATURAL

Chapter 6
SKEPTICISM, SCIENCE, AND THE PARANORMAL

The term *paranormal* was not invented by the Committee for the Scientific Investigation of Claims of the Paranormal but has been widely used, first by parapsychologists and later by others, to refer to anomalous phenomena that allegedly could not be explained in terms of the existing categories of science. "Paranormal" refers to that which is "beside" or even "beyond" the range of normal experience and explanation. It is used to depict phenomena like clairvoyance, precognition, telepathy, psychokinesis, levitation, poltergeists, astral projection, automatic writing, communication with discarnate spirits, and so on.

Most skeptics deny that the term *paranormal* has any clearly identifiable meaning. Like the "noumenal," "occult," or even "supernatural," its precise referents are vague and ambiguous. The boundaries of human knowledge are constantly expanding and being refined, and what was unknowable yesterday may become scientifically explicable the next day; thus the DNA code, the concept of black holes, and newly postulated subatomic particles surely cannot be said to have been "paranormal" when they were initially proposed. Is the paranormal simply equivalent to that

["Debunking, Neutrality, and Skepticism in Science" *Skeptical Inquirer* 8, no. 3 (Spring 1984): 239–46]

which is unfamiliar or strange at one state in the development of human knowledge? If so, that would not make it unusual. The term *paranormal* has also been stretched far beyond parapsychology to other so-called mysterious powers within the universe not contained within the parameters of our existing conceptual framework. It has been used to refer to such disparate phenomena as reincarnation, life after life, biorhythms, astrology, UFOs, Chariots of the Gods, the Bermuda Triangle, monsters of the deep (whether Nessie, Chessie, or Champie), Bigfoot, cattle mutilations, human spontaneous combustion, psychic archaeology, and faith healing—in short, almost anything that comes within the range of human imagination and is thought to be "incredible."

On the current world scene, belief in the paranormal is fed and reinforced by a vast media industry that profits from it, and it has been transformed into a folk religion, perhaps the dominant one today. Curiously, it is often presented as "scientifically warranted" and as a new, if bizarre, conception of reality that is breaking down our naturalistic-materialistic view of the universe.

Contemporary science is rapidly expanding in many directions. On the macro level, astronomy reports exciting new discoveries. The quest for extraterrestrial life is one of the most dramatic adventures of our time. This is grist for science fiction and the poetic imagination, outstripping that which has been verified or is technologically feasible today. On the micro level, physicists postulate new particles in an attempt to unravel the nature of physical reality. And in the life sciences, biologists are decoding the genetic basis of life and are on the threshold of creating new forms. At the same time, the information revolution unfolds stunning new applications.

Men and women have always been fascinated by the depths of the unknown. As far back as we can trace there has been an interest in the occult and the magical. The persistence and growth of ancient paranormal beliefs in our highly educated scientific-technological civilization is a puzzling phenomenon to many of us. There are many reasons for this, not the least of which are the fast pace of scientific progress, the role of science fiction in stimulating the imagination, and the breakthrough into space beyond our planet. And so people ask, for example, why is it not possible for the mind to engage in remote viewing of far-distant scenes and events, precognate or retrocognate, or to exist in some form separate from the body? Present-day science for many seems to demonstrate that virtually *anything* is possible, and that what was once thought to be impractical or unreal can later be found to be perfectly real. And they think perhaps psi phenomena, biorhythms and horoscopes, faith healing and extraterrestrial UFOs are genuine. There is some confusion in the public mind between the possible and the actual, and for many people the fact that something is possible converts it into the actual.

Some skeptics have dissented, maintaining that since paranormal concepts contradict the basic conceptual categories by which we understand and interpret the world, they may be rejected on a priori grounds. In my view, it is difficult to impose preconceived limits on inquiry or to rule out such claims as logically "impossible." The history of science is littered with such vain attempts. Whether or not paranormal phenomena exist and, if they do, how they may be interpreted can only be determined in the last analysis within the process of scientific verification and validation and not antecedent to it.

WHAT SHOULD BE THE ROLE OF SCIENCE?

Now the question is often raised: How should science deal with the paranormal? One familiar response is that science should ignore the paranormal entirely. Many scientists until recently considered it beneath their dignity to become involved in what they viewed as patent nonsense. This has not been the response of those scientists and scholars associated with CSICOP. We believe that such claims ought to be investigated because of the widespread public interest and also because some paranormalists on the borderlands of science claim to have made significant discoveries.

If one decides to examine such claims, how does one proceed? One way is to debunk nonsensical paranormal beliefs. Martin Gardner quotes H. L. Mencken to the effect that "one horse-laugh is worth a thousand syllogisms." Some people have insisted that debunking is not an appropriate activity, particularly for academic scientists. To "debunk" means "to correct a misapprehension, to disabuse, set right, put straight, open the eyes or clear the mind, disenchant, or dispose of illusion, unfoil, unmask, or tell the truth" (*Roget's Thesaurus*). Some of the claims that are made—even by scientists and scholars—are preposterous, and debunking is not an illegitimate activity in dealing with them. Sometimes the best way to refute such a claim is to show how foolish it is, and to do so graphically. Indeed, debunking, in its place, is a perfectly respectable intellectual activity that any number of great writers have engaged in with wit and wisdom: Plato, Socrates, Voltaire, Shaw, and Mencken, to mention only some. Surely it has a place within philosophy, politics, religion, and on the borderlands of science and pseudoscience. It should not, however, be abused but should be used with caution, and it should be based upon a careful examination of the facts.

But there are dangers here: Sometimes what appears to be bunkum because it does not accord with the existing level of "common sense" may turn out to be true. Mere prejudice and dogma may supplant inquiry. If one debunks, he had better command an arsenal of facts and marshal evidence to show *why* something is improbable or even downright false.

We can ask: Does sleeping under a pyramid increase sexual potency? Do plants have ESP and will talking to them enhance their growth? Do tape recorders really pick up voices of the dead? All of these claims have been proposed by paranormalists within the past decades. They should not be rejected out of hand. On the other hand, at some point—after inquiry, not before—they may deserve forceful debunking; this is particularly the case when scholarly critiques of inflated claims go unnoticed by the public. Jeane Dixon and Uri Geller, for example, seem as unsinkable as rubber ducks—though some of us have attempted to make duck soup out of them. Thus we are concerned not simply with paranormal beliefs in the laboratory but with their dramatization in the media.

Another response to the paranormalists is to maintain that we should examine each and every claim—however far-fetched—that anyone makes, and to give it equal and impartial hearing. There are literally thousands of claims pouring forth each year. One cannot possibly deal with them all. We receive a goodly number of calls and letters every week at the offices of CSICOP from people who claim that they have prophetic powers, are reincarnated, or have been abducted aboard UFOs. Some of our critics nevertheless have insisted that this is the only appropriate response for science to make: to be neutral about them all. After all, were not Galileo and Semmelweis, and even Velikovsky, suppressed by the scientific and intellectual establishments of their day? And might not we in our day likewise reject an unconventional or heretical point of view simply because it is not in accord with the prevailing intellectual fashion? I repeat: this is a danger that we need especially to avoid. For the history of science is full of radical departures from established principles. Thus we must keep an open mind about unsuspected possibilities still to be discovered.

However, one should make a distinction between the open mind and the open sink. The former uses certain critical standards of inquiry and employs rigorous methodological criteria that enable one to separate the genuine from the patently specious, and yet to give a fair hearing to the serious heretic within the domain of science. Isaac Asimov has made a useful distinction between *endoheresies*, which are deviations made *within* science, and *exoheresies*, which are deviations made *outside* of science by those who do not use objective methods of inquiry and whose theories cannot be submitted to test, replication, validation, or corroboration. Even here one must be extremely cautious, for an exoheretic may be founding a new science. A protoscience may thus be emerging that deserves careful appraisal by the scientific and intellectual community. Or the exoheretic may simply be a crank—even though he or she may have a wide public following and be encouraged by the powerful effects of extensive media coverage. Simple neutrality in the face of this may be a form of self-deception.

Philosopher Paul Feyerabend has maintained that there are virtually no standards of scientific objectivity and that one theory can be as true as the next. But I submit that he is mistaken. If we cannot always easily demarcate antecedent to inquiry, pseudo from genuine science, we can after the fact apply critical standards of evaluation. Within these limited confines, then, I submit that some debunking is not only useful but necessary, particularly if we are to deal with the realities of belief in our media-coddled society. Given the level of ready public acceptance of the "incredible" and a tendency toward gullibility, one horse-laugh in its appropriate setting may be worth a dozen scholarly papers, though never at the price of the latter.

There is still another response to bizarre claims. In the last analysis this is the most important posture to assume: namely, if a paranormal claim is seriously proposed and if some effort is made to support it by responsible research methods, then it does warrant serious examination. I am not talking about antiscientific, religious, subjective, or emotive approaches to the paranormal, which abound, but rather efforts by serious inquirers to present hypotheses or conclusions based upon objective research. This is the case with parapsychology, which today deserves a fair and responsible hearing. Going back at least a century, some of the important thinkers—

philosophers, psychologists, and physical scientists—have investigated the psychical: William James, Henry Sidgwick, H. H. Price, Oliver Lodge, William Crookes, and more recently Gardner Murphy and J. B. Rhine. Their work deserves careful analysis, though it is not immune to strong criticism on methodological and evidential grounds. Similarly for some aspects of recent UFO and astrological research: If there are falsifiable claims and conceptually coherent theories, then they need rigorous testing and careful logical analysis by independent scientific investigation. And here neutrality in the process of evaluation is the only legitimate approach; take a hypothesis, examine the experimental data reported, attempt to replicate the experiment, make predictions, and see if the theories are logically consistent and can be verified. That this same neutrality should apply to fortune-telling, horoscopes, tarot cards, palmistry, fortune cookies, and other popular fields is another matter. Take them into the laboratory to see if you can get results. But if you get no results, then the only response often is to debunk them.

WHAT IS SKEPTICISM?

It is no secret that CSICOP has been identified with the skeptical position. We have said that we do not find adequate support for many or most of the claims of the paranormal that have been made both within and without science. We have been bitterly attacked by paranormal magazines and newspapers (such as *Fate* magazine) for publishing debunking articles at the same time these publications purvey misinformation to the public and seek to sell everything from crystal balls to Ouija boards. We believe that both debunking and careful scientific examination should be done. In regard to the latter, we often find in the parasciences a lack of replication, inadequate experimental design (as in J. B. Rhine's early experiments), and questionable interpretation of statistical data (as in the remote-viewing experiments of Targ and Puthoff). Sometimes—but only sometimes—there is fraud or deceit (as in the case of S. G. Soal, Walter Levy, and others), but underlying it all there is a strong will to believe (as Project Alpha has shown).

Skepticism is among the oldest intellectual traditions in philosophy, and it can be traced back to ancient philosophers like Carneades, Pyrrho, and Sextus Empiricus, and in modern thought to Descartes, Locke,

Berkeley, Hume, and Kant. Today skepticism is essential to the very lifeblood of scientific inquiry.

Skepticism can assume many forms. One form it may take is universal doubt, the attitude that the reality of the senses and the validity of rational inference should be mistrusted. For this form of skepticism one must adopt an *epoche* in regard to all things; that is, one must assume the role of the agnostic and suspend judgment. Since one position is as good as the next, and all positions may be equally false, none can be said to be true. In philosophy, this has led to extreme solipsism, where one doubts not only the reality of the external world but one's own existence. In ethics, it has led to extreme subjectivism, a mistrust of reason, and a denial that there are any objective ethical standards; values, it is held, are rooted in personal taste and caprice. In science, universal skepticism has led to methodological anarchism, the view that all scientific positions depend upon the mere prejudices of the scientific community and the shifts in paradigms that occur. If this is the case, astrology would be as true as astronomy and psychic phenomena as real as subatomic physics. Such a form of skepticism is easily transformed into the kind of "neutralism" discussed above—since all positions may be equally true or false, we have no way of judging their adequacy.

Universal skepticism is negative, self-defeating, and contradictory. One cannot consistently function as a total skeptic but must assume certain principles of inquiry, some of which turn out to be more reliable than others. We must act upon the best evidence we have as our beliefs confront the external world independent of our wishes. Moreover, we do have well-tested hypotheses that may be held with varying degrees of probability and incorporated into the body of knowledge. The skeptic's own universal principle that there is no reliable knowledge must apply to itself, and if so, we are led to doubt its range of applicability. A universal skepticism is limited by its own criteria. If we assume it to be true, then it is false (since if it applies to everything, it applies to itself), and hence universal skepticism cannot be universal. I do not wish to become impaled by the logic of types. The point I want to make is simply that the most meaningful form of skepticism is a *selective* one. This maintains that doubt is limited to the context of inquiry. We cannot at the same time doubt all of our presuppositions, though we may in other contexts examine each in turn. The doubt that properly emerges is within a problematic context of inquiry and thus can be settled only by the relevant evidence—though perhaps not completely.

What I mean is that the scientific community is always faced with new research problems, and it seeks solutions to these problems (a) in the theoretical sciences, through explanations of what is happening and why, and (b) in the technological and applied sciences, by resolving questions of application. There are alternative theories or hypotheses that may be proposed and compete for acceptance. Some of them may fall by the wayside; those that win out seem to accord best with the relevant data and the conceptual framework at hand, though these may in turn be eventually modified.

Clearly, a researcher should suspend judgment until she can confirm his hypothesis and until it is corroborated by other inquirers. However, no one law or theory can be said to be final or absolute, or to have reached its ultimate formulation. Here Charles Peirce's famous "principle of fallibilism" plays a role: for we may be in error, we may uncover new data, or alternative hypotheses may be found to fit the data more adequately. Thus we must be prepared to admit new hypotheses, however novel or unlikely they may at first appear. Science is open to revision of its theories. The self-corrective process is ongoing. We must always be willing to entertain and not rule out new ideas. This applies to the established sciences, but also to newly emerging proto- or parasciences.

CONCLUSION

I am often asked why belief in the paranormal is so strong in the world today, and especially in highly developed and highly educated scientific-technological societies like our own. There are many explanations that can be and have been given. I wish to conclude by mentioning only two.

First is the fact that we exist in a religious culture of long-standing historic traditions, and dissenting points of view in the area of religion are not given a fair hearing. Since belief in the supernatural and occult remains largely unchallenged, the paranormalist finds a receptive audience. There are at least two cultures existing side by side: on the one hand the religious, and on the other the rational-philosophic-scientific. Until the religious is submitted to intellectual critique openly and forthrightly, the paranormal will continue to flourish on the fringe of science.

The second reason is that although we are a scientific culture, we have not thus far succeeded in our curricula of scientific education in conveying the meaning of science. There is a widespread appreciation for the benefits of scientific technology, particularly for its economic value, as new industries are being spawned at a breathtaking pace. But at the same time there exists fear of science and its possible implications for other aspects of life.

Sadly, our elementary and high schools, and colleges and universities, turn out specialists who may be extremely competent in their narrow fields of expertise, but who lack an appreciation for the broader scientific outlook. Within their own fields students are able to master their subject matter and apply the methods of science and critical intelligence, but these methods often do not spill over to other areas of belief. In my view, a major task we face is proper education in science, both in the schools and for the general public. There is a failure to appreciate the importance of skeptical thinking. A truly educated person should come to appreciate the tentative character of much of human knowledge. The burden of proof always rests upon the claimant to warrant his claim. If all the facts do not support it, then we should suspend judgment.

Science surely is not to be taken as infallible, and some of the defects found in the pseudo- and parasciences can be found in the established sciences as well, though on a reduced scale. Scientists are fallible, and they are as prone to error as everyone else—though it is hoped that the self-corrective process of scientific inquiry will bring these errors to the light of day. Similarly, it would be presumptuous to maintain that all intelligence and wisdom is on the side of the skeptic, for he may be as liable to error as the next person. Fortunately, we have our critics and they are only too willing to point that out—for which we should be grateful. We have made mistakes and have sought to correct them. We should not trust anyone to have all the truth, and this applies to ourselves as well.

Whether life can be lived truly rationally and whether all of our beliefs can be tested before we accept them is a topic that philosophers have long debated. Suffice it to say that selective skepticism can have a constructive and positive role in life, that some degree of skepticism is important, and that reflective individuals will learn to appreciate its value.

Chapter 7

SHOULD SKEPTICAL INQUIRY BE APPLIED TO RELIGION?

The relationship between science and religion has engendered heated controversy. This debate has its roots in the historic conflict between the advocates of reason and the disciples of faith. On the current scene, there is a vocal hallelujah chorus singing praises to the mutual harmony and support of these two realms or "magisteria." I have serious misgivings about this alleged rapprochement, but I wish to focus on only one aspect of the controversy, asking: To what extent should we apply skepticism to religious claims?

By the term *skepticism* I do not refer to the classical philosophical position that denies that reliable knowledge is possible. Rather, I use the term to refer to *skeptical inquiry*. There is a contrast between two forms of skepticism, (1) that which emphasizes doubt and the impossibility of knowledge and (2) that which focuses on *inquiry* and the genuine possibility of knowledge; this latter form of skepticism ("the new skepticism," as I have labeled it),[1] skeptical inquiry, is essential in all fields of scientific research. What I have in mind is the fact that scientific inquirers formulate hypotheses to account for data and solve problems; their findings are ten-

---

[*Skeptical Inquirer* 23, no. 4 (July/August 1999): 24–28]

tative; they are accepted because they draw upon a range of confirming evidence and predictions and/or fit into a logically coherent theoretical framework. Reliable hypotheses are adopted because they are corroborated by a community of inquirers and because the tests that confirm them can be replicated. Scientific hypotheses and theories are fallible, and in principle they are open to question in the light of future discoveries and/or the introduction of more comprehensive theories. The point is that we have been able to achieve reliable knowledge in discipline after discipline because of the effective application of skeptical inquiry.

Now the central questions that have been raised concern the range of skeptical inquiry. Are there areas such as religion in which science cannot enter? In particular, should the skeptical movement extend its inquiry to religious questions? Some influential skeptics think we should not. In my view, skeptical inquirers definitely need to investigate religious claims. I do *not* think that CSICOP and the *Skeptical Inquirer*, however, should deal with religious claims; if they do so, it should be only in a limited way. I shall deal with my reasons for these perhaps surprising statements later in this chapter.

Science has always had its critics, those who have insisted that one or another area of human interest is immune to scientific inquiry. At one time it was proclaimed that scientists could never know the outermost reaches of the universe (August Comte), the innermost nature of the atom (John Locke), or human consciousness (Henri Bergson). Critics have also insisted that we could not apply science to one or another aspect of human experience—political, economic, social, or ethical behavior; the arts; human psychology; sexuality; or feeling. I do not think that we should set a priori limits antecedent to inquiry; we should not seek to denigrate the ability of scientific investigators to explain behavior or to extend the frontiers of research into new areas.

CAN THERE BE A SCIENCE OF RELIGION?

Some have argued that religious phenomena—matters of faith—are entirely beyond the ken of science, but this surely is false, because the scientific investigation of religion has already made great strides and there is a vast literature now available. We may talk about religion in at least two senses. First, religion refers to a form of *human behavior* that can be investigated. Second, it is used to refer to the *transcendental,* to that which transcends human experience or reason.

Let us turn to the first area. Religious behavior has been investigated by a wide range of disciplines: Anthropologists deal with the comparative study of primitive religions, examining prayer, ritual, the rites of passage, and the like. Sociologists have investigated the institutional aspects of religious behavior, such as the role of the priestly class in society. Ever since William James, psychologists of religion have studied the varieties of religious experience, such as mysticism, ecstasy, talking in tongues, exorcism, and so forth. Similarly, biologists have postulated a role for religious beliefs and practices in the evolutionary process and their possible adaptive/survival value. They have asked whether religiosity has a genetic or environmental basis. Others have focused on the neurological correlates of religious piety, and still others have attempted to test the efficacy of prayer.

One can deal with religion in contemporary or historical contexts. A great deal of attention has been devoted to the historical analysis of religious claims, especially since the great classical religions are based on ancient documents (the Old and New Testaments and the Koran), as are some of the newer religions (such as the nineteenth-century Book of Mormon). These texts allege that certain miraculous and revelatory events have occurred in the past and these warrant religious belief today, and it is often claimed that belief in them is based upon faith.

I would respond that scientific methodology has been used in historical investigations to examine these alleged events. Archaeologists seek independent corroborating evidence; they examine written or oral accounts that were contemporaneous with the events (for example, by comparing the Dead Sea Scrolls with the New Testament). The fields of "biblical criticism" or "koranic criticism" have attempted to use the best scholarly techniques, historical evidence, and textual and linguistic analysis to ascertain the historical accuracy of these claims.

Paranormal claims are similar to religious claims—both purport to be exceptions to natural laws. Skeptics have asked: Did D. D. Home float out of a window and levitate over a street in London in the late nineteenth century? Did the Fox sisters and Eusapia Palladino possess the ability to communicate with the dead? And they have sought to provide naturalistic interpretations for reports of bizarre events. No doubt it is easier to examine contemporaneous claims where the record is still available rather than ancient ones where the record may be fragmentary. Yet, in principle at least, the religious investigator is similar to the paranormal investigator, attempting to ascertain the accuracy of the historical record. We use similar methods of inquiry to examine prosaic historical questions, such as: Did Washington cross the Delaware? Did Thomas Jefferson sire the children of Sally Heming? The same goes for religious claims: Did the Red Sea part before the fleeing Hebrews? Was there a Great Flood and a Noah's Ark? I don't see how or why we should declare that these historical religious claims are immune to scientific investigation.

Thus I maintain that insofar as religion refers to a form of human behavior, whether in the past or the present, we can, if we can uncover corroborating data or historical records, attempt to authenticate the historical claims and ask whether there were paranormal, occult, or transcendental causes, or whether naturalistic explanations are available. David Hume's arguments against miracles indicate all the reasons we should be skeptical of ancient claims—because they lack adequate documentation, because the eyewitnesses were biased, and so on. And this should apply, in my view, to reports of revelation as well as miracles. Extraordinary claims that violate naturalistic causal regularities should require strong evidence. I don't see how anyone can protest that his or her beliefs ought to be immune to the standards of objective historical investigation, simply by claiming that they are held on the basis of faith.

A good case in point is the alleged burial shroud of Jesus, the Shroud of Turin. Meticulous carbon-14 dating by three renowned laboratories has shown that the cloth is approximately seven hundred years old and therefore most likely a forgery. The fact that believers may seek to shield their belief by proclaiming that they have faith that the shroud is genuine does not make it any more true. The same principle applies to the key miraculous revelations of the past upon which the classical religions are allegedly based. The strength of a hypothesis or belief should be a function of the empirical evidence extant brought to support it, and if the evidence is weak or spotty, then the faith claim should likewise be so regarded.

Religious belief systems are deeply ingrained in human history, culture, and social institutions that predate science, and thus it is often difficult, if not impossible, to insist upon using the standards of objective skeptical inquiry retrospectively. This is especially the case since to *believe* in a religion is more than a question of cognitive assent, for religion has its roots in ethnic or national identity, and to question the empirical or rational grounds for religious belief is to shake at the very foundations of the social order.

HOW TO DEAL WITH THE TRANSCENDENTAL?

There is a second sense of religion that is nonbehavioral. Here the key question concerns the very existence of a "transcendental, supernatural, occult, or paranormal realm" over and beyond the natural world. The scientific naturalist argues that we should seek natural causes and explanations for paranormal and religious phenomena, that we should never abandon scientific methodology, and that we should endeavor to test all claims by reference to justifying evidence and reasons. We may ask, What is the truth value of theistic claims? In the great debate between scientific or philosophical skeptics and theists, agnostics/nontheists/atheists maintain that theists have not adequately justified their case and that their claims are unlikely or implausible. I will not here review the extensive classical argument or the kinds or evidence adduced.

I do wish, however, to focus on one point that has recently emerged in the literature. And this concerns a prior question raised by analytic philosophers about the meaning of "God language." Any scientific inquiry presupposes some clarity about the meaning of its basic terms. Is religious language to be taken literally, descriptively, or cognitively, and if so, are we prepared to assert that there is some "transcendental ground, cause, creator, or purpose" to the universe? Most linguistic skeptics have sought to deconstruct religious language and have had difficulty in determining precisely to what the terms *God* or *divinity* or *transcendental being* refer. Similarly for the vague, often incoherent, use of the term *spirituality*, that is so popular today. They appear to be indefinable, even to theologians, and hence before we can say whether he, she, or it exists, we need to know precisely what is being asserted. Most God talk is nonfalsifiable, in that we would not know how to confirm or disconfirm any claim about his presence or existence. God talk is by definition difficult or impossible insofar as it transcends any possible experience or reason and lurks in a mysterious noumenal realm. There are surely many things that we do not know about the universe; but to describe the unknown as "divine" is to take a leap of faith beyond reasonable evidence.

Linguistic skeptics have held that if we are to make sense of religious language, we must recognize that it has other nondescriptive or noncognitive functions. It does not convey us truth about the world (thus competing with science or ordinary experience), but is evocative, expressive, or emotive in character, or is performatory and celebrative in a social context, or is moral in its imperative function, or it has poetic metaphorical meaning. Thus God talk should be construed primarily as a form of personal and social moral poetry. If this is the case, then religion does not give us knowledge or truth; instead it expresses mood and attitude.

I am not talking about the historical truth of Jesus's alleged resurrection or Joseph Smith's encounter with the angel Moroni or Muhammad's communication with Gabriel—these are concrete historical claims and in principle at least are available to empirical and rational inquiry and have some experiential content (even though the evidence may be fragmentary or incomplete)—but of "divinity" viewed outside of history as a transcendental being or spiritual reality. It is the latter that is incomprehensible almost by definition.

Thus religion should not compete with science about the description and explanation of natural processes in the universe. Science, not religion, deals most effectively with these questions. To claim to believe in the theory of evolution, and yet insist the "human soul" is an exception to evolutionary principles because it is created by a deity, is an illegitimate intrusion of an occult cause. Similarly, to seek to transcend the "big bang" physical theory in science by postulating a creator is to leap beyond the verifiable evidence. To say that this is justified by faith is, in my judgment, unwarranted—the most sensible posture to adopt here is that of the agnostic.

In the last analysis, religion and science are different forms of human behavior and have different functions. We may analogically ask, What is the relationship between science and sports, or science and music? These are different forms of experience, and they play different roles in human behavior. Surely neither sports nor music compete in the range of truth claims. In this sense, religion should not be taken as true or false, but as evocative, expressive, uplifting, performatory, good or bad, beautiful or ugly, socially unifying or disruptive. Historically, the claims of religion were taken as true, but this was a prescientific posture drawing upon myth and metaphor, metaphysics and speculation, not testable claims. Thus "religious truth" cannot be appealed to in order to contest the verified findings of the sciences.

I should add that I do not believe that ethics need be based on religious faith either. To maintain that the proper or exclusive role of religion is within the realm of morality (or meaning) is, I think, likewise questionable, particularly when we examine the concrete ethical recommendations made about sexual morality, divorce, abortion, euthanasia, the role of women, capital punishment, and so on. This is all the more so, given the fact that religions often disagree violently about any number of moral principles. I believe there are alternative humanistic and rational grounds for ethical judgment, based in part on scientific knowledge, but that is a topic for another paper.

SKEPTICAL INQUIRY AND RELIGION

The key question that I wish to address is, Should skeptical inquirers question the regnant sacred cows of religion? There are both theoretical and prudential issues here at stake. I can find no theoretical reason why not, but there may be practical considerations. For one, it requires an extraordinary amount of courage, today as in the past (especially in America!), to critique religion. One can challenge paranormal hucksters, mediums, psychics, alternative therapists, astrologers, and past-life hypnotherapists with abandon, but to question the revered figures of orthodox religion is another matter, for this may still raise the serious public charge of blasphemy and heresy, and this can be dangerous to one's person and career—as Salman Rushdie's fatwa so graphically demonstrates.

History vividly illustrates the hesitancy of skeptics to apply their skepticism to religious questions. In ancient Rome, Sextus Empiricus, author of *Outlines of Pyrrhonism,* defended the suspension of belief in regard to metaphysical, philosophical, and ethical issues. He did not think that reliable knowledge about reality or ethical judgments was possible. He neither affirmed nor denied the existence of the gods, but adopted a neutral stance. Since there was no reliable knowledge, Pyrrho urged that compliance with the customs and religion of his day was the most prudent course to follow. The great skeptic Hume bade his friend Adam Smith publish his iconoclastic *Dialogues concerning Natural Religion* after his death (in 1776), but

Smith declined to do so, disappointing Hume. Hume's nephew David arranged for posthumous publication. The French author Pierre Bayle (1647–1706) perhaps expressed the most thoroughgoing skepticism of his time. In his *Dictionnaire historique et critique*, Bayle presented a scathing indictment of the prevailing theories of his day, finding them full of contradictions. He was highly critical of religious absurdities. He maintained that atheists could be more moral than Christians, and that religion did not necessarily provide a basis for ethical conduct. Nonetheless, Bayle professed that he was a Christian and a Calvinist, and this was based upon pure faith, without any evidence to support it—this is known as *fideism*. Did Bayle genuinely hold these views, or was his fideism a ruse to protect his reputation and his fortune?

This form of fideism, I maintain, on theoretical grounds is illegitimate, even irrational. For if, as skeptical inquirers, we are justified in accepting only those beliefs that are based upon evidence and reason, and if there is no evidence either way or insufficient evidence, should we not suspend judgment, or are we justified in taking a leap of faith? If the latter posture of faith is chosen, one can ask, On what basis? If a person is entitled to choose to believe whatever he or she wishes, *solely* or *largely* because of personal feeling and taste, then "anything goes." But this anarchic epistemological principle can be used to distort honest inquiry. (The implication of this argument is that if we do *not* have a similar feeling, we are entitled *not to believe*.) One may ask, Can one generalize the epistemological rule, and if so, can it apply to paranormal claims? Is someone thus entitled to believe in UFO abductions, angels, or demons on the basis of feeling and fancy? The paranormal skeptic retort is that where there is not evidence to decide the question, we are not justified in believing—though in a democracy we are not entitled to expect others to share our skepticism.

But as a matter of fact, most of those who believe in the traditional religions do not base it on pure fideism alone, but on reasons and evidence. Indeed, no less an authority than Pope John Paul II maintained the same in his encyclical entitled *Fides et Ratio* (Faith and Reason). In this, the pope condemns both fideism and atheism. He attacks the naive faith in "UFOs, astrology, and the New Age." He criticizes "exaggerated rationalism" and pragmatism on the one hand and postmodernism on the other, but he also condemns the exclusive reliance on faith. The pope maintains that reason and scientific inquiry support rather than hinder faith in Christian revelation and Catholic doctrine. Skeptics might agree with the pope's defense of reason and scientific inquiry, but question whether these do indeed support his own beliefs.

Thus, in my judgment, acquiescence by skeptics to the fideist's rationalization for his or her beliefs is profoundly mistaken. Similarly, in answer to those theists who maintain that there is adequate evidence and reasons for their belief, skeptical inquirers should not simply ignore their claims, saying that they are beyond scientific confirmation, but should examine them. Since the burden of proof is always upon the claimant, skeptical inquirers may question both the fideist and the partial evidentialist in religion, if they do not believe that they have provided an adequate justified case.

CONCLUSION

The upshot of this controversy, in my judgment, is that scientific and skeptical inquirers should deal with religious claims. Not to do so is to flee from an important area of human behavior and interest and is irresponsible. Indeed, one reason why paranormal beliefs are so prominent today is because religious beliefs are not being critically examined in the marketplace of ideas.

As I have said, I do not believe, however, that CSICOP or the *Skeptical Inquirer* should in any way except tangentially deal with religious issues. But my reasons are pragmatic, not theoretical. It is simply a question of the division of labor. We lack the resources and expertise to focus on the entire range of scientific questions about religion: biblical archaeological, biblical and koranic criticism, linguistics, psychology, anthropology, sociology, the genetic or environmental roots of religion, and so forth. It would take us too far afield. We have focused on fringe science and specialized in the paranormal, and we have made important contributions here. Skeptical inquiry in principle should apply equally to economics, politics, ethics, and indeed to all fields of human interest. Surely we cannot possibly evaluate each and every claim to truth that arises. My reasons are thus practical.

But at the same time I disagree with those who counsel caution in applying scientific skepticism to the religious domain. In my view science should not be so narrowly construed that it only applies to experimental laboratory work; it should bring in the tools of logical analysis, historical research, and rational investigation. In this sense, I submit, religious claims are amenable to scientific examination and skeptical inquiry.

It is possible for a scientist to apply skeptical scientific inquiry to his or her own specialty with considerable expertise, yet he or she may not be qualified to apply the same methods of rational inquiry to other fields, and indeed may harbor religious beliefs that lack evidential support. Although disbelief about religious claims is higher among scientists (an estimated 60 percent) than the general population (perhaps 10 percent), some scientists fail to rigorously examine their own religious beliefs. They may use rigorous standards of inquiry in their particular fields of expertise, yet throw caution to the wind when they leap into questions of religious faith.

One last issue: to claim that skepticism is committed only to "methodological naturalism" and not scientific naturalism (which sums up the evidence for the naturalistic worldview and critiques the theistic/spiritualistic leap beyond) is, I think, profoundly mistaken. To adopt this neutral stance in the current cultural milieu is a cop-out, for questionable religious claims are proliferating daily and they are not adequately evaluated by skeptical scientists. In my view, we need more skeptical inquirers who possess the requisite expertise and are able to apply their investigative skills to religious claims. Such skeptical inquiry is sorely needed today. It could play a vital role in the debate between religion and science.

NOTE

1. Paul Kurtz, *The New Skepticism: Inquiry and Reliable Knowledge* (Amherst, NY: Prometheus Books, 1992).

Chapter 8

SKEPTICISM AND RELIGION

U nbelievers have debated the proper way to describe their position. Some scientists and philosophers—notably Richard Dawkins and Daniel C. Dennett—have recently been sympathetic to the use of the term *bright*. Proponents thought it a clever idea, hoping that *bright* would overcome the negative connotations that other terms such as *atheist* have aroused in the past. Many find this to be an attractive advantage. Critics of the use of *bright* have commented that it is presumptuous for us to suggest that we are "bright," that is, intelligent, implying that those with whom we disagree are dim-witted or dumb. Clearly, many people have been turned off by the term *atheism*, which they perceive as too negative or dogmatic. Others may seek refuge in some form of popular agnosticism, which suggests that they are simply uncertain about the God question—though this may simply enable them to resort to "faith" or "fideism" as an artful dodge.

I would like to introduce another term into the equation, a description of the religious "unbeliever" that is more appropriate. One may simply say, "I am a *skeptic*." This is a classical philosophical position, yet I submit that it is still relevant today, for many people are deeply skeptical about religious claims.

["Why I Am a Skeptic about Religious Claims," *Free Inquiry* 26, no. 4 (June–July 2006): 30–33]

Skepticism is widely employed in the sciences. Skeptics doubt theories or hypotheses unless they are able to verify them on adequate evidential grounds. The same is true among skeptical inquirers into religion. The skeptic in religion is not dogmatic, nor does he or she reject religious claims a priori; he or she is simply unable to accept the case for God unless it is supported by adequate evidence.

The burden of proof lies upon theists to provide cogent reasons and evidence for their belief that God exists. Faith by itself is hardly sufficient, for faiths collide—in any case, the appeal to faith to support one's creed is irrational in its pretentious claim based on the "will to believe." If it were acceptable to argue in this way, then anyone would be entitled to believe whatever he or she fancied.

The skeptic thus requires evidence and reasons for a hypothesis or belief before it is accepted. Always open to inquiry, skeptical inquirers are prepared to change their beliefs in the light of new evidence or arguments. They will not accept appeals to authority or faith, custom or tradition, intuition or mysticism, reports of miracles or uncorroborated revelations. Skeptical inquirers are willing to suspend judgment about questions for which there is insufficient evidence. Skeptics are in that sense genuinely agnostic, in that they view the question as still open, though they remain unbelievers in proposals for which they think theists offer insufficient evidence and invalid arguments. Hence, they regard the existence of any god as highly improbable.

In this sense, a skeptic is a nontheist or an atheist. The better way to describe this stance, I submit, is to say that such a person is a skeptic about religious claims.

"Skepticism," as a coherent philosophical and scientific posture, has always dealt with religious questions, and it professed to find little scientific or philosophical justification for belief in God. Philosophers in the ancient world such as Pyrrho, Cratylus, Sextus Empiricus, and Carneades questioned metaphysical and theological claims. Modern philosophers, including Descartes, Bacon, Locke, Berkeley, Hume, and Kant, have drawn heavily on classical skepticism in developing their scientific outlook. Many found the "God question" unintelligible; modern science could proceed only by rejecting occult claims as vacuous, as was done by Galileo and other working scientists—and also by latter-day authors such as Freud and Marx, Russell and Dewey, Sartre and Heidegger, Popper and Hook, Crick and Watson, Bunge and Wilson.

The expression "a skeptic about religious claims" is more appropriate in my opinion than the term *atheist*, for it emphasizes inquiry. The concept of inquiry contains an important constructive component, for inquiry leads to scientific wisdom—human understanding of our place in the cosmos and the ever-increasing fund of human knowledge.

In what follows, I will outline some of the evidence and reasons many scientists and philosophers are skeptical of theistic religious claims. I will focus primarily on supernatural theism and especially on monotheistic religions that emphasize command ethics, immortality of the soul, and an eschatology of heaven and hell. Given space limitations, what follows is only a thumbnail sketch of the case against God.

Succinctly, I maintain that the skeptical inquirer is dubious of the claims

1. that God exists;
2. that he is a person;
3. that our ultimate moral principles are derived from God;
4. that faith in God will provide eternal salvation; and
5. that one cannot be good without belief in God.

I reiterate that the burden of proof rests upon those who believe in God. If they are unable to make the case for belief in God, then I have every right to remain a skeptic.

Why do skeptics doubt the existence of God?

First, because the skeptical inquirer does not find the traditional concept of God as "transcendent," "omnipotent," "omnipresent," or "omni-beneficent" to be coherent, intelligible, or meaningful. To postulate a transcendent being who is incomprehensible to the human mind (as theologians maintain) does not explain the world that we encounter. How can we say that such an indefinable being exists, if we do not know in what sense that being is said to exist? How are we to understand a God that exists outside space and time and that transcends our capacity to comprehend his essence? Theists have postulated an unknowable "X." But if his content is unfathomable, then he is little more than an empty, speculative abstraction. Thus, the skeptic in religion presents semantic objections to God language, charging that it is unintelligible and lacks any clear referent.

A popular argument adduced for the existence of this unknowable entity is that he is the first cause, but we can ask of anyone who postulates this, "What is the cause of this first cause?" To say that he is uncaused only pushes our ignorance back one step. To step outside the physical universe is to assume an answer by a leap of faith.

Nor does the claim that the universe manifests intelligent design explain the facts of conflict, the struggle for survival, and the inescapable tragedy, evil, pain, and suffering that is encountered in the world of sentient beings. Regularities and chaos do not necessarily indicate design. The argument from design is reminiscent of Aristotle's teleological argument that there are purposes or ends in nature. But we can find no evidence for purpose in nature. Even if we were to find what appears to be design in the universe, this does not imply a designer for whose existence there is insufficient evidence.

The evolutionary hypothesis provides a more parsimonious explanation of the origins of species. The changes in species through time are better accounted for by chance mutations, differential reproduction, natural selection, and adaptation, rather than by design. Moreover, vestigial features such as the human appendix, tailbone, and male breasts and nipples hardly suggest adequate design; the same is true for vestigial organs in other species. Thus, the doctrine of creation is hardly supported in empirical terms.

Another version of the intelligent design argument is the so-called fine-tuning argument. Its proponents maintain that there is a unique combination of "physical constants" in the universe that possess the only values capable of sustaining life, especially sentient organic systems. This they attribute to a designer God. But this too is inadequate. First, because millions of species are extinct; the alleged "fine-tuning" did nothing to ensure their survival. Second, great numbers of human beings have been extinguished by natural causes such as diseases and disasters. The Indian Ocean tsunami of 2004 that suddenly killed more than two hundred thousand innocent men, women, and children was due to a shift in tectonic plates. This hardly indicates fine-tuning—after all, this tragedy could have been avoided had a supposed fine-tuner troubled to correct defects in the surface strata of the planet. A close variant of the fine-tuning argument is the so-called anthropic principle, which is simply a form of anthropomorphism; that is, it reads into nature the fondest hopes and wishes of believers, which are then imposed upon the universe. But if we are to do this, should we not also attribute the errors and mistakes encountered in nature to the designer?

Related to this, of course, is the classical problem of evil. If an omnipotent, omnipresent, and omnibeneficent God is responsible for the world as we know it, then how to explain evil? Surely, humans cannot be held responsible for a massive flood or plague, for example; we can explain such calamities only by inferring that God is malevolent—because he knew of, yet permitted, terrible destructive events to occur—or by suggesting that God is impotent to prevent evil. This would also suggest an unintelligent, deficient, or faulty designer.

The historic religions maintain that God has revealed himself in history and that he has manifested his presence to selected humans. These revelations are not corroborated by independent, objective observers. They are disclosed, rather, to privileged prophets or mystics, whose claims have not been adequately verified; there is insufficient circumstantial evidence to confirm their authenticity.

To attribute inexplicable events to miracles performed by God, as declared in the so-called sacred literature, is often a substitute for finding their true causes scientifically. Scientific inquiry is generally able to explain alleged "miracles" by discovering natural causes.

The Bible, Qur'an, and other classical documents are full of contradictions and factual errors. They were written by human beings in ancient civilizations, expressing the scientific and moral speculations of their day. They do not convey the eternal word of God, but rather the yearnings of ancient tribes based on oral legends and received doctrines; as such, they are hardly relevant to all cultures and times. The Old and New Testaments are not accurate accounts of historical events. The reliability of the Old Testament is highly questionable in the events and personages it depicts; Moses, Abraham, Joseph, and so on are largely uncorroborated by historical evidence. As for the New Testament, scholarship has shown that none of its authors knew Jesus directly. The four Gospels were not written by eyewitnesses but are products of oral tradition and hearsay. There is but flimsy and contradictory evidence for the virgin birth, the healings of Jesus, and the Resurrection.

Similarly, contrary to Muslim claims that that religion's scriptures passed virtually unmediated from Allah, there have in fact been several versions of the Qur'an; it is no less a product of oral traditions than the Bible. Likewise, the provenance of the Hadith, allegedly passed down by Muhammad's companions, has not been independently confirmed by reliable historical research.

Some claim to believe in God because they say God has entered into their personal lives and has imbued them with new meaning. This is a psychological or phenomenological account of a person's inner experience. It is hardly adequate evidence for the existence of a divine being independent of human beings' internal soliloquies. Appeals to mystical experiences or private subjective states hardly suffice as evidential support that some external being or force caused such altered states of consciousness; skeptical inquirers have a legitimate basis for doubt, unless or until such claims of interior experience can somehow be independently corroborated. Experiences of God or gods, or angels or demons, talking to one may disturb or entrance those persons who undergo such experiences, but the question is whether these internal subjective states have external veracity. This especially applies to those individuals who claim some sort of special revelation from on high, such as the hearing of commandments.

Second, is God a person? Does he take on human form? Has he communicated in discernible form, say, as the Holy Spirit, to Moses, Abraham, Jesus, Muhammad, or other prophets?

These claims again are uncorroborated by objective eyewitnesses. They are rather promulgated by propagandists of the various faith traditions that have been inflicted on societies and enforced by entrenched ecclesiastical authorities and political powers. They are supported by customs and traditions buried for millennia by the sands of time and institutional inertia. They are simply assumed to be true without question.

The ancient documents alleging God's existence are preliterate, prephilosophical, and, in any case, unconfirmed by scientific inquiry. They are often eloquent literary expressions of existential moral poetry, but they are unverified by archeological evidence or careful historical investigation. Moreover, they contradict each other in their claims of authenticity and legitimacy.

The ancient faith that God is a person has not been corroborated by the historical record. Such conceptions of God are anthropomorphic and anthropocentric, reading into the universe human predilections and feelings. "If lions had gods they would be lionlike in character," said Xenophon. Thus, human gods are an extrapolation of human hopes and aspirations, fanciful tales of imaginative fiction.

Third, the claim that our ultimate moral values are derived from God is likewise highly suspect. The so-called sacred moral codes reflect the sociohistorical cultures out of which they emerged. For example, the Old Testament commands that adulterers, blasphemers, disobedient sons, bastards, witches, and homosexuals be stoned to death. It threatens collective guilt: Punishment is inflicted by Jehovah on the children's children of unbelievers. It defends patriarchy and the dominion of men over women. It condones slavery and genocide in the name of God.

The New Testament consigns "unto Caesar the things that are Caesar's"; it demands that women be obedient to their husbands; it accepts faith healing, exorcisms, and miracles; it exalts obedience over independence, fear and trembling over courage, and piety over self-determination.

The Qur'an does not tolerate dissent, freedom of conscience, or the right to unbelief. It denies the rights of women. It exhorts jihad, holy war against infidels. It demands utter submission to the Word of God as revealed by Muhammad. It rejects the separation of mosque and state, thus installing the law of sharia and the theocracy of imams and mullahs.

From the fatherhood of God, contradictory moral commandments have been derived; theists have often lined up on opposite sides of moral issues. Believers have stood for and against war; for and against slavery; for and against capital punishment, some embracing retribution, others mercy and rehabilitation; for and against the divine right of kings, slavery, and patriarchy; for and against the emancipation of women; for and against the absolute prohibition of contraception, euthanasia, and abortion; for and against sexual and gender equality; for and against freedom of scientific research; for and against the libertarian ideals of a free society.

True believers have in the past often found little room for human autonomy, individual freedom, or self-reliance. They have emphasized submission to the word of God instead of self-determination, faith over reason, credulity over doubt. All too often they have had little confidence in the ability of humans to solve problems and create a better future by drawing on their own resources. In the face of tragedy, they supplicate to God through prayer instead of summoning the courage to overcome adversity and build a better future. The skeptic concludes, "No deity will save us; if we are to be saved it must be by our own efforts."

The traditional religions have too often waged wars of intolerance not only against other religions or ideologies that dispute the legitimacy of their divine revelations but even against sects that are mere variants of the same religion (e.g., Catholic versus Protestant, Shiite versus Sunni). Religions claim to speak in the name of God, yet bloodshed, tyranny, and untold horrors have often been justified on behalf of holy creeds. True believers have all too often opposed human progress: the abolition of slavery, the liberation of women, the extension of equal rights to trans-gendered people and gays, the expansion of democracy and human rights.

I realize that liberal religionists generally have rejected the absolutist creeds of fundamentalism. Fortunately, they have been influenced by modern democratic and humanistic values, which mitigate fundamentalism's inherent intolerance. Nevertheless, even many liberal believers embrace a key article of faith in the three major Abrahamic religions, Christianity, Islam, and Judaism: the promise of eternal salvation.

Fourth, we are driven to ask: Will those who believe in God actually achieve immortality of the soul and eternal salvation as promised? The first objection of the skeptic to this claim is that the forms of salvation being offered are highly sectarian. The Hebrew Bible promises salvation for the chosen people; the New Testament, the Rapture to those who have faith in Jesus Christ; the Qur'an, heaven to those who accept the will of Allah as transmitted by Muhammad.

In general, these promises are not universal but apply only to those who acquiesce to a specific creed, as interpreted by priests, ministers, rabbis, or mullahs. Bloody wars have been waged to establish the legitimacy of the papacy (between Protestantism, Roman Catholicism, and Eastern Orthodoxy), the priority of Muhammad and the Qur'an, and the authenticity of the Old Testament.

A second objection is that there is insufficient scientific evidence for the claim that the "soul" can exist separate from the body and that it can survive death as a "discarnate" being, and much less for the claim that it can persist throughout eternity. Science points to the fact that the "mind" or "consciousness" is a function of the brain and nervous system and that with the physical death of the body, the "self" or "person" disappears. Thus, the claim that a person's soul can endure forever is supported by no evidence whatever, only by pious hope.

Along the same line, believers have never succeeded in demonstrating the existence of the disembodied souls of any of the billions who went before us. All efforts to communicate with such discarnate entities have been fruitless. Sightings of alleged ghosts have not been corroborated by reliable eyewitness testimony.

The appeal to near-death experiences simply reports the phenomeno-logical experiences of persons who undergo part of the dying process but ultimately do not die. Of course, we never hear from anyone who has truly died by any clinical standard, gone to "the other side," and returned. In any case, these subjective experiences can be explained in terms of natural, psychological, and physiological causes.

Fifth, theists maintain that one cannot be good unless one believes in God. Skepticism about God's existence and divine plan does not imply pessimism, nihilism, the collapse of all values, or the implication that "any-thing goes." It has been demonstrated time and again, by countless human beings, that it is possible to be morally concerned with the needs of others, to be a good citizen, and to lead a life of nobility and excellence, all without religion. Thus, anyone can be righteous and altruistic, compas-sionate and benevolent, without belief in a deity. A person can develop the common moral virtues and express a goodwill toward others without devo-tion to God. It is possible to be empathetic toward others and at the same time be concerned with one's own well-being. Secular ethical principles and values thus can be supported by evidence and reason, the cultivation of moral growth and development, the finding of common ground that brings people together. Our principles and values can be vindicated as we examine the consequences of our choices and modify them in light of experience. Skeptics who are humanists focus on the good life here and now. They exhort us to live creatively, seeking a life full of happiness, even joyful exuberance. They urge us to face life's tragedies with equanimity, to marshal the courage and stoic forbearance to live meaningfully in spite of adversity, and to take satisfaction in our achievements. Life can be relished and is intrinsically worthwhile for its own sake, without any need for external support.

Though ethical values and principles are relative to human interests and needs, that does not suggest that they are necessarily subjective. Instead, they are amenable to objective, critical evaluation and modifica-tion in the light of reason. A new paradigm has emerged that integrates skepticism with secular humanism, a paradigm based on scientific wisdom, eupraxsophy, and a naturalistic conception of nature. Thus, the skeptic in religion who is also a humanist in ethics can be affirmative and positive about the potentialities for achieving the good life. Such a person can not only live fully but can also be morally concerned about the needs of others.

In summary, the skeptical inquirer finds inconclusive evidence—and thus insufficient reason to believe—that God exists, that God is a person, that all ethical principles must be derived from God, that faith in divinity will enable the soul to achieve eternal salvation, and that ethical conduct is impossible without belief in God.

On the contrary, skepticism based on scientific inquiry leaves room for a naturalistic account of the universe. It can also recommend alternative secular and humanist forms of moral conduct. Accordingly, one can simply affirm, when asked if he or she believes in God, "No, I do not; I am a skeptic," and one may add, "I believe in doing good!"

Chapter 9

ARE SCIENCE AND RELIGION COMPATIBLE?

There have been many conferences recently discussing the relationship between science and religion. The Templeton Foundation, for example, has supported numerous conferences on this theme. Many of those participating in these discussions apparently assume that science and religion are compatible. They argue that there is no contradiction between them, and some even maintain that science confirms the basic principles of religious faith. I suspect that most of the participants of this conference, made up predominantly of skeptics and nontheists, do not agree.

There are many areas where religionists and scientists make radically different truth claims. Some of them are: (1) Does the soul or consciousness exist as a separate and distinct entity, or is it a function of the brain? (2) Does science provide evidence for "intelligent design," or does evolutionary biology suffice without it? (3) Is it possible to influence the healing of persons by praying for them at a distance, or are the tests performed completely unreliable? (4) Is there empirical evidence for the claim that "near-death experiences" enable us to reach "the other side," or are there alternative physiological and psychological explanations for these experi-

[*Skeptical Inquirer* 26, no. 2 (March/April 2002): 42–45]

ences? (5) Can mediums under certain conditions communicate with deceased persons, or are the protocols of such tests too loose? (6) Does the big bang hypothesis in astronomy point to God as the cause of the universe, or is the latter claim beyond science and purely speculative?

In dealing with the above topics various questions emerge: Are coherent theories and testable hypotheses presented? If so, what is the evidence for them? Do paranormal-spiritual-religious explanations survive critical scrutiny? Skeptics have focused on the examination of paranormal claims. They do not deal with religious claims per se, unless they can be examined empirically. Secular humanists, on the other hand, do wish to deal with religious claims, testing them as best they can. Interestingly, in recent years the borderlines between the paranormal and religion have blurred, and it is often difficult to tell when we are dealing with paranormal or religious phenomena. Thus spiritualism, near-death experiences, and communication with dead people interest both paranormal and religious investigators. Similarly for the appeal to intelligent design—a classical philosophical argument now introduced within evolutionary biology and cosmology.

I have proposed that we use the term *paranatural* to refer to religious claims that are capable of some empirical resolution and are not transcendental or supernatural. In this sense they are similar to testable paranormal claims.

A good example of the overlap is in the popular belief that mysterious, intelligent, and beneficent extraterrestrial beings are visiting earthlings and floating them aboard spaceships. This is a quasi-religious phenomenon reminiscent of angels and other divine or semidivine beings of earlier ages. The disappearance of the Roswell aliens is not unlike the empty tomb of the New Testament!

In order to analyze the relationship between science and religion, we need to define and characterize each domain. Many consider that religion offers a special kind of higher spiritual truth. They maintain that there are two truths: (1) the truths of science, employing the methods of scientific inquiry and testing claims empirically, rationally, and experimentally; and (2) the truths of religion, which transcend the categories of empirical fact and logic. Skeptics are rightly dubious of this latter claim.

The most reliable methods, they insist, are those that satisfy the objective standards of verification and justification. The historic claims of revelation in the ancient sacred texts are insufficiently corroborated by reliable eyewitnesses or are based upon questionable oral traditions. These were compiled many decades, even centuries, after the alleged death of the prophets. Many miraculous claims found in the Bible and the Qur'an—for example, the claims of healings and exorcisms within the New Testament or the creationist account in the Old Testament—are unreliable. They express the primitive science of an ancient nomadic and agricultural people, and do not withstand contemporary scientific scrutiny.

Unfortunately, some proponents of the historic religions have often used their creeds in order to block or censor scientific inquiry. Freedom of inquiry within science is essential for human civilization; any effort to limit scientific research is counterproductive.

A good illustration of this is the present effort of some to restrict embryonic stem cell research on moral or religious grounds. It is argued that once a cell begins to divide, even if only six or eight cells, a "soul" of a person is already implanted, and that any effort to experiment with this is "immoral." The postulation of a soul to prohibit scientific inquiry is reminiscent of the suppression of Galileo and the teaching of Darwinism. Thus, insofar as religion claims to provide some overall imprimatur for scientific research, we need a separation of religion and science.

A second area concerns the relationship between science and morality. I raise this question here because many people think that the main function of religion is moral. Stephen Jay Gould in the *Skeptical Inquirer* talked about two magisteria, science and religion, which he says do not compete and do not contradict each other.[1] The domain of science deals with truth, he says, and that of religion with ethics. I think this position is mistaken. Indeed I would argue that there also ought to be a separation between ethics and religion. Religionists have no special competence in framing moral judgments. I say this because a great effort has been expended in the history of ethics—from Aristotle to Spinoza, Kant, John Stuart Mill, and John Dewey—to demonstrate that ethics can be autonomous and that it is possible to frame ethical judgments on the basis of rational inquiry. There are a logic of judgments of practice, rules of effective decision making, and ethical knowledge that we can develop quite independently of a religious framework. Science has a role to play here, for it can expand the means at our disposal (technology) and it can modify value judgments in the light of the facts of the case and their consequences. Many people today mistakenly believe that you cannot be moral without religious foundations. Ever since the Renaissance, the secularization of morality has continued quite independently of religious commandments.

A third area that has been hotly debated in the modern world is the relationship between religion and the state. Most democrats today defend the separation of religion and the state; they say that although religionists have every right to express their point of view in the public square, religion should be primarily a private matter. Religions should not seek to impose their fundamental moral principles on the entire society. Democratic states should be neutral about professing religious principles.

What, then, is the proper domain of religion? Is anything left to religion? My answer is in the affirmative. This may surprise skeptics, but I think religion and science are compatible, depending of course on what is meant by religion. Religion has performed an important function that cannot be simply dismissed. Religions will continue with us in the foreseeable future and will not easily wither away. No doubt my thesis is controversial: Religious language, I submit, is not primarily descriptive; nor is it prescriptive. The descriptive and explanatory functions of language are within the domain of science; the prescriptive and normative are the function of ethics. Both of these domains, science and ethics, have a kind of autonomy. Certainly within the political domain, religionists do not have any special competence, and similarly for the moral domain. It should be left to every citizen of a democracy to express his or her political views. Likewise for the developing moral personality who is able to render moral judgments.

If this is the case, what is appropriate for the religious realm? The domain of the religious, I submit, is evocative, expressive, emotive. It presents moral poetry, aesthetic inspiration, performative ceremonial rituals, which act out and dramatize the human condition and human interests, and seek to slake the thirst for meaning and purpose. Religions—at least the religions of revelation—deal in parables, narratives, metaphors, stories, and myths; they frame the divine in human (anthropomorphic) form. They express the existential yearnings of individuals endeavoring to cope with the world that they encounter and find meaning in the face of death. Religious language in this sense is eschatological. Its primary function is to express *hope*. If science gives us truth; morality, the good and the right; and politics, justice, religion is the realm of promise and expectation. Its main function is to overcome despair and hopelessness in response to human tragedy, adversity, and conflict—the brute, inexplicable, contingent, and fragile facts of the human condition. Under this interpretation religions are not primarily true, nor are they primarily good or right, or even just; they are, if you will, evocative, attempting to transcend contrition, fear, anxiety, and remorse, providing balm for the aching heart—at least for many people, if not all.

I would add to this the fact that religious systems of belief, thought, emotion, and attitude are products of the creative human imagination. They traffic in fantasy and fiction, taking the promises of long-forgotten historical figures and endowing them with eternal cosmic significance.

The role of creative imagination, fantasy, and fiction should not be dismissed. These are among the most powerful expressions of human dreams and hopes, ideals and longings. Who could have imagined that J. K. Rowlings's Harry Potter series of books or J. R. R. Tolkien's *Lord of the Rings* would so entrance young people, or that so many humans would be so fascinated by fictionalized novels, movies, and plays? The creative religious imagination weaves tales of consolation and of expectation. They are dramatic expressions of human longing, enabling humans to overcome grief and depression.

In the above interpretation of religion as dramatic existentialist poetry, science and religion are not necessarily incompatible, for they address different human interests and needs.

A special challenge to naturalism emerges at this point. I think most of us might agree that *methodological naturalism* is the basic epistemological principle of the sciences, namely, that we should seek natural, causal explanations for phenomena, testing these by the methods of science. *Scientific naturalism*, on the other hand, goes beyond this, because it rejects as nonevidential the postulation of occult metaphors, the invoking of divine forces, spirits, ghosts, or souls to explain the universe; and it tries to deal in materialistic, physical-chemical, or nonreductive naturalistic explanations. The frenzied opposition to Darwinism today is clearly based upon fear that scientific naturalism will undermine religious faith.

If this is the case, the great challenge to scientific naturalism is not in the area of truth but in that of hope, not of the good but of promise, not of the just but of expectation—in the light of the tragic character of the human condition. This is in stark contrast with the findings of neo-Darwinism, which recognizes that death is final, not simply the death of each individual but the possible extinction some day in the remote future of the human species itself. Evolutionists have discovered that millions of species have become extinct. Does not the same fate await the human species? Cosmological scientists indicate that at some point it seems likely that our sun will cool down, indeed, looking into the future, that a "big crunch" may overtake the entire universe. Others talk about a deep freeze. Some star trekkers are inspired by science fiction. They say that one day perhaps we will leave Earth to inhabit other planets and galaxies. Nonetheless, at some point the death not only of the individual but of our species, our planet, and our solar system seems likely.

What does this portend for the ultimate human condition? We live in an epoch where the dimensions of the universe have expanded enormously on both the micro and the macro level. We are talking about billions of light years in dimension. Much of this is based on speculative extrapolation. Nonetheless, we can ask, Does the naturalistic picture crush human aspiration? Does it destroy and undermine hope? Does it provide sufficient consolation for the human spirit? From this perspective, the central issue for humans is the question of human courage. Can we live a full life in the face of ultimate human extinction? These are large-scale questions, yet they are central for the religious consciousness. Can scientific naturalism, insofar as it undermines theism, provide an alternative dramatic, poetic rendering of the human condition, offering hope and promise? Countless numbers of brave individuals can live significant lives and even thrive accepting the possible far death of the species and our solar system. But so many other humans—perhaps the bulk of humankind—cannot bear that thought. They crave immortality, and religion satisfies their need. Many others do not stay awake nights worrying what will happen five, ten, or fifteen billion years from now. They find life worthwhile for its own sake here and now.

In conclusion, let me say that we are living through a period of exacerbated religiosity in the United States. There seems to be a new spiritual paradigm emerging, contesting both scientific and methodological naturalism. The United States is an anomaly in this regard, especially in contrast with the decline of religious belief in Europe. Recent scientific polls of belief in European countries—France, Germany, England, and others —as well as Japan indicate that the level of belief in a deistic being and the institutionalized practice of organized religion have declined considerably, yet these highly secular societies exemplify good moral behavior, and are far less violent than the United States. The view that without religion you cannot have a meaningful life or high motivation is thus thrown into question. We should not take the current religious bias regnant in America today as necessarily universal for all cultures.

NOTE

1. Stephen J. Gould, "Non-Overlapping Magisteria," *Skeptical Inquirer* 23, no. 4 (July/August 1999).

Section Three

SKEPTICISM IN THE HUMAN WORLD

Chapter 10

SKEPTICISM AND POLITICAL INQUIRY

THREE KINDS OF SKEPTICISM IN POLITICS

I t is apparent that the ethical choices of individuals cannot be dealt with separately from the political and social institutions that regulate their conduct in terms of how they live and function. Many ethical issues can only be resolved within the public square, yet it is forever rife with controversy. If ever there was an arena that needed skeptical inquiry, it is in the political domain. For in the modern world, political ideology has served as the chief moral inspiration for large sectors of humankind. It is not God or the afterlife, but the building of the just society that has moved men and women to dedication and devotion. Historically, more individuals have benefited from or been abused by the state than perhaps by any other social institution. The emergence of the city-state, the empire, and the nation-state has brought great good, but it also has inflicted great harm: first, because it is the state or government that has the power to make, interpret, and apply the law; and second, because the state generally possesses a preponderance of coercive military and police force. It alone has

[*The New Skepticism* (1992): pp. 303–305, 322–25]

the supreme authority to tax, regulate, and control the lives of its citizens and, if it so wishes, to enforce its decrees and compel obedience to them. It has been primarily the national state that has waged ferocious wars of mass genocide and destruction. Although many positive programs have been enacted to fulfill human needs and to protect the health, safety, welfare, and property of its citizens, often the opposite has occurred. Political ideologies have both inspired unquestioning commitment and engendered skeptical disenchantment. Indeed, political philosophers compete with theologians in spinning out theories of mystification. No wonder that a downright distrust of all ideological programs and politicians has emerged for large sectors of public opinion.

There are three forms of political skepticism that correspond to the kinds of epistemological and ethical skepticism discussed in this book's opening chapters and in the next chapter. The first is *political nihilism, total negative skepticism, and subjectivism.* This position claims that there are no objective standards of judgment by which we may evaluate the policies of statecraft. For this viewpoint, justice, in the last analysis, is simply based upon sentiment, convention, or power—nothing more and nothing less.

If we were to accept this extreme interpretation of political decision making, one form of political rule would be as good as the next. There would be no grounds for criticizing tyrannical laws other than that a person or group finds them emotionally repugnant. Any opposition to or support of fascism or Stalinism, for example, would simply be a question of taste or caprice. Such nihilism in politics, as in ethics, is contradicted by experience, for we constantly formulate political and ethical judgments, and we attempt to justify them by argument and evidence. To deny that any objective considerations are present is to reduce politics to irrational feelings or brute force.

The second is *mitigated skepticism*, which recognizes that in spite of relativity of political power and the rule of sentiment and self-interest, we need to live and work together, and hence some principles of justice need to be developed. Here some rational standards are introduced to justify social polity. This marks a decided advance over political nihilism. Are the criteria to which the mitigated skeptic defers—such as an appeal to the greatest-happiness principle or the common good—based solely upon sentiment, and are these standards without justification? In the last analysis, does everything reduce to subjectivity? I submit that this is not the case, for the mitigated skeptics at the very least recognize that there are principles of prudential rationality and pragmatic effectiveness that they appeal to in order to guide policy, and these are not based solely upon taste or sentiment.

The third is the full application of *skeptical inquiry* to the political domain. Here the method of critical intelligence is relevant to affairs of state and to the formulation of judgments of practice in all social institutions. Nonetheless, skeptical inquiry is based upon a healthy mistrust of leadership and possible abuses of power. Yet it is still possible to work out wise decisions, not only on prudential grounds but even concerning our ends and goals, which are not *simply* a matter of sentiment and can be modified in the light of reason and practice.

SKEPTICAL INQUIRY

At this point, let me return to the key challenge that I raise elsewhere in this book: Can skepticism help us to frame judgments of practice? My answer is in the affirmative. Skepticism need not be totally negative. It can be used as a tool of inquiry applicable to a wide range of practical concerns, including politics and economics. Thus a constructive skepticism can employ objective methods of inquiry and can draw upon the sciences to frame wise decisions. Matters are thus not hopelessly muddled beyond repair, in spite of the human tendency to illusion. Some *political and economic skepticism* serves as an antidote. It should be an essential ingredient of any educated mind. Without honest critics of the dominant shibboleths of the age, there is always the danger that ideological and political nostrums will be swallowed, with disastrous consequences.

There is something banal about the nonsense masked as received doctrine that often dominates political discourse. Every society needs leaders with long-range visions, able to analyze social conditions and provide thoughtful policies. Yet at the same time there is the familiar lure of a Pied Piper, who tempts lemmings into following him as he marches into the sea. The beginning of public wisdom is the development of some intelligent mistrust of leaders and of skepticism about easy ideological solutions and quick fixes. This need not be overly negative or so destructive that it would be impossible for anyone to assume the mantle of leadership. There ought to be an end to excessively parochial party politics—the belief that Our

Party has discovered Truth, Justice, and Piety, and that other parties are made of fools. No one is perfect. Statesmen ought to be able to admit that they have made mistakes. They need a touch of humility and a sense of their own fallibility. We need reflective men and women in positions of leadership who are willing to learn from experience and to modify programs in the light of criticism or altered circumstances, without being castigated as being contradictory or hypocritical. But to develop such leadership entails some capacity for reflective intelligence in the public at large and an educated approach to social problems. Skeptical inquiry cannot work unless there is an appreciation for how it works.

Let us turn our attention to what I think is the constructive use of skeptical inquiry on the level of political decision making, but not without reminding the reader of the special pitfall of unexamined political abstractions perverting public discourse, and that it is necessary to see through the sacred cows of the day. I have mentioned only some that have inordinate roles, particularly in recent history; but there are many others that we have not examined. There is always the danger that new and even more virulent ideologies able to seize the imagination will emerge, become mass movements, and inundate human civilization with new forms of nonsense. The best therapy for all of this, I reiterate, is a sufficient dose of skepticism.

How can skeptical inquiry function in the political domain? First, the claims to political truths should be considered as *hypotheses*. Second, they ought to be tested within the process of inquiry by appraising the evidence brought to bear in their support. They should to be judged by their *consequences*—that is, how they work out in practice. Third, they should be related to other policies and rules of conduct that we have adopted and consider reasonable. Here, the criterion is *logical coherence*. Fourth, policies should be evaluated on a *comparative scale*, weighed in balance with other alternatives. If and when such policies are judged as reliable, they then may become incorporated into the body of knowledge and may serve as guides to future conduct. We already possess a large fund of technological knowledge and applied expert opinion. In economic matters we draw upon the prescriptions of economists, financial consultants, auditors, and accountants. In political questions we may consult political scientists, sociologists, and policy advisers. In other fields, educators, psychologists, psychiatrists, doctors, or social scientists may be called upon for advice. The point is that there are teams of specialists who can assist us in making wise choices.

There is, however, some danger in believing that experts, philosopher-kings, technocrats, behavioral engineers, and bureaucratic planners can relieve us of the burden of deciding. This would be unfortunate, for entrusting the powers of decision making to the authorities may lead to rule by elites. No one can claim infallible knowledge. In many fields the experts differ among themselves. We need to exercise some healthy skepticism of what the authorities declare to be true. The history of science illustrates the fact that scientific opinion fixed at one stage of inquiry can be easily transformed into dogmatic assertion in the next. The fact that authorities may declare something to be true does not necessarily make it so. In principle, any claim to truth, even by the highest scientific authorities, must be open to challenge, and the grounds of the assertions must be independently corroborated. Open peer review by researchers in every field of inquiry is essential for the testing of knowledge.

We may generalize from this: In the last analysis, the best community is the open one, in which alternative hypotheses can be examined and the views of dissenters can receive a hearing. The democratic society is open to a wide range of viewpoints, and it allows for criticism of the decisions of political leaders and bureaucrats. *The justification of democracy is based on methodological grounds.* It is presupposed by the method of inquiry itself. If no one class, party, or group can be said to have the Absolute Truth, then they cannot be entrusted with the power to decide the fate of everyone else. Power is thus widely shared by all of the citizens of the commonwealth. The underlying premise is that the truth is difficult to achieve and that a free market of ideas will be most receptive to pluralistic claims to knowledge. Only with open dialogue may we draw upon alternative conceptions and perhaps better approximate truth. In an open market of ideas, no group can demand immunity from criticism. This allows for the emergence of responsible leadership and it also holds them accountable to the will of the electorate.

The democratic method of inquiry itself need not be justified by reference to metaphysical abstractions, nor is it deduced from first principles, themselves in need of further justification. Rather, it is tested experimentally. In the long run those societies that are open will tend to have less duplicity and cruelty and there is less likelihood that injustice will remain hidden. In opening the public square to debate, new discoveries and new ideas are likely to emerge.

Chapter 11

SKEPTICISM AND ETHICAL INQUIRY

W e have analyzed in other chapters the role of skepticism in developing true beliefs about the world. But as we have seen, men and women do not live by knowledge alone, nor do they always seek truth for its own sake. On the contrary, knowledge is desired for the ends that it will enable us to achieve: whether fame or fortune, power or love, happiness or God. Which ends ought we seek? Can we say what is ultimately good? Can we develop normative knowledge? Does it make any sense to talk meaningfully about "good," "bad," "right," "wrong," "justice," and "responsibility"? Is there such a thing as "ethical truth"?

There is a long historical tradition, from Protagoras and the Sophists down to Hume and the emotivists, that denies the possibility of a rational or scientific ethics and that reduces ethical judgments to subjective sentiment. These skeptics deny that values are amenable to cognitive criticism or that standards of objectivity can be discovered. I think that they are profoundly mistaken and that a modified naturalistic and situational theory can provide some basis for rationality and objectivity in ethics.

In what follows, I wish to review the key arguments brought by clas-

[*The New Skepticism* (1992), pp. 277–90]

sical skepticism against the possibility of ethical knowledge, and my responses to them. We may distinguish three types of ethical skepticism, corresponding to the three types of epistemological skepticism.

ETHICAL NIHILISM

The first kind of skepticism is that of *ethical nihilism*, that is, total negative skepticism. This is the claim that it is not possible to test ethical judgments empirically or by an appeal to reason. This argument assumes various forms. Let us begin with the critique of ontological value. Ethical skeptics, I submit, correctly observe that it is impossible to discover any framework for morality in the universe at large, independent of human experience. The converse is likely the case, namely, human beings are disposed to read into nature their fondest hopes and to attribute moral qualities to the universe, but these represent the expression of their own yearnings to find an eternal place for their values in the scheme of things.

The most common illustration of fallacious moral extrapolation is the postulation of a divine being (or beings) and the attribution to him or her (or them) of the highest good. For Aristotle, the unmoved movers were engaged in *nous*, or pure thought; they were thinking about thinking. This was considered the noblest form of excellence that Man could attain, and it was what Aristotle himself prized as the highest good. The Old Testament had Man created in the image of God, though in reality God is fashioned out of the human imagination and assumes human form, possessed of all of the qualities that we cherish, but in extended form: power, omniscience, immortality. Yahweh is prone to anger and is vindictive and unremitting in his demands for obedience to the moral rules. He is a lawgiver who issues commandments (through his emissaries, the priests and prophets) that men and women are required to submit to if they are to escape punishment, but these rules in actuality reflect the social structure of the times. The New Testament continues the same kind of moral deception, for it deifies certain moral imperatives found desirable: for example, to love one another as God loves us. In the case of Jesus, this divine form of morality is embodied in human flesh at some point in history. Muhammad has given the Muslim moral code endurance and strength by claiming that it was Allah who defined and proclaimed the code.

Thus theistic creeds that attempt to ground the moral life in ultimate theological truths simply mask the tendencies of humans to attribute their own moral purposes to the universe at large, and to use this postulation to insist that those divine commandments ought to be obeyed. Skeptics have identified the implicit self-deception intrinsic to theological foundationalism. They have pointed out that mutually contradictory injunctions have been derived from the same deity. God has been used to defend both slavery and freedom, monogamy and polygamy, abortion and laws against abortion, war and peace, depending on the religious tradition and the social context in which it was revealed or interpreted. The divine commandments are made to fulfill eminently practical purposes, and the universe is endowed with moral qualities. These ultimately have their source in existential despair, which is transferred into hope by means of religious faith. God is invoked to enable people to endure death and tragedy, to provide some consolation and resolution of the human condition and to guarantee a future existence *in saecula, saeculorum.*

Skeptics have rightly demonstrated that all human values and ethical principles are intrinsically related to the human condition. "Man is the measure of all things, of things that are that they are, and of things that are not that they are not," observed Protagoras, the great Sophist who denied the reality of moral ideas independent of human existence. Theological moral systems do not depart from this, for their moral beliefs and Gods are drenched in human significance and relative to human concerns, although believers may deny that this is the case. Indeed, theism holds that God is a person much like a human being, which only emphasizes the anthropomorphic basis of theistic morality.

A similar indictment can be brought against any kind of Platonic moral realism, that is, the notion that eternal moral ideas are implicit in a realm of being and that the task of human reason is to discover and apply these essences of life. Socrates attempted to define "justice" and "the good," hoping his definitions of absolute ideas would provide a beacon for both the individual soul and the polis. For Plato, nature is interpreted as the basis for "the good" over and beyond convention. Skeptics have rightly rejected this theory as pure postulate, without reasonable justification or proof. The reification of essences makes an unwarranted epistemological leap. According to Protagoras, ethics has a relativistic basis: "Whatever is seen just to a city is just for that city so long as it seems so."

A similar critique has been brought against naturalistic theories, that is, any effort to find an ultimate ground for ethics in "human nature," "natural law," "the march of history," or "evolutionary progress." Surely these naturalistic forces are not without human content, for they are related to human institutions. Accordingly, relativism would seem to be necessary as a starting point for any conception of value.

An important distinction must be made, however, between *relativism* and *subjectivism*, for to say that morality is related to human beings does not necessarily mean that it is irreducibly subjective. Relativism and subjectivism are not the same, and the former does not imply the latter. One can be a relativist and an objectivist. Total negative skeptics argue that there are no objective standards that can be used to appraise what the individual or city deems to be just or good. They maintain that to say that something is good or right means simply that we feel this to be the case, and that our sentiments are disposed either to like or dislike. Some forms of subjectivism reduce to nihilism, for if moral beliefs in the last analysis are nothing but an expression of tastes, feelings, and sentiments—*de gustibus non disputandem est*—then we cannot really demonstrate the moral excellence of one belief over another. If, from the standpoint of the state, whatever is just is relative to convention, custom, or power, then there are no normative criteria for adjudicating differences. "Justice is the interest of the stronger," affirmed the nihilist Thrasymachus in the *Republic*; therefore "might makes right." It is the strongest faction of society that defines moral rectitude and lays down laws to adjudicate conflicting interests. Ethics is nothing more or nothing less than that.

The emotive theory, introduced in the twentieth century by the logical positivists, also expresses a strong form of ethical skepticism. The emotivists distinguish between three kinds of sentences: (1) descriptive statements, which they said could be verified directly or indirectly by factual observations or experiment; (2) analytic statements, which are tautological and established as formally true by deductive inferences; and (3) emotive utterances, which have no cognitive or literal significance, but are expressive and imperative in force. To say that "rape is wrong," for the emotivists, merely means that I (or we) are repulsed by it and that I (or we) condemn it and command others to do so as well. These sentences cannot be verified in any objective manner, for they violate the principles of verifiability and analyticity.

Extreme subjectivity thus leads us to an impasse, because we need to get on with the business of living with others in the community. Nihilism is a posture that we can hardly afford to adopt in practical life. There is therefore a serious question as to whether or not the reduction of ethics to subjectivity is true to our ethical experiences. For to maintain that there are no cognitive criteria that can be brought to bear in ethical questions, and that in the last analysis it is simply a question of feeling or force, seems to impose a tremendous strain on credulity. For example, if there are no objective standards of ethical value, is the statement that "the policies of Hitler and Stalin were evil" without any basis other than that I or we do not like them? Is the ethical principle "Mothers ought not to torture their children" similarly without any merit? If so, subjectivity reduces human morality either to the toleration of barbarism (for there is no meaningful ground to oppose it) or utter absurdity, in which anything is as good as anything else, and right and wrong have no signification. Under this theory, monsters may be equivalent to martyrs, sinners to saints, egoists to altruists. But if no ethical distinctions are allowed, social life would become impossible. Why doesn't a person steal, murder, torture, or rape? Is it simply a question of sentiment or the fear that one will be punished by the police (or God)? This position is contradicted by the evidence of the ethical life: We *do* make ethical judgments, and some are considered warranted. We criticize moral monsters and tyrants and applaud altruists and humanitarians, and with some justification. Ethical nihilism is infantile, and those who vehemently proclaim it in all ethical situations have not fully developed their moral sensibilities. They are concealing their own moral ignorance, and by their total negative skepticism reveal that they have not achieved mature moral growth.

To argue the position of the ethical neutralist—that is, that one must be "morally neutral" about *all* moral questions—is similarly mistaken. I would agree that *some* moral quandaries are difficult to resolve, particularly where there are conflicts between rights and goods, both of which we cannot have, or the choice between the lesser of two evils, one of which we must choose. To urge the *universal* suspension of ethical judgment, as the ethical nihilist advocates, however, does not follow. If a skeptic cannot decide between two sides of *any* moral issue, and thereby refuses to choose or to act, is he or she not confessing a similar blind spot concerning the phenomenological character of moral experience and reflection? Or, if one does act, but only from feeling or because one thinks that following conventional custom is the safest course, is one not insensitive to the deeper nuances of the moral life? Such a position, if consistently defended, reduces to a perverse kind of moral dogmatism.

Agnostic skepticism is not without some redeeming virtues, however. For in opposing moral absolutism or fanaticism, and in seeing through the sham of self-righteous claims that one's moral theories are the ultimate truth, skepticism may be a useful antidote for paternalistic or authoritarian claptrap. Moral absolutists assume that their views are intrinsic to reality, and they are all too readily prepared to suppress those who dissent. Some will seek to apply Reason or Progress or Virtue or God to impose views that simply mask their own preferences. As such, they have substituted dogmatism for inquiry. On the other hand, the persistent denial that there are *any* moral truths at all, if it is consistently asserted, belies its own form of moral intransigence, based largely upon epistemological error: for to deny that there is any kind of moral truth or reliable knowledge is to flout the considerable body of reliable ethical knowledge that we have as a product of the collective wisdom of the race.

MITIGATED ETHICAL SKEPTICISM

A second kind of skeptical theory is less extreme than the first. This we may call *mitigated ethical skepticism*. It assumes various forms. In particular, it states that although sentiment is at the root of all human values, this still leaves some room for rational criticism and control.

One can see this position again first presented by the Sophists. Glaucon, in the *Republic*, outlines the social contract theory, which is later elaborated by modern political philosophers like Thomas Hobbes: All men seek to satisfy their own desires, and self-interest dominates their choices. But they soon see that if individuals had carte blanche to do whatever they wished, there would be "a war of all against all" in which case life would become "solitary, poor, nasty, brutish, and short." Rational persons thus are willing to restrain their passions and enter into a social contract, agree to limit their liberties, and abide by the rule of law. Here the criterion is the social good, and this is justified because it is to the self-interest of every person to establish a framework of peace, law, and order, in which common guarantees and protections are provided by the civil society and the state. One variation of this is the utilitarian theory; namely, we agree to adhere to the moral rules of society because they provide the conditions of happiness for all. This theory does not attempt to ground justice in God, the Absolute, or Nature writ large. Ethical principles are related to human interests, and they have a conventional basis. But they also provide a consequential and experimental test. Although they are relative to the individual, it is not subjectivity alone that rules, for ethical judgments are still open to rational criticism and may be justified in terms of their instrumental effectiveness.

Hume was critical of certain assumptions implicit in classical ethical theory, for he argued that a moral judgment intrinsically involves feelings: When we judge an act or trait of a character as good or bad, we are saying that we approve or disapprove, and we do so because we have sentiments of pleasure or displeasure and/or we consider it to be useful or harmful. Hume argued that there were basic differences between judgments of fact and judgments of value. Judgments of fact can be ascertained to be true or false. On the contrary, judgments of morality, like judgments of taste, cannot. Hume inferred from this that reason by itself cannot decide moral judgments, nor can it alone make moral distinctions or resolve moral quandaries. It is "moral sentiment," not rationality, that is the wellspring of action. What we consider good or bad is dependent on whether moral sentiment is attached to it, and by this he meant the feeling that something is pleasant or useful. Hume was thus a skeptic in ethics, for he held that reason by itself cannot resolve moral questions. His statement "Reason is, and ought only to be, the slave of passions" is both provocative and controversial. The point he wished to make was that moral judgments are neither like factual statements, tested by observation, nor like the logical inferences, concerned with the relationships of ideas.

In his *Treatise on Human Nature*,[1] Hume observed that in all "systems of morality" that have been enunciated, the proponent would begin with "ordinary ways of reasoning." For example, he might attempt to prove that God exists, or he might describe human society, but at one point he makes a leap, going from what "is" or "is not" to be the case. Here something not contained in the premise is suddenly introduced into the conclusion. There is an unwarranted gap in the argument. The "ought" is not deduced from the "is," but is arrived at by the surreptitious introduction of the author's sentiment or feeling. The conclusion Hume drew from his analysis is that we cannot deduce the "ought" from the "is" and that any effort to do so is fallacious. Interestingly, given his skepticism, Hume ended up a conservative, for if there are no ultimate guides or moral truths, then we ought to abide by the customary rules of conduct.

In the twentieth century, a great deal of effort has been expended by philosophers, from G. E. Moore to the emotivists, to analyze moral language. Moore used the term *naturalistic fallacy* to describe all efforts to define "the good." The naturalistic fallacy is similar to Hume's theory of the "is-ought" dualism.[2] Moore thought that any definition of "good" was vulnerable to the open question argument and that it applied to theological as well as naturalistic ethical systems, to John Stuart Mill as well as Thomas Aquinas. He asked, "*Why* should we accept your definition of good?" and he ended up doubtful of any and all attempts to define "good." Moore's own epistemological theory assumed a form of Platonic realism. "Good" was an "indefinable, nonnatural property" by definition, and that was why it could not be defined.

Other twentieth-century neo-Kantians (H. A. Prichard, Henry Sedgwick, and W. D. Ross) agreed that ethical predicates could not be derived from nonethical ones.[3] They thought the basic ethical terms were deontological ("right," "wrong," "obligation," and "duty"), not teleological ("good," "bad," "value" and "disvalue"), and that these were indefinable because they contained an implicit obligatoriness. Even though they could not define ethical terms, neither Moore nor the intuitionists considered themselves to be ethical skeptics. Prichard thought classical ethical inquiry rested on a mistake, for it attempted to prove its first principles, whereas one's moral obligations could be known intuitively and directly within moral situations.

It was the emotivists, to whom we have already referred, especially Charles L. Stevenson, who were ethical skeptics, though some were mitigated.[4] They maintained that the reason *why* we could not define ethical terms was that they were not descriptive, like "hard" or "brittle," but emotive in character. Ethical words were expressive and evocative, much like "ugh" or "whew," and imperative, such as "drop dead" or "kiss me." These terms give vent to our emotional attitudes and they express our desires that other people agree with us and/or do our bidding. Efforts to define such terms are at best "persuasive definitions," the emotivists said, for they simply express our own moral sentiments.

Of special significance is the belief of the emotivists that disagreements in the moral domain often degenerated into disputes between contending parties that could not, even in principle, be resolved. This was due to the fact that the disagreements were "disagreements in attitude," as distinct from "disagreements in belief." As mitigated ethical skeptics, they said that the latter disagreements could be resolved by empirical, rational methods, where two or more parties to a dispute differed about factual claims. These controversies, at least in principle, could be overcome—that is, if the moral dispute was based upon the facts. In some cases, the disputes might be purely analytical and concern the meaning of a term, and these could be clarified by definition and again be overcome. For example, C maintains that a fetus weighs 8 ounces, and D claims that it weighs 6. Presumably they could weigh the fetus and decide the factual issue. Or again, if C and D disagree about the definition of "euthanasia" and whether or not it is voluntary or involuntary, then presumably by clearly defining what they mean, they can possibly overcome some forms of disagreement. However, if the dispute is distinctively *moral*, according to Stevenson, then it is attitudinal, and we may not be able to resolve the differences. For example, if D says that "abortion is *wrong*" because the fetus is a person, and E declares that "abortion is *right*" because it is based upon the principle of freedom of choice for women, then we may not be able to resolve the dispute—for the disagreement is not purely factual, but an attitudinal difference about which principle to accept. Hence an impasse may be reached.

Such moral disputes may not in principle be resolvable. F may think that euthanasia is wrong because we ought never to take the life of another, and suffering is not necessarily evil; and G may think that euthanasia is right if it is voluntary, because unnecessary pain and suffering in terminal cases is evil. Unless both parties can agree in their basic attitudes about suffering and pain or voluntary and involuntary death, they may never be able to resolve their moral controversy.

This second form of ethical skepticism is *mitigated*, because in spite of the ultimate subjective differences in sentiment, feeling, or emotion, the moral life is not entirely bereft of rational considerations, and some moral disagreement may be grounded in belief, not attitude. If, for example, H says that she is in favor of capital punishment because it is a deterrent to future murders, since the belief is contingent on the deterrence issue we can presumably do a factual study to resolve the disagreement. Similarly, if J is against the death penalty because she doesn't think it deters murder, we could again perhaps resolve this by doing a sociological study, examining murder rates in those states or countries that have the death penalty and those that do not, to see if there is any statistical difference. Similarly, we can study those states or countries before and after the imposition or repeal of the death penalty to see whether there is any significant difference. If these moral judgments pro or con were truly a function of the facts, then if they were mistaken about the factual truth, the persons involved might change their beliefs regarding the death penalty.

There are other arguments that mitigated skeptics can introduce in disagreements in an effort to persuade other persons to modify their judgments. They can appeal to the *consistency* criterion. If some persons hold a particular moral principle, and yet make exceptions to it, they are contradicting themselves. For example, they may say they believe in democracy as the best form of government, yet they may exclude one portion of society from exercising the franchise. Presumably, if we show them that they have disenfranchised blacks we would have an argument against apartheid in South Africa, or if they disenfranchised women we could make the case for universal suffrage. And if our moralists believe in consistency, they will change their views, for they would want to order their values in some coherent form.

The same considerations apply to the test of *consequences*; that is, persons who hold a principle, even with intensity, may not appreciate all of the consequences that may ensue from it. They may, for example, be committed to equal legal rights for all adults above the age of eighteen, the age at which an individual can vote or be conscripted into the armed services. Yet they might be willing to make an exception to this general principle and prohibit the serving of alcohol in bars to individuals under the age of twenty-one. They may have changed their views because the dangerous consequences—in the form of high rates of fatal automobile accidents—have been pointed out to them. Here consistency may give way to considerations of consequences, and in weighing the latter they may be willing to override the former.

Therefore, even though values may at root be attitudinal, they may be restructured by rational considerations. We have to live and function in the world and modify our attitudes in the light of these considerations.

The subjectivistic skeptical rejoinder to this, however, is that the reason some individuals believe in deterrence is that they find murder emotionally repulsive. The reason they find drunk driving abhorrent is that accidental death due to negligence is likewise repugnant to their feelings. Likewise, they believe that universal suffrage is right because they approve of it attitudinally. Even the mitigated skeptic agrees that rational criticisms are accepted ultimately only because they rest on nonrational grounds. These moral postulates, they insist, are without any cognitive justification beyond our sentiment.

Aware of the epistemological pitfalls inherent in morality, some skeptics have urged a return to custom, and they have adopted a conservative bias. If no sentiment is ultimately better than any other, we had best choose those that are less dangerous to society and/or those that do not impede individual liberty. Even this stance is mitigated in its justification. Other skeptics, in agreeing that there are *no* rational foundations for ethics or politics, may choose to be liberals or radicals. But this stance, in the final analysis, say the skeptics, is likewise based on taste, and no rational proof is possible.

ETHICAL INQUIRY

This leads to our third form of skepticism, that which is related to inquiry. This position involves a skeptical component that is never fully abandoned: cognition in the course of skeptical inquiry. Our search for ethical judgments is thus continuous with our quest for reliable knowledge in all fields of human endeavor. At the very least, our choices are based upon our knowledge of the world and ourselves. The relationship between knowledge and value is central to the concept of *ethical inquiry*.

If we say that ethical choices may be related to rationality, the question that is immediately raised is whether there are any *ultimate* principles that are foundational to our ethical decisions and to which we must be committed if we are able to make sense of ethical rationality. I must confess an extreme reluctance to assert that there are; at least all such efforts heretofore to find such first principles a priori seem to me to have failed.

The salient point is that ethics is relative to life as lived by specific person or societies, and it is rooted in historical-social conditions and concrete behavior. Ethical principles are thus in the midrange; they are proximate, not ultimate. We do not reason about the moral life *in abstracto* and hope to make sense of it; we always begin *here* and *now*, with *this* individual in *this* society faced with *these* choices. The basic subject matter of ethics is action and conduct. It is not concerned essentially with propositions about practice, as some analytic philosophers thought, but with praxis itself. The knowledge that we seek is practical: what to choose, how to act, and how to evaluate the courses of action that confront us. We are interested in formulating wise, prudential, and effective judgments of practice. This does not deny that we can generalize about human practice and indeed formulate rules of conduct applicable to similar situations or values that have a wider appeal. Still, the contents of our judgments have concrete referents.

Rarely when we engage in ethical inquiry do we begin at the beginning—except perhaps in crisis/existential situations where we are forced to examine our root values. Rather, we find ourselves in the midst of practical demands and conflicts, trying to make sense of the web of decisions and behavior in which we are entangled. And included in our nexus is the considerable fund of normative data that we bring with us: the things we cherish or esteem, or conversely detest or reject, and the principles to which we are committed. Ethical inquiry is initiated when there is some puzzle about what we should do or some conflict between competing values and principles, and to select those that seem approximate. The ethical inquirer in the best sense is committed to the use of reflective intelligence, in which he or she is able to define and clarify his or her values and principles and to search for alternative courses of action that seem most fitting within the context of inquiry.

The ethical inquirer, like the scientist, seeks knowledge, but he or she does not simply describe what is factually the case or explain events by means of causal theories. Nor is he or she interested primarily in arriving at analytic or formal truths. The goal is eminently practical: to choose something that will guide behavior and affect the world.

NOTES

1. David Hume, *Treatise on Human Nature* (1739), book 3, part 1, section 1.
2. G. E. Moore, *Principia Ethica* (Cambridge: Cambridge University Press, 1903).

3. H. A. Prichard, "Does Moral Philosophy Rest on a Mistake?" *Mind* 21 (1921); Henry Sidgwick, *The Methods of Ethics*, 6th ed. (New York: Macmillan, 1901); W. D. Ross, *The Right and the Good* (Oxford: Clarendon Press, 1930).

4. A. J. Ayer, *Language, Truth and Logic* (Oxford: Clarendon Press, 1936); Charles L. Stevenson, *Ethics and Language* (New Haven, CT: Yale University Press, 1943).

Chapter 12

MORAL FAITH AND ETHICAL SKEPTICISM RECONSIDERED

There are two contrasting approaches to the moral life. The first I shall call "moral faith" and the second, "ethical skepticism." Moral faith has been the deepest and most pervasive force in human culture, and the proponents of this approach to the moral life have had the predominant influence. Ethical skepticism has been relatively rare in human history and has been espoused by only a small number of intellectuals. It has been considered by Establishments to be an extremely dangerous position. Its earliest known proponent was Socrates, at least insofar as he questioned the reigning orthodoxy of his age, though his own position later became enshrined as part of a new faith.

Now, there are other possible postures that we may adopt in respect to morality. One can, for example, be largely indifferent to the demands of morality and not take it seriously. One may be a cynic about it, or even assume the role of the nihilist and reject it entirely. These positions, though interesting, I will not attempt to deal with in this paper, though perhaps some verge on ethical skepticism. Rather, I shall focus on the above two alternative views of morality. I will attempt to explicate and also

[*Journal of Value Inquiry* 19, no. 1 (1985): 55–65]

defend one variety of ethical skepticism, though there are many different forms that skepticism may assume.

MORAL FAITH

Now, the term *faith* is usually employed by reference to transcendent beliefs, that is, beliefs that describe, designate, or point to some existent reality that we cannot demonstrate exists. To say that one has faith usually means that one accepts beliefs in a state or reality for which there is insufficient evidence, though there is the conviction that this reality exists in some form. Faith is that portion of one's psychological belief state that transcends the evidence offered for the belief.

A *moral faith*, on the contrary, is normative or prescriptive. It does not simply allege that something is the case, but that it *ought* to be, and it recommends bringing into being a state of affairs that is considered to be "good," "just," "valuable," or "right," or has some other commendable properties. Those who express a moral faith hold it to be true in some sense of the term *true*; that is, they believe that moral values or principles have some reality independent of the person who espouses them, and that therefore we have an obligation to fulfill or obey them. Now, those who espouse a moral faith usually also express some deep-seated commitment to that faith. Indeed, the term *faith* implies some fidelity or loyalty on the part of a person to instate or defend his moral commitment. It implies that there are deep roots within the individual personality or the social institutions that espouse the faith. It is not simply an intellectual commitment on the level of cognition, but involves passion and feeling. It is both *imperative* in the sense that those who hold the faith believe that what it recommends ought to exist, if it does not as yet, and *expressive* in that it evokes an emotional response. But it is not merely emotive, and it is not simply a matter of taste or caprice, for it gives vent to our deepest attitudes and longings. Thus a moral faith is generally grounded in one's first principles.

To talk about a person's faith in the area of morality is analogous to talking about a person's faith in religion. When we probe a person's moral roots, we know that we have touched rock bottom when we are able to elicit a blush or a stammer. Faith is at the core of a person's value structure.

There are at least two fundamental ingredients to a person's moral faith: (1) basic values and (2) moral principles. Though we may distinguish them in kind, values and principles overlap and are intertwined within a personal or social framework. The *values* of a person or a society refer to the things that are found to be good and worthwhile, that are cherished and held dear. In behavioristic terms, values refer to preferential, selective, or teleonomic behavior, the attitudinal-cognitive-conative motives that impel us to achieve goals and purposes. A person has a great number of values, from immediately liking a glass of vodka, a chocolate ice cream sundae, a melody, or an embrace to approving of an intellectual position or the long-range quest for happiness. In philosophical language, teleological theories have focused on the ends and goals that are considered to be most enduring and worthwhile. Now, there has been a wide range of experiences that have been cherished and diverse ends that have been pursued. One's basic value commitments—whether to love, piety, science, or the general happiness—express one's deepest values and the kind of a world that we wish to bring about. For some this refers to ideal ends to be achieved.

A second component of the moral life is *moral principles*. I use the term *principle* here to refer to a rule of conduct, a standard or norm governing action. A principle is usually taken to be universal or general in that it lays down a policy guide for future conduct, or it limits or proscribes other forms of human action. It is clearly prescriptive or prohibitive: recommending, advising, or commending us how to live or behave. Generally, the philosophical schools that have emphasized this are called *deontological*. They emphasize our obligations and responsibilities to obey or fulfill the principles that serve as moral guides. They underscore the demands of justice and fairness. There are any number of moral principles that have been expressed, such as the biblical proverbs: "Love thy neighbor as thyself," "An eye for an eye, tooth for tooth, hand for hand, foot for foot; burning for burning, wound for wound, stripe for stripe," "Do unto others as ye would have them do unto you." But there are many other moral principles that we recognize in conduct: to tell the truth; not cheat, steal, kill, or injure another; to keep your promises and be sincere. Moral principles are often revised and new ones introduced. Two recently enunciated moral principles have aroused intense debate and commitment in democratic societies. There is, for example, the libertarian principle that "all individuals are equal in dignity and worth and entitled to equality of opportunity, ethical consideration, or equal deserts." Still other moral principles have emerged today involving the recognition of human rights.

There are a great variety of moral values and principles that have prevailed in history, and there are alternative moral codes: the Samurai warrior, Christian priest, bourgeois entrepreneur, Bohemian poet, scientific investigator, and Marxist revolutionary express different values and principles. Thus there is the familiar problem of cultural relativity. Each social group seeks to inculcate its cherished values and principles. It provides sanctions for those who flout them and rewards those who conform and are considered to be paragons of virtue.

Moral systems that are rooted in faith generally take their basic values and central moral principles as universal; these are held to express deep truths about the universe of humankind. Values and principles are not taken as subjective nor are they considered merely to be a matter of taste or caprice; they are allegedly grounded in the nature of things. Thus there are efforts to derive them from religious, metaphysical, ideological, or scientific doctrines. Moral values and principles are not made to justify them by an appeal to reason and to defend them against their critics. All of these codes, however, have religious or semireligious qualities and elements of faith attached to them.

There are no doubt differences in the degrees of faith with which moral systems are held. On the one extreme is moral absolutism. Here moral principles are considered to be absolute commandments, and they are enforced by the threat of punishment, whether from Jehovah or the state. There is apprehension about flouting them. Moral phobias develop. Principles become inviolable. Orthodox religious moralities have absolute prohibitions against divorce, adultery, or homosexuality. Such systems can be highly repressive, even tyrannical.

A strongly held faith more often than not involves some self-righteousness. There is a fear of heretics, disbelievers, or aliens, who are taken as "immoral" or "wicked" and are condemned as corrupters of the true morality. And there is a sense that one has a duty to further the moral faith and to oppose or even destroy offending adversaries. There may be a heightened sense of a cosmic struggle between the forces of good and evil and a conviction that our side needs all the support it can get in its holy crusade against those benighted souls who reject our moral point of view or choose to live differently. While these attitudes apply to religious believers—whether orthodox defenders of the holy faith or the disciples of a new cult—they also may characterize entirely secular movements, which may likewise be engulfed by ardor and the need to sacrifice for the cause.

One's moral faith may be considered to be far more important than one's religious belief, for often it is not what you believe in that counts, but what you do, how you bring up your children, and how your women are treated. These matters touch at the very core of one's sense of propriety, and they can arouse intense hatred if they offend it. Public approbation or disapprobation may not be sufficient to support the moral code. If so, other institutions emerge to enforce compliance. A priestly class employs the symbols of God's power and the threat of excommunication or damnation. Or it is the state that becomes the ultimate guardian of morality, for it can enact and enforce the laws. Although it is the state that may legislate morality, all of the institutions of society may be charged with inculcating and reinforcing moral conduct: the family, schools, economic institutions, even voluntary associations.

Appeals to the fatherhood of God are a familiar psychological device for sanctifying one's moral principles, but there are secular equivalents of divinity. The twentieth century is all too familiar with secular ideologies, which involve ethical-political doctrines and principles that we held to be implicit within the womb of nature. Instead of God, Marxists appeal to the dialectical laws of history in which higher forms of social relations struggle to emerge, and in which one's highest duty is said to be to assist the oppressed or to achieve a classless society. Following Darwinism, Herbert Spencer and others sought to defend free enterprise and the struggle of the fittest for survival. Others defended the idea of inevitable human progress. Gobineau and Chamberlin later provided the basis for Nazi racist policies, but these were based upon the mistaken notions of biologically superior and inferior races. No doubt one can indict such simplistic approaches—we ought not to commit science to a dogmatic moral faith. Perhaps the above theories were not verified, but were forms of pseudo-science. The above illustrates, however, that scientific theories can be translated into ethical prescriptions of the uses of science in moral persuasions: the debate about IQ and race, sociobiology and the instinct for aggression, and so on. Is science relevant to ethics? Can it function not as a faith, but in another way?

One fault in the above systems, I submit, is that they present a hierarchical structure of values and principles; that is, they take one value or principle and seek to make it all-controlling. This is a common approach in any system of faith. But one should guard against the tyranny of principles, that is, using a principle as an absolute and not admitting any exception to it. To illustrate: those who argue that it is wrong to take an innocent human life—the fetus is held to be a form of human life and innocent—maintain that any form of abortion is always wrong under any circumstance, even when the fetus is grossly retarded or the pregnancy is due to rape or incest. Conversely, the libertarian defends the principle that an individual should be permitted to do whatever he or she wants, so long as the action doesn't harm others. Thus Thomas Szasz comes out against any involuntary commitment to mental hospitals, even if a patient is seriously disturbed or schizophrenic. He denies any evidence of the latter. To be consistent, we are told, the principle means that heroin and other addictive drugs should be legalized—even if this would mean the death and debilitation of a large sector of the population. Thus for dedicated moral faith, root values and first principles cannot be held in contradiction. Consistency is the ultimate test as to whether one is true to his principles. A deeply held moral faith pursued to its ultimate conclusion, can become ludicrous if it is applied without distinction.

Now, in the above cases, one's faith is often the product of one's unexamined assumptions. We imbibe our moral faith at our mother's knee and it persists without reflection. It is nourished and fed in the sociocultural context in which we grow and function. It is prerational and affective-conative in character. Some justification for our moral-faith state is sought when challenged by others. At that point, appeals may be made to one's higher religious faith, or our moral faith may be derived from an elaborate ideological system. Or we may seek to justify our faith by reference to science, and to use that to support it by reference to its research findings. Should we equate a moral faith based upon religion or ideology with one based upon science? Is that not stretching it too far? Are there not important differences? I think there are. Yet I fear that some degree of self-deception lurks under the mantle of science. In its most extreme form there is worship of the faith that "science will save us." The scientific intellectual is not unlike the religious intellectuals waiting in expectation of Godot, who never arrives. For the scientific believer, we are waiting for our own Godot, the salvation promised by science.

We should not deceive ourselves into believing that scientific intellectuals are any more fair-minded or impartial than others when it comes to their own cherished values and moral principles. These often reflect their own deepest prejudices. This can be seen vividly in the area of political belief. For many intellectuals, politics often functions religiously. I am often struck by the deep partisan bias—in most cases to a liberal-left orientation—and the intense animosity displayed toward individuals or parties that oppose it. Intellectuals are not unique in this regard. Their emotive bias is similar to those who have a conservative right-wing faith, especially business or corporate executives. Alas, all too few intellectuals recognize their political faith for what it is. There is some need for political skepticism about all strongly held partisan positions, whether of the left or the right.

I do not mean to suggest that all moral faiths are intransigent or non-self-critical. There are periods of conversion in history when there are radical paradigm shifts and when new values and principles emerge. Some moral faiths are unyielding; others are receptive to modification in the light of intellectual criticism. And that, as I view it, is the essential role that ethical skepticism can play in reforming and liberalizing preexisting systems and making them responsive to alternative conceptions of the good life or the just society.

ETHICAL SKEPTICISM

Now, I do not wish to deny that science is relevant to ethics. But it is important that we be clear about what scientific inquiry can and cannot do. It can never, in my judgment, free us entirely from ethical indeterminacy. Some skepticism is essential to the lifeblood of the scientific enterprise itself.

What is ethical skepticism? Let me describe it as it developed in the field of twentieth-century metaethics. Interestingly, it has been used most directly against naturalistic and scientific ethics, that is, the confident expectations of philosophers and scientists that we might develop a science of ethics and value.

Now, there are three parts of the skeptics' critique:

(1) there are inherent logical difficulties in defining our basic ethical terms and concepts;

(2) there are epistemological difficulties in testing ethical principles and judgments or deriving "ought" statements from "is" statements, values from facts; and

(3) there are existential difficulties in justifying first principles and root values.

G. E. Moore was among the first to raise some serious questions about the meaning of ethical terms and concepts. In particular, he argued that the "good" was indefinable, and that all previous ethical theories that had attempted to provide a definition or theory of the good had committed a logical fallacy, which he labeled as the *naturalistic fallacy*. This fallacy applied to any effort to derive the good or other normative concepts from nonnormative equivalents. Moore leveled his attack upon the utilitarians (especially John Stuart Mill), who were influential at the turn of the century. The utilitarians had attempted to create a science of ethics. They sought to derive normative ethics (in which the good was defined as pleasure or happiness) from a descriptive theory of motivation (psychological hedonism, i.e., that all humans seek to maximize pleasure and avoid pain). It was a mistake, said Moore, to try to find a nonnormative substitute for "good." He offered his famous "open question argument": For any definition that you proposed, one could ask, But *is* it good and *why* should I accept your definition? "Good" is "good," said Moore, a "simple, nonnatural quality." It is "indefinable," like yellow, though we can know what it is directly and intuitively. Moore's objection applied not only to scientific naturalism but to any and all efforts at definition. It applied equally to metaphysical or theological definitions: to those in which the good is identified with "God's will," "human progress," the "general happiness," or anything else.

I think Moore was mistaken about much of this. His reasons for rejecting normative definitions were questionable. He thought that the property "good" was a floating, "nonnatural" Platonic essence; that is why it was indefinable. We can raise the open-question argument against Moore himself: Why accept his epistemological definitions of "good"? If Moore is correct, then a definist's fallacy might apply to *all* scientific efforts at descriptive definition. One could not provide rigorous operational definitions in the sciences for anything. A thing is what it is and not something else.

Other neo-Kantian intuitionists in twentieth-century ethics (Sidgwick, Prichard, Ross, etc.) did not focus on teleological terms, such as *good* or *value*, which they thought were derivative and definable, but upon deonto-logical terms such as *right, wrong*, or *justice*. These they found nonreductive and indefinable. Although such ethical predicates are knowable, they argued, these are not translatable into nonethical terminology. Neither Moore nor the deontological intuitionists were skeptics or subjectivists. They believed that ethical knowledge was meaningful and possible and that there was such a thing as ethical truth.

Of special interest to scientific naturalists are the further perplexing questions they raised: What is the proof of axioms, postulates, and first principles? Mill thought that he could not prove his first principles. For him, the basic point of utilitarianism was that all moral rules are to be tested by their consequences, by whether or not they contribute to the greatest happiness. Mill committed a logical blunder: The only proof we could give that something is visible is that it can be seen, or audible is that it can be heard, and therefore the only proof that something is desirable is that it can be desired. The fallacy here is figure of speech, for in the con-clusion the suffix "able" implies that it *ought* to be desired—not that it *can* be—and this has *normative* force. Thus, Mill's attempted proof of the basic premise of utilitarianism was formally invalid. Whether Mill, one of the leading logicians of the day, had his tongue in cheek when he wrote that is open to debate. The key conclusion the critics of scientific naturalism drew was that normative judgments could not be derived from descriptive premises. No less an authority than David Hume, the leading skeptic of modern philosophy, is responsible for recognizing the fallacy in attempting to derive an imperative statement from a descriptive one.

There are two key issues here. First, can we define ethical terms and concepts? Second, how can we test ethical judgments? The two additional schools in twentieth-century philosophy—logical positivism and existentialism—have further assaulted the foundations of classical philos-ophy, undermining our confidence in reason and conviction that we could create a science of ethics or values based on science. The logical positivists agreed with Moore and the intuitionists that we could not define ethical terms and concepts. The reasons for this, they argued, are different from Moore's: Normative terms were nondescriptive and nondesignative. Eth-ical language had other functions. It was expressive or emotive in character and imperative in function. The reason we could not define ethical terms was that they had no identifiable empirical referents in the world, no sense data to which they referred. Being evocative, they gave vent to our feelings and attitudes and sought to arouse similar responses in others. Any effort to provide objective definitions were thus bound to fail and were in the last analysis "persuasive."

The emotivists in ethics drew a threefold distinction between (1) descriptive, (2) analytic, and (3) emotive sentences. The first could be tested by some empirical verification, at least in principle. The second were tautological and formally valid in terms of the rules that governed their use. The third had no identifiable means by which we might confirm them. There were no criteria by which we could determine their truth values. Thus value judgments and ethical sentences had no intersubjective methods of confirmation. They were often prey to indeterminable disputes. This question became pivotal: How could we resolve normative disagreements?

C. L. Stevenson provided us with a modified emotive theory. Many disagreements, he said, were rooted in beliefs. These could be resolved, at least in principle, where factual matters are at issue. Presumably disagreements in the descriptive sciences could be overcome by reference to empirical confirmation or disconfirmation, indirectly if not directly. Ethical disputes, where they are grounded in cognitive beliefs, could be resolved by pointing out the mistakes about factual conditions or the consequences of proposed policies. But ethical disagreements that are rooted in attitudes may be difficult or impossible to resolve. It all depends upon whether or not we share similar attitudes. A science of value thus might reach a hopeless impasse, for whether or not we can solve a moral dispute depends upon whether we share the same moral faith. And when we hit rock bottom, we may not hold the same ethical convictions.

On this last point existentialism is especially pertinent. For it has maintained that there is a kind of absurdity concerning first principles, and that how we choose to live in the last analysis may depend upon a leap of faith. At crucial turning points in life we may be confronted with a radical freedom—to choose or not to choose—and there are no ultimate guidelines. Our first principles are beyond proof. They grow out of and are validated in the process of living, and there is no deductive proof that can be given for one style of life rather than another.

Now, there has been a lot of water over the dam since the emotive theory and existentialism burst upon the scene. And there is an extensive critical literature that has examined their claims and shown them to be excessive. First, although we may not define ethical terms arbitrarily, their meanings are embedded in our language, and they have a wide variety of uses, and it is by reference to descriptive properties that we apply value terms to objects. For example, if we say, "This chair is comfortable," we may attribute the term *comfortable* because the chair as a matter of fact is "soft" or "supportive" and has other descriptive properties.

Second, although value judgments cannot be deduced from descriptive sentences, descriptive sentences are relevant to their verification. There is a logic of judgments of practice. For example, we employ these in applied sciences, such as medicine, engineering, psychiatry, or pedagogy. Value disagreements are not primarily a question of feeling or caprice; there are objective considerations that are relevant to the context under analysis and the decision-making procedures.

Third, in an ethical dilemma we usually do not have to trace ourselves back to first principles, but we resolve our moral problems by dealing with the values and principles that are relevant. The situation provides some guidelines and parameters for our choice. A return to first principles occurs only in special crisis situations. Normally we deal with principles of the middle range. Thus there is a kind of practical wisdom that we discover in experience, a kind of objective relativism. What we do is relative to the situation in which we have to make a choice, and these are amenable to some intelligent criticism. Thus there are objective considerations and standards in the field of ethical judgment.

Yet in spite of the above, *some* degree of ethical skepticism still remains, and I do not see how we can transcend it entirely. There are, however, two kinds of ethical skepticism. First, there are those who maintain that ethics is entirely capricious and emotive and that no knowledge is relevant to choice. This kind of nihilistic and negative skepticism is self-contradictory and belied by life itself. Some intelligent basis for criticism is necessary if we are to live and function. Second, there is a kind of modified ethical skepticism, which uses knowledge and data but is never entirely able to prove its first principles or find a decisive verification for its values or principles, for those who do not already accept them. Although it rejects moral faith as self-deceptive, it recognizes that the ultimate act of choosing a way of life and the form of being already embedded in a context of values and principles—as the de facto given—are beyond decisive confirmation. We can at best vindicate our basic principles and values and make them seem reasonable to other humans; it is difficult to prove or verify them in any conclusive way.

A MODIFIED FORM OF ETHICAL NATURALISM

In what follows I wish to outline a modified form of ethical naturalism. Let me indicate, however, what it can and cannot do: (1) It cannot hope to derive or deduce from our scientific study of nature, society, or human nature a complete set of moral values or principles that everywhere applies. (2) It cannot hope to derive universal values or principles that are objectively verified in the same way that descriptive hypotheses and theories are. What I wish to suggest is a weaker form of ethical naturalism. Simply stated it is as follows: *Scientific knowledge is relevant to our choices and values and should be part of the evidential and valuational base from which we can formulate ethical judgments.*

Now, my underlying premise, which no doubt some will question, is that human beings are free, autonomous, and creative agents: at least, in the sense that we face problems and are capable of choosing between alternatives. As decision makers, individuals or communities can be assisted by knowledge to make wiser or more effective choices.

The basic questions we face are: How shall we choose? and What values and principles should guide us? I would suggest the following range of relevant facts:

(1) We first have to consider the *factual knowledge* that we have, as drawn from everyday life and the sciences. This refers to:
   a) the particular facts of the case and the specific circumstances in which we are involved;
   b) the *casual* conditions that are operative, the social conditions that have led to the present state, the invariant casual irregularities;
   c) the *means* at our disposal, the techniques that are available;
   d) the likely *consequences* that might ensue, the results or effects of various courses of action; and
   e) the *common needs* of human beings, as preconditions of survival, health, and functioning.

The above are value neutral.

(2) We also need knowledge of preexisting *values* (teleological ethics):
  a) comparative knowledge of values that other humans have had, whether in the past or in the present; and
  b) those that we are now committed to or find controlling in our lives.

(3) We need knowledge of *moral principles* (deontological ethics):
  a) comparative knowledge of the rules and norms that have governed mankind, empirically based data, about the rules of the game; and
  b) the moral principles that are now relevant to the individual and/or the society in which he believes.

What we ought to do is a function of the above three conditions: knowledge of (1) facts, (2) values, and (3) principles. The second and third considerations suggest a kind of de facto involvement. These are in one sense contingent and relative to our particular existential situations in history. What we ought to do, how we ought to live, is conditioned by our past. But it is also a function of creative inquiry in the present and it entails a balancing of facts, values, and principles in the concrete contexts of choice. I believe that there is a role for objectivity; it is not universal or a priori, but contingent and existential. There is no ultimate justification for the framework in which we happen to exist, or our basic sociocultural perspective. These are semiarbitrary givens. They may be revised or reconstructed, but we are limited by the range of possibilities. Hence my skepticism about universalistic ethical systems that ignore actual phenomenological contexts in the lifeworld. There is a kind of irreducible pluralism about human reality and the human condition. Ethics is thus relational to the frames of reference in which we find ourselves. Knowledge is relevant to human choices, but our choices are not simply deducible from propositions or principles. Life precedes thought. Cognition is only one phase of our conative-affective or sociocultural existence.

The universe of man is thus open and uncharted. It is changing, not fixed or final. Life is full of striving and endeavor. It is in part precarious, uncertain, indeterminate. Knowledge can serve us in the ongoing process of living, but it is not a substitute for life. Science is a tool, no doubt the most important that we have, but it is not always infallible or reliable. Our existence precedes our essence. Alas, some faith is always present in the act of living—animal faith, if you will. Hence, we need some skepticism about even the reaches of science or the possibilities it provides for reforming our moral life, let alone the pitfalls of religion or ontology or ideology.

Critical scientific inquiry nevertheless, I submit, has high value as a human enterprise. Comparatively it still provides the greatest promise for solving our problems. In particular, it should provide us with a powerful critique of the methodologies and orthodoxies that reign in every age, the chauvinistic delusions, the systems of narrow moral faith that lord over human behavior or suppress freedom.

Ethical skepticism is not only an epistemological position. It no doubt presupposes a number of moral values. It prefers clarity to confusion, truth to illusion. Skepticism also can contribute to a sense of humility and an awareness of the fallible and problematic character of all human efforts. It enables us to appreciate other points of view. It cultivates a willingness to negotiate differences and to reach compromises. Ethical skepticism tends to liberate us from vain pretensions. It enables us to moderate and humanize intolerant doctrines. It says no to those who would sacrifice us to their excessive moral faiths. There is nothing as unprincipled as men of principles. Get out of their way, since they are all too prone to consume others in the name of their moral dogmas. Their most intense hatred is often directed against heretics, dissenters, or skeptics. Indeed, all sides loathe them the most, for they see through their shame and pretensions and do not take their shallow intensity seriously. Hopefully, some skepticism can chasten moral impatience somewhat. Perhaps it can reduce the level of moral hysteria and protect us from the worst excesses of faiths, whether in the name of religion or ideology or science.

The sad truth is that no person can live without some moral faith, not even the skeptic. The difference is that the skeptic is aware of the limits and pitfalls of his or her own cherished principles and values. The paradox for skeptics is that we too need some motivation and enthusiasm for our values and principles, else life would be empty and devoid of zest: hence the role of faith. Skepticism is vital, however, for it gives us pause; it restrains our zeal; it moderates our passions; it civilizes our follies. It is both the beginning and the end of wisdom. It calls us back. It is a corrective, an antidote to the morally intoxicated of every age.

Chapter 13

SKEPTICISM AND EUPRAXSOPHY

THE NEED TO INTEGRATE KNOWLEDGE

W e are now brought full circle back to the original question of this book. If skepticism has a vital role to play in the development of reliable knowledge, and if it need not be totally negative, nor simply mitigated, what relevance does it have for human affairs? Can it leave room for genuine commitment and strong convictions in ethics, politics, and life—or do any such attitudes betray the skeptical attitude itself? Does skeptical inquiry presuppose any first principles, and are these, like all other first principles, beyond proof? If so, does skeptical inquiry, if turned upon itself, entail an illegitimate leap of faith and a violation of its own program?

We face a unique crisis on the frontiers of knowledge today, and this is not necessarily due to the paucity of knowledge, but, on the contrary, to an embarrassment of riches, for scientific discoveries have grown so rapidly that it has become difficult to assimilate and interpret this vast body of knowledge. Concomitant with this is the extreme specialization that has

[*The New Skepticism* (1992), pp. 331–44]

developed. It is a truism to say that the advancement of scientific knowledge can best be achieved by a division of labor; that is, complex theoretical and technological problems can best be solved by the intensive concentration of efforts. Great progress has resulted, often by a relatively small number of workers in a field who follow the technical literature and are versed in its conceptual framework and the use of mathematical methods, and whose contributions are reviewed by their peers. This departmentalization of knowledge has had enormous success, yet at the same time specialists have so divided their subject matter that members of the same profession often are unable to communicate with one another as fields and subfields proliferate. The dilemma can be readily illustrated by reference to medicine, where general practitioners have declined in influence and where patients are referred to specialists for the diagnosis and treatment of most illnesses. The gap we face is that we do not always know how discoveries in one field relate to those in others. Nicholas Murray Butler, a former president of Columbia University, once defined an expert as "one who knows more and more about less and less." Clearly specialists within the same profession interact with their peers, and there is some interdisciplinary communication. But other scientists and the educated public at large are looking for generalizations that cut across specialties; they are seeking concepts, hypotheses, and theories of broader significance.

It was possible to provide such general interpretations on the frontiers of knowledge in earlier centuries. This often was the task of the philosopher, who had special analytic and interpretive skills. Aristotle summed up the main scientific, ethical, and political wisdom of his day—at least in broad outline—and he was able to synthesize this by means of his metaphysical categories. His doctrine of four causes—substance, form and matter, potentiality, and actuality—gave a comprehensive overview of how nature operated and how we experience and understand it. His idea of nature was organismic: Species were fixed, and the universe was intelligible to the human mind. The Greek idea of nature was modified drastically by latter-day theologians, who viewed the universe as God's creation, fulfilling a plan in which humanity played a central role. The Newtonian-Galilean world-view rejected teleology and overthrew Aristotle and the organismic universe. The new idea of nature was that it was materialistic, mechanistic, and deterministic. The great philosophers of the modern period—Spinoza, Hobbes, Descartes, Locke, Leibniz, and Kant—attempted to interpret nature in the light of the Newtonian scheme. In the nineteenth century a historical focus emerged, and this led to the sweeping theories of history of Hegel and Marx. This was also the century in which there was a great leap forward in biology, and in which Darwin's evolutionary hypothesis replaced the doctrine of fixed species. There were also important developments in the social and behavioral sciences, which attempted to understand and study human psychology and social behavior. The twentieth century saw the expansion of quantum mechanics, the modification of Newtonian theories by relativity physics, and the dramatic advance in our knowledge on the cosmic scale in astronomy and on the microlevel in nuclear physics, chemistry, genetics, and biology. Moreover, the new technologies that have been created have enabled unparalleled scientific advances: for example, computer science, space technology, and biogenetic engineering.

Today it is increasingly difficult to develop a comprehensive, unified view of nature and of the human species. The philosophy of science has focused more on epistemological issues than on interpreting what we know. So the central questions are: What does science tell us about nature and life? Can we develop a larger cosmic weltanshauung? For any one mind to do so today would require an enormous capacity to understand conceptual and theoretical developments on the frontiers of knowledge. There are literally hundreds of thousands of scientific journals today, and they are expanding at an exponential rate. We would need a super-Aristotle to do so. Are there enough brain cells in any one mind to ingest and comprehend this massive amount of information?

But the need for such knowledge is as pressing as ever. Perhaps we do not need to store the megatrillion bits of information or even to sort or catalog it; we need only to program and interpret it. What we need to develop today, as in the past, is some *sophia*, or wisdom. This means an ability to coordinate what we know and/or to synthesize it. Now clearly there has to be an effort within the sciences to develop higher-level unifying theories, from which lower-level theories and hypotheses can be deduced. Efforts have been made to develop highly generalized theories in a number of fields: in physics, astronomy, psychology, biology, sociology, anthropology, and history. Such theories attempt to integrate all that is known in one particular area, and some creative scientists have attempted to do that. We see the bold insights of such endeavors, but also the possible snares: Hegelian, Marxist, and Toynbeean theories of history; generalized

Freudian explanations of sexual behavior; Whitehead's *Process or Reality*, and so on. All of these were ambitious programs and all of them had pitfalls. Nonetheless, there is still a need for more comprehensive interpretations of what we know. These may serve for a time during an epoch when certain general paradigms dominate the scientific imagination, but these unifications may eventually give way as unexpected discoveries and unsettling new theories are introduced.

The postmodern intellectual world is in a state of disarray in comparison with previous periods, for we have not found a grand synthesis, and indeed we may never succeed in creating one. To place the burden of providing some integrated cosmic outlook on the philosopher today is inordinately difficult. The special problem with contemporary philosophy is that it has itself become highly specialized and fragmented into separate schools with their own gurus and literatures. Often, great divides have been erected across which there is little communication. It was considered to be the task of metaphysicians classically to provide integrative systems of knowledge, but the classical metaphysical enterprise has been thrown into disrepute, for most metaphysicians attempted to spin out speculative theories of reality quite independent of the discoveries of the empirical sciences. They thought that it was possible to analyze the logical and ontological structures of nature without relating their conceptual schemes to perceptual experience. Many philosophical systems were purely formal and had no relationship to the real world or to the concrete findings of the sciences. Many philosophers indeed were, or still are, antiscientific or at best nonscientific, drawing on formal logic, or literature, or the arts, quite independently of scientific inquiry. Existentialists, phenomenologists, postmodern deconstructionists, and analytic philosophers have attempted to plumb the depths of reality or the relationship between language and the external world without considering essentially what science was discovering about it. Some philosophers, such as Heidegger, have disdained any contamination with science or technology, urging a return to the call of Being in a prelinguistic sense. Some have reverted to the literature of theology and mythology to fathom the nature of reality. Yet for any thinker to persistently ignore scientific interpretations of the world is difficult to comprehend today. For it is the methods of scientific inquiry that have been the most effective in developing reliable knowledge, and it is the concepts, hypotheses, and theories of the sciences that should be our starting point.

Nature is encountered by us as pluralistic. We discover what appears to be both order and disorder, chance and chaos. Hence we may never develop a reductive, unified theory comprising all of the processes of nature. Corresponding to the variety and multiplicity that we find, however, are levels of description and explanation, and unifying theories in specific sciences. The quest for a comprehensive theory accounting for everything is faced with perhaps insuperable obstacles. Not only is it not possible for any one mind to absorb, let alone understand, the complex, kaleidoscopic range of knowledge that we possess, but each of us is limited by the particular spatiotemporal slab in which we exist. We are each culture bound, confined as it were by the intellectual, philosophical, and scientific paradigms that dominate our age. Yet in spite of the herculean dimensions of the task and the complexity and finitude of a person's life, there is still some compelling urgency that we at least attempt to make some sense of our collective knowledge.

Any adequate interpretation of the body of knowledge cannot be focused only on our own present temporocultural framework, for we need some historical perspective that defines where we were in the past in comparison with where we are in the present. This requires some appreciation for the great literature of history to be knowledgeable about the struggles men and women underwent in seeking to explore and learn the world. This would include some reckoning of their breakthroughs and discoveries as well as their failures and blind alleys. Alchemy, bloodletting, numerology, psychical research, phrenology, and astrology are testimonies to the failed pseudosciences of the past, fields in which countless generations of investigators were engaged, and in some cases still are. Any effort to integrate knowledge must be made with the knowledge of the great conceptual systems of history, many or most of which have been replaced, and of the great civilizations that have had their day in the sun and have also disappeared. But we also need to know of the great achievements that have remained and been incorporated into the body of tested knowledge today. In addition, we also need to have some sense of future prospects of the expanding frontiers of knowledge and the widening horizons of the new ideas, goals, and ends to which we may aspire. These are all part of the human adventure in which we can collectively participate. But any worldview we work out will be *ours* at this particular nexus in history, and this will most likely give way in future generations that are faced with new challenges and opportunities.

No matter what the epoch, however, the demand of humans for meaning is perennial. And so we ask: What does it all mean and how does it fit together? What is my (or our) place in the scheme of things? What does this portend for me (or us)?

Unfortunately, some cultural lag is ever-present, for it takes time to digest and assimilate the knowledge we already possess. It is a paradox that many of the integrative schemes that still dominate belief hark back one, two, or three millennia. The explanatory tales and parables of God and spiritual forces, woven out of human imagination by our nomadic-agricultural forebears, still sustain the bulk of humankind. They are the myths of consolation, spawned by the yearnings for the sacred and fed by the transcendental temptation.

The overwhelming fact of life is its finitude and fragility. It passes so quickly. We are each destined to be buried by the sands of time. In the desperate effort to cope with the contingencies and ambiguities intrinsic to the human condition, men and women are led to postulate hidden sources outside of nature. Life in any age is uncertain and indeterminate, fraught with tragedies, and so there is a deceptive quest for eternity, a search for moorings for our otherwise rudderless vessels in the uncharged seas of existence. That is apparently one explanation of why human beings cling to myths long since discredited, and why they are still fixated on their promises. What else do they have to make sense of what they perceive as an otherwise meaningless world? At the present moment, we have progressed rather far in what we know about the universe. We understand full well that eschatological divinity tales are mere illusions that have no foundation in fact. Those who wish comfort can seek out priests and prophets to make their passage through life more bearable. Those who wish truth can find no consolation in self-deception. Skepticism has shattered the idols of the temple.

But if God is dead, what is the human prospect? Must it remain forlorn in a bleak universe? Is it possible to develop an authentic alternative that has some rational support? But to whom shall we turn for guidance? Unfortunately, not to the scientific specialist who has divided up the world, investigates only his or her small portion, and does not know how it fits together. Shall we look to the philosopher who takes as his or her task cosmic *sophia*? Alas, the philosopher, in being committed to examining all sides of the questions in the process, is often unable to make up his or her mind or resolve any of them. Philosophy from the earliest has been interested in analyzing meanings and unraveling mysteries, but the philosopher is often hesitant and indecisive, unable to solve quandaries, unwilling to stimulate motivation or action. Human beings want to know—not only for the intrinsic pleasure of knowing but so that they may act. And it is the business of life that demands answers. We go to practical men and women to help us solve our concrete problems: doctors and lawyers, bakers and tailors, engineers and architects, business people and politicians.

But we need something more. We need generalists, who have a broader view of how the sciences interrelate. We need historians, who have an understanding of past human civilizations. We also need idealists, men and women of inventive imagination who have some sense of possible future worlds to create. Surely we are mere mortals, not gods. Who among us can claim to encapsulate or plan the entire human prospect? We need to be skeptical of utopianists who offer unreliable totalistic visions of other worlds and strive to take us there. We need some ideals, but we also need to protect ourselves from the miscalculations and misadventures of visionaries.

THE EUPRAXSOPHERS

At this point, it seems to me, we need to make room for *eupraxsophy*, a new field of knowledge and a craft.[1] Eupraxsophers will strive to be generalists, able to understand, as best they can, what the sciences tell us about nature and life. Eupraxsophers will thus study the sciences carefully—anthropology and paleontology, psychology and sociology, economics and politics, genetics and biology, physics and astronomy. They will attempt to work with other generalists in developing general-systems theory and in finding common concepts and theories that cut across fields and seem most reliable. They will attempt to incorporate the skills of the historian and the futurist at the same time. But they will also be skeptics, in that they will be critical of pretentious untested claims. They will be able to analyze the meanings of terms and concepts and examine the evidential ground for belief. They will attempt to be objective in their inquiries.

Eupraxsophers will concentrate on two tasks: (1) They will seek *sophia*, or wisdom, a summing-up in a synoptic view of what the most reliable knowledge of the day tells us about nature and humankind. (2) They will also be concerned with *eupraxia*, that is, with *eu* (good) and *praxis* (conduct)—succinctly, good conduct. They will, in other words, attempt to draw the normative implications of *sophia* for living our practical life.

How will eupraxsophers proceed? In the first sense, by applying the principle of *coduction*. If they cannot find a unified-field theory, incorporating all of the sciences, they can at least develop a factorial analysis. They can, in other words, seek to comprehend or explain nature by reference to pluralistic sets of causal hypotheses. There are levels of inquiry in which specific kinds of factual data are described and accounted for. These are drawn from the micro and macro levels, and apply to physical-chemical, biological, psychological, and sociocultural systems of events. They refer to subatomic particles, atoms, molecules, cells, organs, organisms, persons, cultures, social institutions, and the global system. They are related to our planet, solar system, and galaxy, to other galaxies, and to the universe at large. I have introduced the term *coduction* to describe such an approach to understanding.[2] Clearly the logic of conductive explanation would allow for both reductionistic and holistic theories. In the human domain they would allow for both physicalistic and intentional explanations of human and social behavior.

As a methodological program, coduction encourages the quest for general physicalistic explanatory principles, but it would also allow for teleonomic explanations. For it must deal with the various levels of data under observation and the concepts that are introduced to interpret the complexities of higher-order systems. Coduction thus leaves a place for both biochemical explanations and psychological, behavioral, and sociocultural explanations on the level of human behavior. We must always be prepared to exercise our skeptical criticisms about any such theories that are proposed. Selective skepticism within the sciences is essential to inquiry. Nonetheless we recognize that we have many well-tested hypotheses and theories, and that our cosmic outlook is best informed and constantly transformed by reference to this body of reliable knowledge. Here our *sophia* is not fixed but is a function of the historical-cultural epoch in which we live.

Eupraxsophers will also have a deep interest in ethical and social questions, and will help us to frame reliable judgments of practice. Both individual and public choices can best be *act-duced* in the light of empirical knowledge. Our evaluations of good or bad, right or wrong, are most effectively formulated by reference to a valuational base. Included in the base are factual and technological hypotheses and theories about the world and ourselves. This includes causal knowledge, knowledge of means/ends, and predictions of the consequences of our choices. The valuation base also includes value-laden norms and ethical principles. This incorporates our own de facto prizings and appraisings, and our understanding of the normal needs of the human species, the common moral decencies, and the civic virtues that may prevail in our own sociocultural historical context. What we will decide to do in any context of moral decision making is open to ongoing criticism. All choices are tentative and hypothetical. Thus some degree of constructive ethical skepticism is intrinsic to our life as reflective members of the community. Nonetheless we can reach some measure of reliable ethical knowledge. Our *eupraxia*—the things we consider worthwhile—is related to our cosmic *sophia*—our understanding of the universe in which we live.

Are there a sufficient number of eupraxsophers in our midst? Regrettably, they are all too few in number. Philosophers like John Dewey, Sidney Hook, and Bertrand Russell exemplified the eupraxsophic life; they were interested not only in knowledge, but in action. It was not simply the love of wisdom (*philo*) that they sought, but good ethical practice (*eupraxia*). They were skeptical of occult, theological, and transcendental theories. As free thinkers they drew upon the sciences to understand the world; they espoused humanistic values and defended the free society.

I submit that there is an identifiable need for universities and colleges to develop a new profession, that of eupraxsophy. In addition to training scientists or technocrats, economists or philosophers, we need men and women interested in the quest for wisdom and its application to the good life. Eupraxsophers are concerned with questions concerning the meaning of life and the relevance of the sciences and the arts to the life of practical judgment. This is surely one of the tasks of liberal education. Students are exposed to a wide range of fields of human knowledge in the arts and sciences so that they can expand their horizons of appreciation and understanding. Unfortunately, the university curriculum today has been emasculated by the demands of the narrow specialty professions. Students have been given a smorgasbord of subjective electives. They are unable to interpret what they have learned or reconcile it with their system of values. Moreover, few students really appreciate the methods of critical and skeptical inquiry or the nature of reliable knowledge. All too often, in the name of liberal arts education, students graduate as scientific illiterates. Eupraxsophy should be the mark of every educated person: the capacity for reflective judgment and skeptical inquiry, some understanding of the universe in which he or she lives, and some ability to formulate judgments of practice.

CONVICTIONS

The final question I wish to address is whether persons committed to skeptical inquiry in all areas of knowledge can live fully. Will they be sufficiently stimulated to undertake great tasks, or will skepticism corrode their judgment, undermine their zest for life, deaden their desire for exploration and discovery?

This is a crucial issue that is often raised, but its solution is *psychological* as much as it is theoretical. It deals with the question of human motivation and how to untap the vital potentialities for living exuberantly. The real test of eupraxsophy is whether it can arouse conviction. Will it have sufficient motivational force so that people will consider their lives interesting and exciting, and will they readily embark upon robust Promethean adventures?

What is pivotal here is the recognition that in stimulating great actions, we must go beyond purely cognitive thought. Human beings are not empty intellectual shells, but passionate centers for feeling, profoundly influenced by the intensity of their inner everything. We have the capacity to be moved by aesthetic beauty and the arts, and to be inspired by ethical choice. This is testified to by the fact that humans are not only interested in ascertaining whether or not their beliefs are true, but in how to satisfy their passionate desires. A full life is infused with intensity and emotions. It is moved by love and affection, anger and pride, fear and hope, glory and despair. In both our private soliloquies and public expression, we need to interrelate our thoughts and feelings, our beliefs and attitudes. But although we need to savor the immediacies of the emotional life—the exciting thrills and the subtle delicacies—skeptical inquirers ask that personal beliefs not be deceptively influenced by feelings, and that beliefs be amenable to modification in the light of inquiry. There are constant temptations to sacrifice thought to other passionate interests. At some point we need to regain our cognitive composure. There should therefore be limits placed upon unrestrained temperament and, in the contest between true belief and deceptive passion, the former must eventually win out.

Plato observed that the "chariot of the soul" is pulled by three horses: reason, ambition, and passion. The goal of the wise person is not to allow either passion or ambition to lunge out beyond the lead horse, reason, and to so entangle the chariot that it is overturned, but we need to have all three horses work together in unison. The chariot of the soul should be guided by reason if harmony is to be reached, but ambition and passion still have a place in the full life. For we still are irreducibly men and women of feeling. We fall deeply in love, are moved to laughter or aroused by victory. We need to taste and enjoy the hedonic pleasures of life. We need to be committed to helping others, to be involved in beloved causes. Sometimes our illusions may cloud our clarity of thought. Sometimes we may be overwhelmed by false prophets, grandiose schemes, or illusory projects. We need to be critical of mythic systems of fantasy and illusion and of unbounded goals that are destructive to ourselves and others.

We need a realistic appraisal of the human condition. This includes an appreciation for the positive reaches of life—and here optimism is warranted. But there are also the sometimes tragic components of death, failure, disease, and suffering—and here are some realistic pessimism is relevant. Secular humanists are impressed by the unbounded potentialities of the Promethean spirit and the opportunities for experiencing joyful living, yet we must not overlook the tears and sorrow that we sometimes experience. Eupraxsophers need to offer some consolation to the bereaved, or else they will be outdistanced by the theological purveyors of empty promises of eternal life. The Old Testament admonishes us to remember: "Mine afflictions and my misery, the wormwood and the gall" (Lam. 3:19). Or again, the tragedian reminds us: "Preach to the storm, and reason with despair. But tell not Misery's son that life is fair."[3]

Life must go on, responds the practical person, and we should try our best. No doubt we need a realistic appraisal of the human condition, but it needs always to be infused with some underlying optimism, or else the fainthearted may be tempted to give up, exclaiming, "What's the use?" Thus there is a basic principle of motivation that the skeptical humanist insists upon: that life is good, or can be good, and that living is better than dying. Indeed, it can be exciting, full of joy and zest. The empirical evidence that life can be intensely significant has been attested by the lives of countless men and women who have been skeptical, yet were passionately committed to the achievement of great ideals or to the robust fulfillment of joyful living. No doubt this is the first principle of the skeptical humanist: *Life itself needs no justification beyond itself.* The question, "*Why life?*" has no cognitive significance. Skeptical humanists and atheists need not be devoid of some form of natural piety, an appreciation of the wonder and magnificence of the cosmic scene—particularly as they stare into the heavens at night. "My atheism, like that of Spinoza," says the humanist philosopher George Santayana, "is true piety towards the universe and denies only gods fashioned by men in their own image, to be servants of their human interests."[4]

The decisive response to the nihilistic skeptic is that we encounter life head on, and we find it good in the *living of it.* The basic problem of life is not *whether* to live, but *how* to live. The problem of whether to go on living may be raised in some existential situations, such as by persons suffering a painful terminal illness. Here voluntary euthanasia may be a meaningful option. Despair may also overtake individuals living in any overly oppressive society. Here revolt may be the only option. Still, the basic question we face is not whether to live, but *how to live*, and *how to live well.* The lust for life must precede everything else; if it is absent, there is little that can be said. Courage, motivation, affirmation, the intense desire to live is thus the first premise, but this is not imposed on life but is natural to it and at all stages—for the infant, the child, the adolescent, the mature adult, the aging person (providing that the person is not suffering some biochemically induced state of depression).

Skeptical inquiry is our second premise, but it grows out of the first. Life precedes reason, and reason can only minister to it as its servant. Skeptical critics will say, "Aha! Another assumed principle! What is the justification for this?" To which I respond: *If* we wish to live and to live well, *then* the methods of skeptical intelligence and the quest for reliable knowledge are the most effective instruments of our desires. Knowledge can only modify and transform our interests, but the lust for life itself must come first.

Knowledge is surely a good in itself, in that it can give us intrinsic pleasure. But more directly, it has high pragmatic value in helping us to define and explain who and what we are and what is happening in nature, and it best provides us with instruments for resolving our problems. Knowledge can uncover the limiting conditions within the natural world; it can also discover creative new potentialities, and it can evaluate the consequences of our choices. The justification for knowing is found in the process of living, in helping us to cope with the obstacles that confront us. Practical reason is thus embedded in the very fabric of life. It defines what it means to be a civilized being.

We cannot demonstrate that the kind of skeptical inquiry that I have defended is ultimately provable to the nihilist. Yet it has become central to our lives. To abandon it is to slip back to brute biological existence; to expand its use in all areas of life is to advance the cause of civilized living. Beyond that, perhaps nothing more can or need be said.

NOTES

1. I have outlined this concept in detail in my book *Eupraxsophy: Living without Religion* (Amherst, NY: Prometheus Books, 1990).

2. For an extended discussion of conduction, see my *Decision and the Condition of Man* (Seattle: University of Washington Press, 1965), chap. 5.

3. From *Lines on Reading*, by the young English poet Henry Kirke White (1785–1806).

4. George Santayana, *Soliloquies in England* (New York: Scribner's, 1922).

Section Four

THE SKEPTICAL MOVEMENT, PAST AND FUTURE

Chapter 14

THE NEW SKEPTICISM
A Worldwide Movement

I

The contemporary skeptical movement may be said to have been initiated with the founding of the Committee for the Scientific Investigation of Claims of the Paranormal (CSICOP) in 1976. This movement is now growing worldwide and it provides a much-needed antidote to the persistence of irrational, paranormal, and occult systems of belief.

Skepticism is an ancient philosophical and scientific outlook that traces its origins to Greece and Rome. Sextus Empiricus, Pyrrho, Carneades, and others advanced the skeptical outlook in the ancient Greco-Roman world. Skepticism went into eclipse in Christian Europe for over a thousand years, but it was revived during the modern period when thinkers as diverse as Bayle, Descartes, Montaigne, and Hume advocated it. Indeed, in no small measure the revival of modern skepticism led to the development of the scientific revolution in the sixteenth century. Scientific discovery rapidly advanced when men and women were liberated from the blind hold of authority, faith, custom, revelation, and mysticism, and when

[*Skeptical Briefs* 8, no. 2 (June 1998): 1–3, 9–11]

they sought to appeal to inductive evidence and experiment to test hypotheses and to deductive reason and mathematics to develop more comprehensive theories.

There are at least three kinds of skepticism that may be distinguished. The first, in its extreme form, is negative and nihilistic. It has had both classical and modern defenders. It holds that no knowledge is possible, and this applies not only to scientific and philosophical theories, but to any kind of moral or political principles. This form of skepticism is totally unreliable. A person cannot hope to function in the world if he or she is in a state of utter doubt and indecision. A second form of skepticism, which developed in ancient times and came to fruition in the modern world, was called "mitigated skepticism" by David Hume. This approach said that we needed to act in the world and to formulate beliefs about it. Yet it still presupposed an underlying gnawing skepticism about the reliability of knowledge. Still a third kind of skepticism had emerged on the philosophical scene in the early part of the twentieth century. Charles Peirce and the American pragmatists argued that skeptical doubt is but one phase within a process of inquiry, but it can be overcome when hypotheses are tested by adequate evidence and justifying reasons. This form of skepticism is positive and constructive and is limited to specific contexts under inquiry. Scientific inquirers realize that their formulations may not be fixed or final and may be modified in the future by future observations and theories. Nonetheless, science presupposes the conviction that reliable knowledge is possible and can be attained by persistent efforts.

The kind of skepticism CSICOP presents is continuous with the third kind above. I have called this "the new skepticism" in my book by that name.[1] This form of skepticism is based on the realization that the progress of science is the result of the continuing application of the methods of science, and that skepticism is an intrinsic part of the process of inquiry.

Permit me to say something about the reasons why I decided to create such a movement. I had long been a critic of paranormal (and supernatural) claims that could not be supported by the evidence. I was astonished that many or most of the claims continued to enjoy widespread public support, even though they had been refuted. Moreover, the mass media latched onto paranormal claims, which they discovered were profitable at the box office. Uri Geller, Jeane Dixon, and others were enjoying a huge following with hardly a dissent. This occurred despite the fact that scientific inquiry, which investigated their claims, had rejected them for lack of

evidence. Astrology is a good case in point, for it was refuted by astrono-
mers, physicists, statisticians, psychologists, and other scientists. There is
no empirical basis for horoscopes or sun-sign astrology: Its cosmology is
based on the discredited Ptolemaic system; moreover, it is possible to test
its predictions and forecasts, and the results are invariably negative. Yet
very few in the general public are aware of these criticisms, and indeed
often confuse astronomy with astrology.

With this in mind, I helped to draft and issue a statement, "Objections
to Astrology," with the assistance of Bart Bok, a noted astronomer, and
Lawrence Jerome, a science writer. This statement was endorsed by 186
leading scientists, including nineteen Nobel laureates. It received immediate worldwide attention, especially after the *New York Times* did a front-
page story. It seemed to me that the success of this effort, especially within
the scientific community, called for the need for a more organized response
by the academic and scientific community. I decided to create a new coali-
tion comprised of scientists, skeptics, philosophers, magicians, and others.
Hence, I invited several dozen critics of the paranormal to Amherst, New
York, to an open conference to develop an organized opposition to the
uncontested growth of belief in the paranormal. These included some well-
known popular critics, such as Martin Gardner, Milbourne Christopher,
Marcello Truzzi, Ray Hyman, and James Randi. I also invited some distinguished philosophers and scientists, such as Ernest Nagel, Sidney Hook,
and W. V. Quine, to endorse the statement of purpose I had drafted.

The conference was held at the new campus of the State University of
New York at Buffalo, in Amherst, New York. At that time, I was editor of
the *Humanist* magazine, one of the leading journals critical of religion. At
the inaugural meeting of CSICOP, in my opening address ("The Scientific
Attitude versus Antiscience and Pseudoscience"), I said that there was a
long-standing conflict in the history of culture between religion and science, but that today a new challenge to science has come to the fore
because of the growth of pseudoscientific and paranormal claims. The
apparent popular belief in exorcism,[2] nouveau witches, and Satanism were
symptomatic of the Aquarian consciousness then being proclaimed. The
mass media also presented as true (and usually without any dissent)
accounts of Kirlian photography, the wonders of ESP and psychokinesis,
UFO sightings, the Bermuda Triangle, Bigfoot, von Däniken's *Chariots of
the Gods?* and so on. A great number of quasi-religious organizations had

emerged at that time, including the Hare Krishna, Reverend Moon's Unification Church, and the Scientologists. These were symptomatic of a countercultural opposition to science that had begun to appear, and it needed, in my judgment, to be responded to—for the public had a right to hear the scientific critique of pseudoscientific and fringe claims.

I raised the following questions: Should we assume that the scientific revolution, which began in the sixteenth century, is continuous? Or will it be overwhelmed by the forces of unreason?

And I replied: We ought not to assume, simply because ours is an advanced scientific-technological society, that irrational thinking will be overcome. The evidence suggests that this is far from being the case. Indeed, there is always the danger that science itself may be engulfed by the forces of unreason.[3]

Since that time, postmodernism has emerged, denying the possibility of scientific objectivity and considering science as only one mythic narrative among others. And much to everyone's surprise, there have been widespread attacks on the Enlightenment and the ideals of the scientific revolution.

Today these antiscientific protests are accompanied by a resurgence of fundamentalist religions. So the challenge to science is not simply from propagandists for the paranormal, but also from the disciples of many religions. I should point out that although I personally believe that skeptics need to deal with religious claims as well as with paranormal claims, I recommended that CSICOP concentrate on paranormal and pseudoscientific claims. The British and American Societies for Psychical Research, founded in 1882 and 1885, respectively, were basically made up of those committed to the psychical point of view, as was J. B. Rhine's laboratory founded at Duke University in 1927. Hence, CSICOP would concentrate on paranormal investigations, though hopefully from a neutral and impartial framework, and it would examine religious claims only insofar as they were testable. I founded *Free Inquiry* in 1980 explicitly to deal with religious claims, for the new skepticism needs to be applied across the board.

As is well known, the first meeting of CSICOP had an enormous impact. There was extensive press coverage from the *Washington Post* and *New York Times* to the *New Scientist* and *Pravda*, with virtually all of the major science magazines welcoming the formation of CSICOP. We had crystallized a perceived need that both the scientific community and many in the general public thought had to be satisfied: a response to the growth of paranormal claims. Within a year our new magazine was launched, at first called the *Zetetic* (under the editorship of Marcello Truzzi), and thence the *Skeptical Inquirer* (under the editorship of Kendrick Frazier, who had been the editor of *Science News*). Much to our pleasure, skeptical groups began forming all over the world, so that today there are over seventy-five such groups from Germany, England, and the Netherlands to China, Russia, Spain, and Mexico; and there are networks of such groups in Europe and Latin America. Moreover, some fifty magazines and newsletters have appeared. Indeed, we have worked closely with national groups to help get their organizations and magazines started.

All of these developments have contributed to the formation of a worldwide New Skepticism Movement. There is now a vibrant and growing international network affiliated with CSICOP and the *Skeptical Inquirer*. We are all committed to the scientific program; we are skeptical of paranormal and occult claims, unless they have been corroborated and replicated by independent investigators.

One may ask, After more than two decades of inquiry, what can be learned about this entire phenomenon? In the rest of this chapter I wish to sum up many of the basic findings and conclusions that the skeptical movement has reached about paranormal beliefs and claims.

II

First, the term *paranormal* itself is highly questionable. We decided to use the term only because proponents (such as J. B. Rhine) had used it. We doubt that it is possible to find a paranormal realm separate from or independent of the natural universe. We are seeking normal and natural explanations for phenomena. The best meaning of the term *paranormal* is that there are sometimes bizarre, unexpected anomalies that we encounter (as Charles Fort described them), and we are willing to examine them with an open mind and do not wish to reject them a priori and antecedent to inquiry. Murray Gell-Mann, a Nobel Prize winner and Fellow of CSICOP, at a conference at the University of Colorado in 1986, observed that in one sense we deny the paranormal entirely, because once we find that phenomena can be explained by reference to prosaic causes, then these explanations are incorporated into the natural scientific worldview and are not separated from it. I reiterate: we have an open mind and are willing to examine anomalies without prejudgment, provided the claims made by the proponents are responsible.

Anecdotal Reports

What we have found is that many reports of anomalous events are based on anecdotal accounts. While these reports cannot be dismissed out of hand or without a fair hearing, especially if they are seriously offered, skeptics hold that inquirers should go beyond mere anecdotes to a more systematic examination of the phenomena. Many anecdotal narratives are based upon private experiences, subjective and introspective in character, or upon memory of past events, which may be unreliable, or made upon second- or thirdhand hearsay.

It is important that all such reports be carefully sifted through, if possible, before they are accepted. Anecdotes may have a grain of truth and they may bring new and important data that has been otherwise overlooked. On the other hand, they may involve serious misperception or faulty memory, they may involve stories embellished upon beyond their original meaning, or they may be incidents blown out of proportion to what actually happened or the deception of the senses colored by suggestion. Many of these alleged anecdotes, if reported secondhand, take on the character of gossip, folktales, or urban legends. There is a tendency for people who believe in the occult to read mysterious nuances into otherwise prosaic experiences or to exaggerate the significance of random events. This commonly occurs, for example, in reports of ghostly apparitions, crisis premonitions of death, visitations by extraterrestrial beings, or the accuracy of psychic prophecies. Skeptics ask, Did the event occur as the person states, and is the interpretation placed on the event the most likely cause?

Unless an anecdotal account can be corroborated independently, investigators urge caution about its authenticity. This not only applies to the truth of the event alleged to have actually occurred, but to the occult explanation that is imposed on it because of ignorance of the real causes.

The skeptic says that the report may or may not be true and that if it did occur there may be alternative causal explanations to be made of it. Are we dealing with a real event or a misperception, hallucinatory experience, fantasy, and/or misinterpretation of what happened?

Eyewitness Testimony

The appeal to eyewitness testimony is the bedrock of our knowledge about the world and ourselves. The data are drawn from direct, firsthand experience. It is important, however, that such testimony not be accepted on face value without careful inspection. This is especially the case when the testimony is about anomalous, unexpected, or bizarre events. If a person reports that it is raining heavily outside and he supports the claim with the fact that he is soaking wet, and if this report does not conflict with our common knowledge about the world, it need not demand weighty evidence (though he may have been squirted with a hose or had a bucket of water dumped on him). We can corroborate such claims by looking outside, receiving reports from other bystanders, and/or consulting a barometer. If, on the contrary, a person reports that it is raining pink fairies, skeptical inquirers request that his extraordinary account be corroborated by independent and impartial observers.

Psychologist Elizabeth Loftus of the University of Washington (Fellow of CSICOP and a speaker at its 1994 convention) has performed numerous experiments to demonstrate the often fallible and deceptive character of memory. She found that bystanders at a robbery or accident often offer conflicting reports, especially where the incident is emotionally charged. This tendency to misperceive may be compounded when someone claims to have seen a statue of the Virgin Mary weep or a miraculous cure by a faith healer. Not only must the report of an observer be carefully analyzed, but the interpretation that is placed upon it must be evaluated. Thus skeptical inquirers ask that wherever possible there be two or more witnesses to an event, that these witnesses be careful observers, and that what they have said can be independently corroborated. Reports of UFO visitations are common throughout the world, and these reports often come in waves, often depending on sensationalistic media exploitation. The investigator asks: What did these people really see? Can these interpretations be verified? Skeptical inquirers have sought to provide prosaic explanations for unidentified flying objects, which are often identified as planets, meteors, weather balloons, terrestrial rockets, aircraft, or other phenomena.

Extraordinary Claims Need Extraordinary Evidence

This principle has been adduced for anomalous accounts. If it is the case that a paranormal event, if confirmed, would overthrow the known laws of science, then one would need abundant evidence to accept it. The evidence must not be skimpy or haphazard, but so strong that its denial would require more credulity than its acceptance. The claim has been made that psychokinesis is genuine—that the mind can move matter without an intervening physical object or material force—or that precognitive events can be known before they happen. Helmut Schmidt has claimed experimental evidence that persons in the present can retrogressively affect past events in a random generator. This unusual anomaly would seem to violate the laws of physics, and/or it would require that physics be revised to account for it. We would need several lines of independent replication before we could accept the claim.

Burden-of-Proof Argument

Some parapsychologists, such as John Beloff, have argued that the strongest evidence for paranormal events is in the historical cases of famous mediums and psychics. Eusapia Palladino, for example, was tested by numerous scientific bodies. Many found that she had cheated in some cases; others could find no evidence of cheating, hence they attributed the event to paranormal causes.[4] Similarly, it is claimed that D. D. Home, a well-known medium, allegedly floated out a London window above the street and performed other strange feats, and that those feats could not be accounted for in normal terms. Beloff maintains that unless skeptical inquirers can explain how these mediums performed what they did in all cases, then these accounts should be accepted as veridical. The skeptical inquirer responds that the burden of proof rests upon the paranormal claimant. It is he or she who must be able to account for such cases with sufficient evidence; unless this is done, one should suspend judgment and remain skeptical. This is particularly the case in regard to historical claims, where it is difficult to reconstruct the situation under which the alleged effect occurred. That is why skeptics ask for replication in the present before they can accept the phenomenon.

The burden-of-proof argument has been used in religion. Is a believer entitled to believe whatever he or she wishes about God, unless the skeptic can disprove God's existence or demonstrate that the properties attributed to him do not exist? The skeptic criticizes the logic of the argument in the following manner: If someone were to claim that mermaids exist, the burden of proof is upon the claimant to prove the fact, not the skeptic to disprove it.

Fraud

The resort to fraud is notorious in human affairs, including cases in orthodox science (for example, the Piltdown Man hoax). It is especially widespread in the paranormal area. Many mediums and psychics have been found cheating. Although some of the deception might be inadvertent, considerable intentional trickery has been uncovered. It is thus important that every precaution against deception be used. In the design of an experiment, safeguards ought to be built in so that the subjects under study cannot fudge the data, whether inadvertently or intentionally. C. E. M. Hansel has pointed out that many of the earlier experiments of J. B. Rhine were suspect, since the conditions of the experiments were loose. In the famous Pearce-Pratt experiment for telepathy, Pratt could easily have peeked at the Zener cards by sneaking out of the library to the sender's office, or by using an accomplice. Many scientists have been easily deceived by children. For example, physicist John Taylor, when observing children through a two-way mirror, found that they were bending spoons and forks manually, and not by paranormal means as was claimed. Suzie Cottrell was shown to be using the Shulein forced card trick to deceive observers. In a clever test of her powers conducted by fellows of CSICOP, she was seen on a hidden camera to use sleight of hand in shuffling the cards and to peek at them when no one was observing. It is also important that experimental fraud not intervene. A notable case in J. B. Rhine's parapsychology lab dramatizes the problem. Walter Levy was said to have tampered with the evidence for precognitive tests of chicks by altering the data.

There have been blatant illustrations of hoaxing in the UFO field. Billy Meier in Switzerland is one infamous example. The hoaxing of crop circles as evidence of extraterrestrial visitations in Great Britain has been exposed. Similarly for the unmasking of Philippine psychic surgeons and evangelical faith healers by James Randi and the Committee for the Scientific Examination of Religion.

A key point that has been made is that scientists who are accomplished in their own disciplines are not necessarily the most careful observers in other domains, and they can often be deceived by clever conjurers posing as psychics.

Experimenter Bias

The role of unconscious bias by an experimenter poses a problem in virtually all fields of science. Those who propose a theory are often not the best or most competent judges of the evidential basis in support of it. Experimenter bias may be conscious or unconscious. It may creep in by inadvertent sensory leakage or in assessment techniques. A good case is Michel Gauquelin, who was hailed by many as the founder of a new science of "astrobiology." Gauquelin claimed to have found a correlation between planetary configurations and professional achievement. He said that when Mars was in certain portions of the sky (key sectors 1 and 4) there was a tendency for greater sports champions to be born. There is considerable evidence that Gauquelin selected his sample based on prior knowledge of whether they were born with Mars in key sectors. Hence the effect found was due less to any Mars Effect than to Gauquelin's biased samples. Independent scientific inquiries were unable to replicate the efforts.

Noted parapsychologist Gertrude Schmeidler has said that there is a difference between sheep (believers) and goats (skeptics), and that the former are more likely to believe than the latter. Whether sheep can consistently show the existence of ESP is questionable. It is the case, however, that experimenters who are sheep may be more disposed to accept as positive any nuances in the data. On the other hand, the reverse may be the case and experimenters who are goats may dismiss evidence because of their antibias. In a debate with Charles Honorton, Ray Hyman has pointed to the need for tightening the experimental design in the Ganzfeld tests by the proper randomization of trials and careful grading techniques. Others have pointed to the questionable grading techniques in the remote-viewing tests of by Targ and Puthoff at the Stanford Research Institute.

Demand for Replication

The key argument of skeptical inquirers, not only in the paranormal field but in orthodox sciences as well, is the need for replicable experiments. Until psychical researchers can specify antecedent laboratory conditions under which an effect can be observed by independent observers, skeptics have the right to be cautious. The great controversy in parapsychology is precisely on this point: Is there a standard replicable experiment that can demonstrate the existence of psi to the neutral investigator? Unless that condition is satisfied, skeptics remain dubious about the reality of the phenomena.

Magical Thinking

Many skeptical inquirers have been puzzled by the ready tendency of many human beings to resort to magical thinking, that is, to accept without sufficient evidence contracausal explanations. This includes the capacity for adopting paranormal interpretations and/or reading occult forces into nature. There is a tendency to attribute miraculous powers to some individuals. Historically, this applies to the prophets who claim to have had revelations from on high and to be endowed with supernatural abilities. This also applies to gurus, shamans, medicine men, psychics, and faith healers, all of whom are believed to be possessed of magical powers. The person who resorts to magical thinking is more likely to accept the occult and/or psychic explanation without critical skepticism. The miracle worker is taken as an authority and the facts are stretched to validate the healing claim.

Psychological Interpretations of the Paranormal

Many skeptical inquirers maintain that the key to understanding paranormal phenomena is in human psychology and human nature. This has many dimensions: being amenable to suggestibility, being fantasy-prone and given to magical thinking, and having the general tendency to allow one's personal propensities, desires, and hopes to color the data. Ray Hyman has demonstrated the power of "cold reading" and how many people are taken in by it. But this can be generalized to many other paranormal fields.

The popularity of astrological horoscopes provides considerable support for a psychological interpretation. There is little or no evidence to support astrology, and it has failed virtually all the tests adduced to validate it.[5] All efforts to find a statistical correlation between the moment and place of birth and the position of the heavenly bodies have had negative results. Yet many people claim that astrological sun signs and horoscopes are true. For the skeptic the more likely explanation is that truth is in the eye of the beholder. Palm readers, astrologers, or psychics are often so general in their readings that their diagnoses and prognostications are stretched by the subject so that they are personally validated. Thus, in my view the key to the paranormal is that it is within the *eye of the beholder*. This is what I have labeled the "stretched-sock syndrome," for they can be stretched to fit any feet.

The Transcendental Temptation

Why is this so? I have postulated a "transcendental temptation" in human culture and human nature as a possible explanation for the tendency to accept a paranormal or occult universe.[6] This perhaps has its roots in the long evolutionary history of the species and it may have even a genetic basis. Some, such as E. O. Wilson, have claimed sociobiological roots for religiosity, though many skeptics have criticized this theory as not being sufficiently tested. John Schumaker, an Australian psychologist, believes that some illusions are necessary for sanity, and that "the corruption of reality" is an essential ingredient of mental health.[7] To face death or existential nothingness, he said, is difficult for most people, and so they achieve consolation by reading hidden meanings into nature, including belief in the afterlife or the ability to communicate with dead persons. The same explanation can be applied to many other areas of the paranormal. Gullibility is thus fed by the hunger for transcendence.

Hypnosis

One topic that has aroused considerable skeptical controversy concerns the reliability of hypnosis as a source of knowledge. Is hypnosis a special "trance state" induced in a subject, or is he or she simply acting out the suggestions of the hypnotist? It is clear that hypnosis is a useful technique in many areas of practice. It does have its pitfalls, however, concerning a whole range of paranormal phenomena, allegedly verified by hypnotic regression. This is the case in regard to "past-life regressions" used by some researchers as evidence for reincarnation. Budd Hopkins, David Jacobs, and John Mack have introduced hypnotic regressions as evidence for abductions by alien beings, who are allegedly engaged in sexual or genetic experiments.[8] Skeptics have argued that a more likely explanation for such bizarre tales is that the evidence is contaminated by the hypnotherapist, who, using suggestion, tends to implant the ideas in a person and/or assists in conjuring fantasies. The skeptic maintains that we need not postulate prior lives or extraterrestrial abductions in the paranormal realm, for there are still other possible alternative explanations. For example, some otherwise normal, fantasy-prone individuals are likely to weave tales from their imaginations. Often cryptomnesia is at work and ideas or experiences deeply embedded in the unconscious are embellished upon and taken as real. The skeptic is highly dubious of such uses of hypnosis.

Pseudoscience versus Protoscience

It is important that a distinction between pseudoscience and genuine science be drawn. Unfortunately, it is not always possible to find a clear demarcation line, and sometimes what is labeled as "pseudoscience" may really be a new protoscience. Marcello Truzzi has pointed out that there is some danger that skeptical inquirers will reject new ideas—protosciences—because they do not fit into the prevailing paradigm. Some criteria for distinguishing a pseudoscience are available: For example, its concepts should be clearly defined and noncontradictory, its theories should be falsifiable, there should be tests available that would enable us to ascertain whether the hypotheses and theories are warranted. Phrenology and biorhythms were two alleged sciences that, after exhaustive testing, were found to warrant the label "pseudoscience." One has to be careful, since many new fields of inquiry have often had an uphill battle against the scientific establishment. The same is true for many established disciplines. Critics point out that psychology, sociology, anthropology, and political science are riddled with inadequate experimental designs and questionable studies. The better part of prudence is for skeptics to be skeptical not only of pseudosciences, but of orthodox science as well, and to be willing to revise even the most revered principles if they do not succeed under criticism by the community of inquirers. The key point of skepticism is not doubt, however, but *inquiry*; skepticism is only one element in the process of inquiry. It is not the belief or disbelief that is the main issue, but the facts, theories, and methods of verification.

Ridicule

Many of those whom skeptics have criticized resent what they consider to be unfair ridicule. Martin Gardner has pointed out that "a horse-laugh may be worth a thousand syllogisms" and that skeptics may rightfully debunk or lampoon outlandish paranormal claims. In the public domain, particularly in the mass media, paranormal claims are most often inflated out of proportion to the evidential basis. The claim is sensationalized and the public is led to believe it has been verified or documented by scientists, when this may not be the case. In such situations, a dispassionate appraisal may not get public attention, and an outrageous claim may need to be deflated by skeptics by some kind of humorous debunking. Here skeptics have entered the domain of rhetoric and persuasion. It is clear that ridicule is not a substitute for genuine inquiry and that such a resort can only occur *after* an extensive process of investigation. For skeptical inquirers, their commitment is to objective standards of responsible inquiry. How to convince the public that there is insufficient evidence for a claim and/or that they ought to suspend judgment, or that the claim is improbable, is an important question for those committed to advancing the program of science. All skeptics concede that their first obligation is to inquiry, and that any debunking must come as a conclusion to their investigations.

Alternative Causal Explanations

The ultimate goal of all scientific inquiry is not only to describe what has happened or is happening (descriptive knowledge) but to interpret phenomena by means of causal explanations. Here the best talents and creative ingenuity of inquirers must be brought to bear. It is often the case that an anomaly can best be explained in prosaic terms. Events that seem inexplicable may be due to coincidence; a miraculous cure may be due to the power of suggestion or the placebo effect; a statistical correlation may only be an artifact of the data; and so on. The program of science can proceed only when someone is sensitive to "the damn facts." One need not deny that anomalies exist; the challenge is to search for deeper causal correlations in order to account for why the facts are occurring. There is continual scientific success in this latter regard, for that which appeared at one time to be mysterious or inexplicable may be explained by reference to general principles or unique historical circumstances. Thus skeptical inquiry is related to the ultimate goal of all scientific research: to adequately describe and account for data and to explain, where possible, how and why they have occurred.

The Unsinkable Rubber Duck Syndrome

After more than two decades of investigation by skeptical inquirers, we are continually astonished by the fact that no matter how often we criticize paranormal belief claims, they still persist. Indeed, even if they are thoroughly examined and refuted in one age, they seem to reemerge within the next, and people will continue to believe them in spite of evidence to the contrary. This is what I have called the "unsinkable rubber duck" syndrome. No doubt many are familiar with a carnival shooting gallery, where customers are induced to shoot down moving ducks. Here, even if the ducks are successfully knocked down, they pop right back up again.

Given the tendency for magical thinking, the transcendental temptation, and gullibility, skeptics have their work cut out for them. We cannot silently steal away once we have investigated and debunked an outrageous claim. There will always be a need for skeptical inquiry in society. Not only do the old myths that crop up to entice a new generation need responses, but new, often more fanciful claims may be introduced and become fashionable. Thus, I submit that there is a continuing need for skeptical inquiry, and skeptics will always serve as the gadflies of society. Standing in the wings of the theater of life, unable to accept the prevailing nonsense on stage, skeptics keep alive the spirit of free inquiry and ask probing questions—even if those they criticize are deeply offended, and/or in spite of the calumny that may descend upon the skeptics for their criticisms.

The New Skepticism Movement thus has an ongoing positive and constructive task in worldwide society, and as long as human credulity persists, there is a need for skeptics to raise unsettling questions about it. We should continue to provide responsible explanations for paranormal and occult claims and, whatever our findings, to publish our views and make them known to the general public. We should not despair at the tidal wave of irrational beliefs that sometimes confront us. We are committed to the quest for knowledge and truth. In the last analysis, our main goal is *inquiry*, not skepticism, and in this regard the skeptical movement will always have a vital role to play in human culture.

NOTES

1. See Paul Kurtz, *The New Skepticism: Inquiry and Reliable Knowledge* (Amherst, NY: Prometheus Books, 1992).

2. This was no doubt stimulated by *The Exorcist*, by William Peter Blatty, and later by a film of that name.

3. "The Scientific Attitude vs. Pseudoscience and Antiscience," *Humanist* 36, no. 4 (July/August 1976): 131.

4. E. Fielding, W. W. Baggally, and H. Carrington, "Report on a Series of Sittings with Eusapia Palladino," *Proceedings of the SPR* 23 (1909): 306–569.

5. Roger B. Culver and Philip A. Ianna, *Astrology: True or False?* (Amherst, NY: Prometheus Books, 1988).

6. Paul Kurtz, *The Transcendental Temptation: A Critique of Religion and the Paranormal* (Amherst, NY: Prometheus Books, 1986).

7. John Schumaker, *The Corruption of Reality* (Amherst, NY: Prometheus Books, 1995).

8. Philip J. Klass, *UFO Abductions: A Dangerous Game* (Amherst, NY: Prometheus Books, 1989).

Chapter 15

SKEPTICAL INQUIRY
My Personal Involvement

I

In this essay I will focus on only one part of my personal skeptical odyssey. I wish to reflect primarily upon what happened in the years following CSICOP's inception. As chairman of the committee, I can only highlight some aspects of this eventful odyssey. As I have said, we got off to a rousing start. The journey has been exhilarating ever since.

PERSONAL BACKGROUND

I should say by way of background that I have always been a skeptic, at least since my early teens. Like others in my generation, I questioned the regnant orthodoxy in religion and politics, and I flirted with Marxism as a young man, though I abandoned any illusions of Communism during the Second World War when I served in the US Army on the western front. I saw that so

---

["My Personal Involvement: A Quarter Century of Skeptical Inquiry," in *Skeptical Odysseys* (2001), pp. 62–81. Section II is inserted from an article of the same name in *Skeptical Briefs* 25, no. 4 (July/August 2001): 42–43.]

many of the freed Soviet laborers in Germany—who had been forced into indentured servitude—refused to go back to Russia. I became an antitotalitarian early, though I remained sympathetic to the social democratic agenda.

Although I flirted with mysticism and Catholicism for a brief period in my late teens, I was turned on to philosophy as a young GI after the war in the American army of occupation. I got a chance to go to a red-brick university in Shrivenham, England, taught by both English and American professors. I took an introductory course in philosophy with Professor Charles W. Hendel of Yale University; the book that turned me on to skeptical inquiry was Plato's *Republic*, and in particular Socrates. I was intrigued by the arguments that Thrasymachus, a Sophist, laid down, and especially the effort by Socrates to respond to the challenge: "Why ought I to be moral?" Socrates was a gadfly, condemned to death by the Athenians for denying the gods, making the better appear the worse, and corrupting the youth of Athens. He took philosophy into the agora, the public square, raising difficult questions and pursuing the life of reason. I resolved at that time to pursue a philosophical career, and after the war continued my studies on my return to the United States.

The most powerful intellectual influence on my life was Sidney Hook, who exemplified the Socratic method of inquiry. Hook was a student of John Dewey and was influenced by Karl Marx. Knowledge for him was relative to praxis: Truth claims can be tested only by the consequences of beliefs in experience and practice. I was impressed by Hook's course "The Philosophy of Democracy" and enthralled by his ability to raise unsettling questions. He was the finest teacher I had. He demonstrated the importance of the method of intelligence and the use of scientific inquiry, especially in dealing with social and political problems. Hook also disabused me of any lingering belief in Marxism, and I became a committed democrat. I had taken a triple major at NYU—in philosophy, political science, and economics. I accepted pragmatic naturalism in both epistemology and metaphysics. I decided to go to Columbia University for my doctorate to study under other students of John Dewey, including Ernest Nagel, Herbert W. Schneider, and John Hermann Randall Jr.

I taught at a number of colleges, beginning with the conservative Episcopal Trinity College in Hartford, Connecticut (we called this the "Episcopal Party at Republican prayer"); Vassar; and Union College, and also for a period of time at the New School for Social Research (where I taught joint courses with Paul Edwards on atheism, agnosticism, and skepticism). Throughout my teaching career, I focused on the philosophy of the behavioral and social sciences, ethics, and value theory, but I had to teach a wide range of courses. At that time pragmatic naturalism involving a commitment to science and reason dominated American philosophy, but it went into eclipse for at least three decades as European imports began to dominate American faculties, especially analytic philosophy, but also phenomenology, existentialism, and even Marxism. For years I taught courses in the philosophy of religion and debated the existence of God—pro and con—and the immortality of the soul, and was a skeptic about both. One reason why I founded Prometheus Books in 1969 was that I thought the country needed a dissenting press that would defend a thoroughgoing naturalistic and scientific-rationalist outlook.

My interest in the paranormal began especially in the early 1960s after meeting with and reading the works of Curt J. Ducasse of Brown University and H. H. Price of Oxford, both of whom were involved in psychical research. I was intrigued by the possibility of ESP and communication with the dead. Although I was doubtful of postmortem survival, the possibility of ESP seemed real. This was enhanced by my own personal experiences, because I thought my wife, Claudine, whom I married in 1960, may have possessed telepathic powers (much like Upton Sinclair's wife). I was intrigued by the fact that she seemed to be able to read my mind. Perhaps I was causing certain perceptions or thoughts in her? I attempted some haphazard card-reading tests and was surprised by the number that she guessed correctly. Although I did not myself investigate this phenomenon systematically, I was not unsympathetic to the claims of psychical research.

A development that disturbed me in the late 1960s and early 1970s was the emergence on American campuses in the wake of the New Left of a series of bizarre cults. I have in mind the Lyndon LaRouche's US Labor Party, which pursued me with a vengeance because of my commitment to democratic humanism; Hare Krishna; Reverend Moon's Church of Unification; and the Scientologists. This led me further into a concern with paranormal beliefs that were proliferating—from astrology and parapsychology to UFOlogy.

At that time, I was uncertain in my own mind about any number of issues. Although skeptical of astrology, I was not sure as to whether or not Michel Gauquelin's claims for a new science of astrobiology were true, and this inquiry occupied me for over twenty years. Similarly, like everyone else, I had been exposed to reports of UFOs and thought it most likely that they were extraterrestrial in origin. Indeed, I once devoted an entire issue of the *Humanist* magazine (May/June 1976), which I edited, to the question, "What should be our reaction to extraterrestrial beings should we ever encounter them on the planet Earth or in outer space?" My very first recognition that UFOlogy was mistaken was when I heard Philip J. Klass at the inaugural session of CSICOP. He provided alternative prosaic explanations of phenomena that seemed reasonable and led me to question my former beliefs in them.

Hence, at the inception of the skeptics movement, I had an open mind about the possibility of telepathy, the claims of Gauquelin, and the likelihood of UFOlogical visitations.

II

It is well known that I am the culprit responsible for the founding of the Committee for the Scientific Investigation of Claims of the Paranormal. Why did I do so? Because I was dismayed in 1976 by the rising tide of belief in the paranormal and the lack of adequate scientific examinations of these claims. At that time a wide range of claims were everywhere present. Books such as Erich von Däniken's *Chariots of the Gods?* Immanuel Velikovsky's *Worlds in Collision*, and Charles Berlin's *The Bermuda Triangle* were widely popular; and self-proclaimed gurus and soothsayers—from Uri Geller to Jeane Dixon—were stalking the media. I was distressed that my students confused astrology with astronomy and accepted pyramid power, Bigfoot, the Loch Ness monster, Kirlian photography, and psychic surgery without the benefit of a scientific critique. Most of my scientific colleagues were equally perplexed by what was happening, but they were focused on their own narrow specialties—interdisciplinary efforts were frowned upon—and they did not know what the facts of the case were. Martin Gardner's *Fads and Fallacies in the Name of Science* was available, but aside from that there were all too few skeptical studies in the literature for open-minded inquirers, let alone the general public.

It is within this cultural milieu that I decided to convene a special conference to discuss "The New Irrationalisms: Antiscience and Pseudoscience." This was held on the newly built Amherst campus of the State University of New York at Buffalo (where I was a professor) between April 30 and May 2, 1976. I drafted a call inviting a number of leading scholars to the inaugural session of the proposed new organization. This was endorsed by many philosophers, including W. V. Quine, Sidney Hook, Ernest Nagel, Brand Blanshard, and Antony Flew. And I invited many of the well-known skeptical critics to this opening session—Martin Gardner, Ray Hyman, Philip J. Klass, Marcello Truzzi, James Randi, L. Sprague de Camp, and Milbourne Christopher. The new organization, which I co-chaired with Truzzi, was to be called the Committee for the Scientific Investigation of Claims of the Paranormal. Our long-range goal was public education of the aims of science, particularly an appreciation for scientific methods of inquiry and critical thinking.

There had been other scientific efforts historically to investigate paranormal claims, such as the Society for Psychical Research founded in Great Britain in 1882 and in the United States in 1885 (by William James). And there had been many UFO groups that came into being in the post–World War II period. But most of these groups mainly attracted believers who were predisposed to accept the phenomena; the skeptics in their midst were few and far between. Thus CSICOP was the first body made up predominantly of skeptics who were willing to investigate the alleged paranormal phenomena. We had been attacked by believers for being "closed minded" and by other skeptics who claimed that we were dignifying phenomena that did not deserve special attention. But we thought we had an important task to fulfill.

THE AGENDA

There were four strategic issues that CSICOP had to address at its founding. First, what would be our approach to such phenomena? Would we simply be debunkers out to show by ridicule the folly of the claims that were made, or would we be serious investigators concerned with research into claims—dispassionate, open-minded inquirers? The answer was clear: Our chief focus would be on inquiry, not doubt. Where we had investigated a claim and found it wanting, we would express our doubt and perhaps even debunk it, but this would be only after careful investigation.

Second, we asked, what would be our relationship to pro-paranormal believers? We observed that there were by now hundreds, perhaps even thousands, of pro-paranormal magazines and publications in the world, and that we were virtually the lone dissenting voice in the wilderness, as it were. We would be glad to engage believers in debate, but it would be our agenda, not theirs. Accordingly, we decided that we wished by and large to pursue our own research strategy, namely, to encourage scientific and skeptical inquiry. Marcello Truzzi, cochairman and editor of the *Zetetic* (founded by him but which we took over), insisted that we present both believers and nonbelievers in dialogue in the pages of the magazine, and this he proceeded to do. Although members of the CSICOP Executive Council found this interesting and perhaps useful, they demurred because they felt that there was already tremendous exposure of the pro-paranormalists' viewpoint, and we really wished to focus on the neglected skeptical case. Truzzi resigned from the editorship of the magazine, and indeed from the Executive Council, and the *Skeptical Inquirer* came into being, edited by veteran science writer Kendrick Frazier, who had covered the first meeting of CSICOP for *Science News*.

Third, one of the most difficult questions we faced was, What was the relationship of the paranormal to religion? Would CSICOP deal with religious questions? Our position has been from the start that we would not investigate religious claims unless there were empirical or experimental means for evaluating them. We were not concerned with religious faith, theology, or morality, but only with scientific evidence adduced for the religious claims.

Fourth, a most interesting and unexpected development occurred: immediately after CSICOP was formed, many concerned scientists and skeptics said they wanted to establish similar local groups in their areas in the United States. We helped them to do so by providing our subscription lists and sending speakers. Similarly, researchers in other countries said they wished to do the same. We assisted this effort in any way we could. I personally visited virtually all of the nascent national organizations or sent other members of CSICOP (especially James Randi, Mark Plummer, and Barry Karr). This included groups in Canada, England, France, Belgium, Italy, Germany, the Netherlands, Hungary, Mexico, and Russia. Thus skeptical organizations began forming throughout the world. This meant CSICOP had become an international organization. Since science was international in scope, the critical examination of paranormal claims was also a matter for the international scientific community. This became all the more evident as the years went by, as the media became further globalized and paranormal programs produced, for example, in Hollywood, were exported virtually everywhere. Today there are approximately one hundred skeptics' organizations in thirty-eight countries and a great number of magazines and newsletters published worldwide, and these numbers continue to grow.

Needless to say the mainstay of the skeptics movement has been the *Skeptical Inquirer*. Its development and influence grew under the brilliant editorship of Kendrick Frazier.

III

After launching CSICOP, we immediately became embroiled in controversy; claims and counterclaims were bandied about. Whatever we did as skeptics was intensely followed. Although we received a warm reception by mainstream science magazines, we were bitterly attacked by believers. They accused us of being "the gatekeepers of science." They said we blocked any consideration of new ideas and that we were suppressing new Galileos waiting in the wings to be discovered.

Astrology

This was particularly the case in regard to the Gauquelin affair. After issuing "Objections to Astrology" (in *Humanist* in 1975), which detailed an attack on astrology, the Gauquelins threatened to sue the magazine for libel because of an article by Lawrence E. Jerome, who had criticized Michel Gauquelin in one brief paragraph. I decided to invite Michel and Françoise Gauquelin to visit the campus of SUNY (even before the founding of CSICOP), and I asked my colleague Marvin Zelen, head of the Department of Statistics (who later joined the Harvard faculty), to resolve the statistical issues; I also invited George O. Abell, noted astronomer at UCLA, to take part in the inquiry. We proposed, as CSICOP was being founded, to carefully examine the Gauquelins' results.

The Gauquelins had claimed to have found an anomaly in the birth statistics of European—especially French and Belgian—athletes, such that Mars seemed to be in the first and fourth sectors as it traversed the twelve sectors of the heavenly sky at the time of birth, and that this was beyond chance. Since my wife was French, we visited the Gauquelins in Paris on several occasions, and we invited them to visit us in the United States.

Zelen had proposed an experiment, later called "the Zelen test," to check the hypothesis of the Comité Para in Belgium. This committee had investigated Michel Gauquelin and disagreed with him because it differed about the baseline of probability of the birth of sports champions in relation to the path of Mars through space. Gauquelin was to go back to Paris and perform the Zelen test to see whether or not the Comité Para was correct. He was supposed to randomly select data and to determine what the normal path of Mars should be. The result of the test, according to Gauquelin, was that the Comité Para was wrong, and he concluded the Mars effect was real. Zelen, Abell, and I examined his work and found that he did not select the sample randomly, nor did he tell us, until we discovered it ourselves, that he had not included all the data from Paris. We thus thought that before anything further should be said, we needed to try to get another replication of his thesis, and so we resolved mutually that we would attempt an independent sample of US athletes. Gauquelin cooperated with us in this inquiry.

We attempted a careful compilation of data, and we ended up with 408 US champions. The statistical calculations were done by Dennis Rawlins, a member of the Executive Council. Gauquelin disputed the results of the American test, and he was able to arouse a sympathetic hearing from scattered scientists who thought his work had been carefully done. This was especially the case with Marcello Truzzi, who, once having left CSICOP, made a career of attacking us for not being "fair-minded." The controversy was exacerbated when Rawlins split with the committee, primarily because George Abell was concerned about his academic qualifications and began to check his background. When Rawlins learned about this he resigned in a huff, but not before others came to believe we had indeed used chicanery in the American sample. The results had been negative (Rawlins agreed here)—though Gauquelin sought to reinterpret the data post hoc and insisted they were positive. Hans Eysenck, a noted psychologist and a friend and colleague with whom I had worked on other issues in the past, agreed with Gauquelin's critique, though he had never himself directly inspected Gauquelin's data.

Several articles on this research were published in the *Skeptical Inquirer* over the years, with responses by Gauquelin and Rawlins. The controversy became heated. Little did I know that this controversy would continue on both sides of the Atlantic for about two decades. We decided that we needed still another effort at replication, and thus we proceeded to work with a newly formed French committee of scientists. They were reluctant to take the time to perform the test, since they said that Gauquelin was not respected in France and that his work had little influence on French scientists. Nevertheless, at our urging they decided to go ahead. Phillippe Cousin, the editor of *Science & Vie* (one of France's leading scientific magazines), said that he thought such a test would be useful, and he called a meeting of Michel Rouzé (a veteran skeptic and editor of the journal *AFIS*), Gauquelin, and me to lay out the protocol for such a test. This was a lengthy process: The French committee, working with an official scientific body, would send out for all the names in two French directories of sports figures, with an independent compilation of the data, not using Gauquelin's own data, which we suspected of some selective bias. This study took many, many years to complete. Led by Jean-Claude Pecker, Michel Rouzé, and other scientists, it was finally completed with the assistance of Jan Willem Nienhuys, a Dutch mathematician. The French committee concluded that the results were negative, that there was no Mars effect, and that the statistical deviations that Gauquelin observed were attributed to selective bias (whether conscious or unconscious). Others, such as Geoffrey Dean, have since suggested still other explanations for Gauquelin's erroneous results (see *Skeptical Odysseys* [2001], chapter 15).

Shortly after the French committee completed its study, Gauquelin committed suicide, with instructions that all of his data be destroyed. I should point out that we endeavored to maintain cordial relations with Gauquelin all during his life and indeed invited him to address CSICOP at Stanford University and on other occasions. There were other proponents of his hypothesis, such as Suitbert Ertel of Germany, who still defended the Gauquelin thesis, but we concluded after many years of hard inquiry that efforts at independent replications in the United States and France failed to sustain the hypothesis. The skeptics who performed these tests—namely, Kurtz, Abell, and Zelen and the French committee—did not engage in debunking, but submitted the claims to a very laborious process of investigation.

I think one of the chief contributions of CSICOP is that it led to demands that other claims of astrologers be tested. Indeed, perhaps more scientific effort has been devoted to testing astrology since the inception of CSICOP than ever in the history of the subject, and many of these papers were published in the *Skeptical Inquirer*. All of the results were negative.

We did at the same time conduct a public campaign in an effort to get newspapers to carry disclaimers to the effect that the daily astrological columns, which were based on sun signs, had no factual scientific support, but should be read for entertainment value only. Many professional astrologers agreed with this appraisal. We have managed to convince some sixty newspapers to carry such disclaimers. The conclusions of our efforts are: first, that intensive scientific study has found no evidence for the claims of classical astrology or its horoscopes, and, second, that the latter-day effort by Gauquelin to develop a new astrobiology has also failed to amass sufficient confirming evidence to support it.

Parapsychology

A good part of CSICOP's efforts were devoted to examining the claims of parapsychologists. We had an excellent parapsychological subcommittee, headed by Professor Ray Hyman of the University of Oregon, and including James Alcock, Barry Beyerstein, and others. This committee worked with other psychologists in the United Kingdom, including Susan Blackmore, Christopher French, Richard Wiseman, and David Marks.

The first alleged psychical claim that CSICOP agreed to investigate was that of Suzie Cottrell, a young teenager who had appeared on Johnny Carson's *Tonight Show*. Suzie was able to read cards in the hands of the players around a table, including Carson and Ed McMahon. Carson said he was mystified. We received so many calls nationwide about her "powers" that we decided to challenge Suzie to a test in March 1978. Her own father said he was puzzled about her abilities, and he agreed that she should be tested by an independent panel. The question was whether she possessed extraordinary abilities enabling her to read what was in other people's minds. The Cottrells sent an advance man to make arrangements. He arrived wearing a bowler hat, spats, and a nifty suit. Apparently there was some interest in developing a national showbiz career for Suzie. He told me that he had had a sore on his nose that would not heal, and that after

Suzie touched it, the wound was cured instantly. I immediately became suspicious of what was afoot.

We used the facilities of the Department of Psychology laboratory at the State University of New York at Buffalo's Amherst campus as a setting for the test, and we invited both Martin Gardner and James Randi to monitor the proceedings. There were several other observers present. ABC Television got wind of the experiment and sent a film crew. Martin Gardner was convinced that Suzie was using a standard card trick perfected by the Chicago card shark Matt Shulein; that is, in dealing the cards she was able to force a target card that she had peeked at to one of the assembled, and then later read the card in the recipient's hand.

Randi began by allowing her to display her feats. The controls at first were lax—she was allowed to deal the cards herself. Her performance was impressive. There was a TV camera on her at all times. Next it was announced that she would not be permitted to deal the cards. All of the subsequent results were negative. She failed every test run. Randi skillfully arranged a ten-minute break and told her that she could relax. There was immediate bedlam in the room. There was also a secret camera in the room hidden behind a screen. Unbeknownst to her, the camera recorded her peeking during the intermission at the top card. The next time she guessed correctly, but we knew why. We also invited Eddie Fechner, a well-known close-up magician, to duplicate her trick. He was able to palm five cards in his huge fist and call them out later, at which point Suzie Cottrell broke into tears, crying, "That's not the way I did it." After Suzie was exposed, little was heard from her again.

I should say that although I realized that there was intense trickery or self-deception afoot in many of these cases, I still was not certain whether psi phenomena existed. My skeptical colleagues insisted that such phenomena were unlikely, but I decided to investigate for myself, to satisfy my own curiosity. I did this by teaching a course entitled, "Philosophy, Parapsychology, and the Paranormal" at the university. Most of the students who registered for the course were believers—I gave them a poll on the first day to determine their level of credulity. My plan was to work closely with students on various experiments in order to test psychic and other claims.

We did two things. First, we used the Zener cards to test for precognition, ESP, and telepathy, doing thousands of trials in class. Second, students would break down into teams of two to five investigators, conceive of a research project, and devote the rest of the term to performing tests. They would report on the design of the project, their progress, and the results. The students were extremely creative in what they proposed. Several well-known psychics were tested to see if they possessed any special abilities. There were also tests of Tarot card readers and astrologers. The students investigated such things as whether psychics could influence the roll of dice (psychokinesis), reports of ghost hauntings, UFO sightings, and other phenomena. I repeated this course four times over eight years, and had over 250 students enroll. They conducted almost one hundred independent tests.

The most creative test was the Ganzfeld experiment conducted in the early 1980s, which I designed with two top engineering students, using a Faraday cage in the Engineering Department. In this test we brought in at least a dozen well-known psychics from upstate New York and elsewhere.

The thing that absolutely stunned me was the fact that we never had positive results in any of the many tests conducted; they were always negative. I have never published these findings, for I did them basically to satisfy my desire (and my students') to ascertain whether anything paranormal could be uncovered. Betty Markwick did much to expose the Soal experiment in the British *Proceedings of the Society of Psychical Research*. After I told her about my testing experience, she remarked that chance dictates we should have had some positive results. Was the so-called goat effect suppressing the evidence? I doubt it. What I do know is that with rigorous protocol we invariably had negative results. Indeed, although 90 percent of the students began the course as believers, by the end 90 percent became extremely skeptical because of the failure to demonstrate the paranormal in their own experiments.

In any case, aside from my own involvement in this area, I think parapsychologists have learned much from CSICOP's critiques, and they have attempted to tighten up their protocol, especially after the criticisms of Ray Hyman, Susan Blackmore, Jim Alcock, Barry Beyerstein, Richard Wiseman, and others.

In my view, if we are to accept any psi factor—and we should always be open to further inquiry—we need simply to insist upon three things: first, that any results be replicated in laboratories in which neutral and/or skeptical inquirers are involved; second, that tight protocols be used so there can be no sensory leakage; and third, that careful and rigorous grading standards be adhered to, for what constitutes a hit is often questionable.

One of my most memorable experiences in the earlier years was my debate with J. B. Rhine on April 19, 1978, at the Smithsonian Institution in Washington, DC. One amusing incident that occurred was that we were both wearing the same color and style of suit. I asked Rhine whether this was of paranormal significance or due to chance. I thought he was a kindly gentleman but rather naive. When I mentioned the chicanery at his laboratory of Walter Levy, who was caught cheating, he said that he was deeply hurt by the scandal, and was sorry that I brought it up.

Uri Geller

From the late 1980s till the mid-1990s CSICOP was confronted with legal suits brought by Uri Geller, who claimed he had been libeled by James Randi and CSICOP. These legal battles took almost a decade to resolve. Geller was unable to prove his case, and CSICOP was awarded court costs. Geller also sued Prometheus Books for publishing books by James Randi (*The Truth about Uri Geller*) and Victor Stenger (*Physics and Psychics*), who had quoted Randi, and me for a passage I had published in *The Transcendental Temptation* that also drew upon Randi's account. We agreed to modify these passages. At the present moment, suits still continue in Great Britain, and threats are constant from Geller, who has sued many others.

In any case, the courts refused to find in favor of Uri Geller, who claimed he has special psychic powers, which he refused to have tested in a court of law. The amount of time and effort spent in defending ourselves against Geller was exhausting. We were gratified that our readers rallied to the cause. They were deeply concerned about these harassing suits against a scientific body. Any time a new suit was leveled against us, contributions poured in, which enabled us to fight back.

One humorous incident stands out: I happened to be in London with my wife and daughter a few years ago, in an ice-cream parlor just off of Piccadilly Circus. The three of us were seated consuming our cones when I suddenly heard, "Paul Kurtz! Paul Kurtz!" A man approached me. He looked familiar. He said, "I'm Uri Geller! I'm Uri Geller! Paul Kurtz, how nice to see you!" I looked up and reciprocated the welcome. He introduced me to his wife, Hannah, and his son, who spoke French with my wife and daughter; and his colleague, Shipi Strang. Geller remarked, "I know that you don't believe in Jungian theories, particularly the theory of synchronicity, but the fact that Paul Kurtz should run into Uri Geller in London is too great an event beyond probability; therefore there must be something in the nature of things, something paranormal, to explain this." I smiled and said, "Well, most likely it was coincidental. I don't know that you can prove that there is a paranormal cause at work." Geller invited me to visit him in his home outside of London the next day, but unfortunately we had to catch an early plane for the Continent. Throughout the legal proceedings with Geller over the years, I tried to remain friendly with him, though I must say it was trying. When I first met him in Maryland during a legal contest, I shook his hand. Of course, I remain convinced that he possesses no special powers.

It is important, however, that we distinguish the antics of psychics and gurus and the vast media hype about the paranormal from the serious work of parapsychologists. I have appeared on hundreds, perhaps thousands, of radio and TV shows over the years and have criticized the exaggerated claims made on behalf of the paranormal. But I have always insisted, and still do today, that any responsible claims made in parapsychology deserve a fair hearing, and I support the endeavor of serious parapsychologists to investigate anomalous phenomena.

UFOlogy

UFOlogy has proven to be especially fascinating. Philip J. Klass, a veteran UFO investigator, became chairman of a new UFO subcommittee that was made up of about nineteen skeptical investigators, including Robert Sheaffer, Gary Posner, and James Oberg. We each were numbered with a 00 before our name; by chance I happened to have the number 007, reminiscent of James Bond. There were so many claims proliferating in the public domain and in the media that the most this committee could do was selectively attempt to explain those that were most prominent. Philip J. Klass did a yeoman's job especially in seeking out alternative causal explanations. I myself was particularly intrigued by the ETI hypothesis, because, as I said, I thought it was entirely possible that intelligent life existed elsewhere in the universe (even though it was sometimes difficult to find it on the planet Earth!). But whether we were being visited or had been visited by extraterrestrial beings manning advanced-state technological spacecraft was the issue. We needed to find some hard physical evidence to corroborate these claims. The one thing that perplexed me was that eyewitnesses were so often deceived. Given the cultural milieu and the prominence of such reports—almost daily at that time—many people looking at the sky thought they had seen UFOs. Obviously they had seen something in the sky, but whether it was a planet, entering rockets from Soviet or US space probes, meteors, weather balloons, advertising planes, or something else was unclear. I had met many people who claimed to have seen UFOs and were intrigued by what I suspected to be the will to believe, or the transcendental temptation at work.

One case particularly stands out. It occurred in Voronezh in the former Soviet Union, a city about two hundred miles from Moscow. We heard one morning on the radio and on television that a UFO sighting had occurred in the public square of Voronezh on October 9, 1989, and that creatures some eight to ten feet tall had descended, kidnapped two young lads, and taken off. The report said that the public square was contaminated with a substance where the landing pads had descended and was "unlike any substance seen on earth." They quoted a Russian geologist. The CSICOP office was besieged with many, many calls. Apparently the TASS news agency had sent out a press release about this. I remember well one reporter who asked me, "Now that the Russians have seen a UFO, do you accept it?" And my response was, "Well, this is a TASS report that we've not been able to confirm." "But TASS would not have lied," was the reply. And I asked, "Do you accept TASS reports about other matters?" The response was, "No, of course not." Then I said, "Why accept this at face value?" In any case, I began to work with a journalist for the *New York Times* and was able to place calls to Voronezh and to a nearby geology department to find out whether or not the scientist who said that the substance was unlike any seen on earth actually saw what was alleged. He denied the quotation attributed to him. It turned out after thorough investigation that the report was based upon hearsay and rumor spread by young children and that there was no objective evidence that such a UFO had landed. So much for the TASS report.

One area that really shocked us was the growth of reports of UFO abductions. Although Barney and Betty Hill in the famous 1961 New Hampshire case claimed they had been abducted aboard a UFO, most

UFOlogical investigators were dubious of this report. The psychiatrist on the case, Dr. Benjamin Simon, put Betty and Barney Hill under hypnosis. He said that he did not believe such an event occurred, though the Hills themselves were convinced they had seen something. Similarly for other popular abductee cases, a possible exception being that of Travis Walton, which many skeptics considered to be a complete fabrication.

Accordingly, it came as a complete surprise to us when reports of abductions not only began to proliferate but were taken seriously. A number of popular books by Budd Hopkins,[1] Professor David Jacobs,[2] and John Mack,[3] a psychologist on the Harvard faculty, appeared. We were puzzled by the claims. I debated each of the proponents on television or radio. Carl Sagan wrote me to say that given the intense public interest, we really ought to look into this phenomenon carefully to see if anything is there. With this in mind we invited John Mack to our national convention in Seattle in 1994, at a special session on UFO abductions. Mack said he was convinced that these abductions were real; he had a number of otherwise trustworthy people who reported such experiences under hypnosis, and he had to accept their claims as true. At an open meeting Phil Klass and John Mack tangled, but we allowed Mack every opportunity to present his point of view. What was at issue was whether psychiatrists should accept at face value the subjective reports of their patients. Would John Mack accept the hallucinations of schizophrenics who believe deeply in the worlds of fantasy that they concoct? If not, then why accept the uncorroborated reports of UFO abductees? Abduction reports were everywhere in the air, and indeed it was estimated by proponents that millions of people began to believe that they too had been abducted.

An interesting sidelight: I headed a delegation of the CSICOP Executive Council to China in 1988. We spoke to several large audiences in Shanghai and Beijing. I invariably raised the open questions: "Has anyone in the audience ever been abducted aboard a UFO?" or "Does anyone know of anyone who has been abducted?" The response was always in the negative. What were we to conclude from this: that the ETs are prejudiced against Chinese and only kidnap Westerners, or a more likely explanation that the Western media hype at that time had not penetrated the Chinese mainland?

CSICOP investigated many other famous cases, most recently during the fiftieth anniversary of the Roswell incident, which allegedly occurred in 1947, and the Gulf Breeze case in Florida, which we exposed as a hoax.

Where we stand at the moment is that there is insufficient evidence to corroborate the claim that UFOs are extraterrestrial in origin.

I must say that in my own empirical inquiry I was especially influenced by meeting and then reading a book published by Allen Hendry at the Center for UFO Studies.[4] Hendry was a colleague of Allen Hynek, a leading astronomer who accepted UFO reports as genuine. Hendry's book detailed over one thousand cases that came into Hynek's UFO Center during a year. The author, an astronomer, made exhaustive efforts to investigate each case. He concluded that there was no hard corroborative evidence for the claims and, as nearly as he could tell, virtually all sightings for which there was sufficient data could be explained in perfectly prosaic and natural terms. I have yet to find a UFO case that withstood critical scrutiny. "What would it take for you to accept an ET visit as genuine?" I was often asked, and I replied: "I would like to see them flush a commode from outer space." At least that would give some corroboration of what otherwise seemed to be largely conjecture.

Hynek once said to me at a meeting at the Smithsonian that he agreed that there was no single case that withstood rigorous examination. However, he said that the great number of sightings worldwide were of sociological and psychological significance. I concurred with this fully, though the "sightings" in my view were not evidence for ET visitations; rather they were most likely in the "eyes of the beholders" and they told us something about ourselves. Isaac Asimov complained on a radio program on which we jointly appeared that when he wrote science-fiction novels he never imagined that people would believe in this bullshit!

IV

Perhaps the most surprising thing that has occurred over the past few years is that as increasing waves of media sensationalism have inundated the public, what was formerly considered to be *unbelievable* is suddenly accepted as true by wide sectors of the public. Added to this is the "unsinkable rubber duck" phenomenon—namely, although skeptical investigators may thoroughly refute a claim in one generation, it may come back to haunt us in the next—as a Hydra-headed monster—with new intensity and attraction. I wish to briefly illustrate this by reference to other weird claims.

Communicating with the Dead

In the late nineteenth and early twentieth centuries, spiritualism was very strong. Beginning with the Fox sisters in 1848, it was widely believed that some sensitives could communicate with discarnate spirits on the other side. Tens of thousands of spiritualists convened séances all across the land, and many in the scientific community attempted to test these claims. They would put the mediums in darkened séance rooms and wait for some physical manifestation that could be observed by independent bystanders, such as rappings, table levitations, materializations, voices, and other such phenomena. The scientific community was very serious about evaluating these claims, and so a whole series of mediums, such as Eusapia Palladino, were carefully tested. In the end the preponderance of scientific judgment was that these mediums were fraudulent, that the so-called manifestations had no basis in empirical fact, and that efforts to communicate with the dead had failed. By and large, then, postmortem survival lacked intellectual respectability and all but disappeared from the landscape.

In the decade of the 1980s, using such names as Ramtha, a latter-day form of spiritualism reemerged. The mediums were often called "channelers." These individuals claimed to have immediate contact with other dimensions from which they received messages of self-help, empowerment, and becoming one with the astral plane. Beginning in the 1990s a spate of best-selling books by a new generation of spirit mediums have appeared, and their authors were prominently interviewed on television. I have in mind especially John Edward (*One Last Time*), James Van Praagh (*Talking to Heaven* and *Reaching to Heaven*), Sylvia Browne (*The Other Side and Back*), and Rosemary Altea (*You Own the Power*). These mediums claim to have immediate communication with the dead in which they bring messages to bereaved relatives and friends. Unfortunately, there are virtually no efforts to corroborate what they have said by any kind of independent tests. Their subjective phenomenological readings are accepted at face value by publishers, popular television hosts, and the general public. This phenomenon is startling to skeptical inquirers who have been willing to investigate carefully the question of postmortem survival, but find this kind of "evidence" totally unreliable. Actually these so-called mediums are using familiar "cold-reading" techniques, by which they artfully fish for information while giving the impression it comes from a mystical source.

What is so apparent is that gullibility and nincompoopery overtake critical common sense and all safeguards are abandoned in the face of guile, deception, and self-deception.

Lily Dale was the center of spiritualism at the turn of the nineteenth century. A decade ago it was considered to be of historical interest, a quaint remembrance of things past, a haven for white-shoe grandmothers engaged in psychic or spiritualist readings. At the end of the twentieth century, Lily Dale has moved into vogue again as the fires of passion for an afterlife are fed with a new kind of frenzy—but with virtually all epistemological standards abandoned. Intense public fascination today with near-death experiences further illustrate this phenomenon. Phenomenological reports of out-of-body experiences by people who are near death can be given naturalistic, physiological, and psychological explanations without postulating a separable "soul leaving the body" and going to "the other side."

Miracles

Another phenomenon that is equally surprising is the return of miracles. Much of this has been fed by the implicit acquiescence of some within the Catholic Church. By the end of the eighteenth century the belief in miracles had been largely discredited by the powerful arguments of David Hume and other skeptical authors. By the nineteenth century it was believed that miracles were a substitute for our ignorance, and that if one examines long enough one can find natural causal explanations for otherwise inexplicable phenomena.

Within the last decade, however, miracle mongers have came to the fore. A good case is Medjugorje, in Bosnia-Herzegovina, which allegedly is a place where some young children were able to see the Virgin Mary and to transmit reports of her messages. Millions of pilgrims visited the site, where it was claimed that miraculous events transpired, such as the changing of rosary beads into gold. (If you rub the silver plating, the brass underneath appears, which is mistaken for gold.) Interestingly, the children at Medjugorje never predicted the terrible wars of ethnic cleansing that ensued in Yugoslavia shortly thereafter. There was no forewarning from Mary. Skeptics were convinced, as were dissident Roman Catholics, that the best explanation for the miracles was that the children were fibbing. The willingness of young teenagers and children to deceive adults with preposterous paranormal claims is a common phenomenon that skeptics have encountered in psychical research and in "poltergeist" cases.

The outbreak of reports of miracles in the United States is especially disturbing, since America is supposed to be educationally advanced. There have been a great number of Jesus and Mary sightings, weeping icons and statues, and even the return of stigmata. All of these claims, which were considered to be medieval superstitions by educated persons, have been moved to center stage by the media, and tens of thousands of devotees throng to places where miracles are proclaimed.

My colleague Joe Nickell, a veteran skeptical investigator, has spent years investigating alleged miracles. He has demonstrated, for example, that the Shroud of Turin was a forgery created in the Middle Ages. Carbon-14 dating by three independent laboratories has confirmed his findings. Yet widespread belief that the Shroud of Turin is genuine is fueled by some prelates of the Catholic Church. On the one hand, church authorities claim to employ rigorous standards in examining miracles, yet they encourage the disciples of the Shroud of Turin and other miraculous wonders to persist in their propaganda to the faithful. Scientific rationalists thought the days of miracle mongering were long gone. Now they have returned with a vengeance. According to a recent poll, some 86 percent of Americans believe that miracles are occurring and that the hand of God intervenes in the course of nature.[5]

Intelligent Design

The case for intelligent design, long thought to have been discredited in the sciences, has been brought to new prominence. The United States is perhaps the only major democracy in which the theory of evolution is hotly contested and in which a significant percentage of the population still believes in biblical creationism. This battle has been going on in the public schools for many years. What is surprising is the sudden reemergence of intelligent design, such as defended by Michael Behe in his book *Darwin's Black Box*.[6] Arguments for intelligent design are also encountered in physics and astronomy. We are beginning to hear statements that the only way the universe can be explained is by postulating a Grand Designer. How else to account for the "fine-tuning" that has occurred? they ask, supposing that life could not have existed unless the proper conditions were present, and only an intelligent being could have arranged that. The arguments against intelligent design go back in the history of science; to wit, there is no evidence for a designer. To read into nature the mind of God in analogy with the mind of Man is a vast postulation, a speculative thesis not based upon scientific evidence. Here we are dealing with a leap of faith, not fact.

Alternative Medicine

One other recent and startling development is the rapid growth of "alternative" or "complementary" medicine. A wide range of alternative therapies—most of them ancient, many of them imported from India and China—has become popular. The list of these therapies is extensive. It includes acupuncture, qigong, therapeutic touch, magnetic therapy, iridology, naturopathy, reflexology, homeopathy, the extensive use of herbal medicines, esoteric cancer cures, crash diets, and the like.

One has to have an open mind about such therapies. They cannot be rejected a priori. Skeptical inquirers have insisted that proposed alternative therapies need to be submitted to double-blind randomized testing. Unfortunately, much of the support for alternative medicine is based on anecdotal hearsay or testimonials by self-proclaimed gurus and healers—such as Andrew Weil and Deepak Chopra—and much of this is spiritual in character.

The reason why skeptical inquirers are dismayed by this development is that scientific evidence-based medicine has made enormous strides in the past century combating illnesses, extending human life, and mitigating suffering—including the development of anesthesia, antibiotics, and modern surgery. Of course, not all diseases have been cured by the medical profession, and so out of desperation many patients turn to alternative therapies. In some cases, if you leave an illness alone, the body will restore itself to health. In others, the placebo effect can have powerful therapeutic value. In any case, the failure of large sectors of the public to appreciate how the scientific method works in medicine is one reason why alternative therapies seem to be gaining ground.

There have been so many other fascinating inquiries that I have been involved in as chairman of CSICOP over the years that I could not possibly hope to describe them all. Among these are our examination of the claims of Indian gurus (such as fire walkers), demonic possession and exorcism (such as the Smurl family in Wilkes Barre, Pennsylvania), poltergeist manifestations (Tina Resch of Columbus, Ohio), faith healers (in cooperation with James Randi), the ongoing creation/evolution controversy, and so much more. All bear striking similarities as a psychosocial phenomenon.

V

I wish to conclude by offering some personal reflections on the development of the skeptics movement in the last quarter of a century. This movement, I submit, is a very significant event in the history of science, for it helped to galvanize for the first time scientific inquirers who were willing to take part in systematic critical evaluations of paranormal claims.

The basic question we need to ask is, Why do paranormal beliefs persist? At the end of the nineteenth century it was widely expected that irrationality and superstitions would decline as education was extended to more people and affluence increased. This has surely not happened, for paranormal and pseudoscience claims continue to proliferate. Although the fruits of science and technology are widely appreciated by the public, unreason still has wide appeal.

I can suggest some possible reasons for this: One explanation is that the claims of religions—old and new—are largely unexamined within present-day American culture. It is considered to be in bad taste to question anyone's religion. Granted, we ought to be tolerant of other points of view. On the other hand, should claims that are patently false be immune to criticism? There are a plethora of religious denominations in the United States and hundreds of bizarre sects and cults. Religious miracles, like paranormal claims, postulate a nonnatural transcendental realm that allegedly cannot be evaluated by evidence or reason. The universe is bifurcated into a natural world, which science deals with, and a transcendent spiritual realm, which allegedly lies beyond our ability to comprehend. Concomitant with these two realms, their proponents insist, are two truths. This dualism is also said to apply to human personality, where we confront a "separate soul."

This classical religious outlook had been eroded by the Copernican and Darwinian revolutions and by steady advances in the behavioral and neurological sciences. In spite of this, the spiritual realm is very rarely questioned. In my view it is impossible to isolate paranormal claims from religious claims. Most skeptical inquirers have said they wished to deal only with those questions that have some empirical grounding. Interestingly, believers in the paranormal/spiritual worldview have blurred the borderlines between the paranormal and the religious. Religious conservatives and fundamentalists have, of course, been highly critical of New Age astrology, UFOlogy, and psychic phenomena, which they consider to be in competition with traditional religion. Nonetheless, paranormal phenomena, which allegedly exist over and beyond or beside normal science, are similar to religious miracles. I have labeled religious miracles as "paranatural," for they lie midway between the supernatural and the natural and are amenable to some evidential examination. In this sense, communication with the dead, the sighting of ghosts, exorcisms, faith healing, prophecies, and prayer at a distance are not unlike UFO abductions, out-of-body experiences, or precognitive predictions—they all are capable of being investigated scientifically.

Unlike many European and Latin American countries, the United States has never had a strong anticlerical tradition. The truths of the Bible, the Koran, or the Book of Mormon are promulgated daily from pulpit, radio, and television, and they are accepted on the basis of faith alone. They are institutionalized and become part of the historical traditions and structures of society. As such, they go largely unchallenged. There are few, if any, objective examinations widely available to the public of the so-called sacred literature. Why should reports of miracles in holy books—faith healing, exorcism, the Virgin Birth and Resurrection, the ascension of Muhammad to heaven, or the visitation to Joseph Smith of the Angel Moroni—be any less amenable to critical scrutiny than any other extraordinary paranormal reports? The fact that these claims appeared in the past is no justification for nontreatment. If similar claims were made by anyone today, we would surely attempt to investigate them. Given the current cultural phobia against the investigation of religion, however, I submit that irrationality will most likely continue strong—unless skeptical inquirers are willing to use the best standards of science, including archaeology, linguistics, history, biology, psychology, and sociology to uncover naturalistic explanations.

Another explanation for the persistence of the paranormal, I submit, is that it is due to "the transcendental temptation." In my book by that name,[7] I present the thesis that paranormal and religious phenomena have similar functions in human experience; they are expressions of a tendency to accept magical thinking. This temptation has such profound roots within human experience and culture that it constantly reasserts itself. Given this, the most outrageous claims are often accepted as gospel truth. If this is the case, then there will always be new forms of transcendental mythology to entice us. And as quickly as one faith system is refuted or dies out (for example, the religion of Isis and Osiris, the Homeric myths, etc.), new forms of irrationality are likely to replace it.

Is there a genetic disposition for this powerful temptation? There is most likely a variety of complex biological, psychological, and sociological causes at work. Transcendental myths offer consolation to bereaved souls who cannot face their own mortality or that of loved ones. They provide psychological succor and social support, enabling them to endure the tragic elements of the human condition and to overcome the fragility of human life in the scheme of things. We need to ask how and in what sense the transcendental temptation can be modified and whether naturalistic moral and poetic equivalents can be found to satisfy it. I am convinced that belief in the paranormal is a religious or quasi-religious phenomenon: Astrology postulates that our destiny lies in the stars. Psychics maintain that there are untapped extrasensory powers that can probe other dimensions of reality. UFOs transport semidivine ETs from other worlds. All of these are efforts to transcend the normal world.

Still another factor in the recent growth of the paranormal is the introduction of new electronic media of communication that are radically altering the way that we view the world. Symbols and concepts are being replaced by signs and images, the abstractions of logic by contrived virtual realities. The culture of books is supplemented by the visual and auditory arts. These media express imagery and sound, form and color. Cinematography transforms intellectual content. Science fiction becomes the Sacred Church of the Paranormal. Soaring flights of imagination distort what is true or false. Instead of explicating a thesis, the immediacy of photography in motion seizes us and renders products of fancy as real.

The special problem that we face today is that the dramatization of spiritual-paranormal claims without adequate criticism now dominates the mass media, which are all too often more interested in box office appeal than accurate information. The general public is exposed to a steady diet of sensationalized claims and is apt to accept them as authentic without sufficient skeptical dissent. Huge media conglomerates find that selling the paranormal by means of books, magazines, TV, and movies is extremely profitable.

Computers are also rapidly transforming the way information is imparted. The Internet is a vast repository of data that presents a huge quantity of unfiltered claims that can be scrolled through without critical analysis. By undermining standards of objectivity, any sentence or utterance is as true as any other, and in this process the methods of logic and science are deemed irrelevant.

I believe that the skeptical and scientific communities have a special responsibility to help redress the current state of misinformation. This becomes difficult, however, for science has become overspecialized. Surely, a division of labor is essential if we are to advance the frontiers of knowledge; we need technical experts focused on specific fields of investigation. Yet one reason why the scientific outlook is continuously undermined by antiscience and pseudoscience is that specialists in one field may not necessarily be competent to judge claims in others, nor do they always understand that science primarily is a method of inquiry. Likewise there is insufficient understanding of the broader implications of scientific discoveries to our conception of the universe and our place within it. We need to state forthrightly the scientific case against intelligent design, the survival of the self after death, or the dearth of evidence for personal salvation. I submit that it is incumbent on us to defend the naturalistic interpretation of reality, a materialistic rather than a spiritual-paranormal account. We need generalists of science who can sum up what science tells us about the human condition in a universe without purpose or design, yet who have the ability to awaken wonder and excitement about the scientific quest itself. Philosophers have performed this task in the past; scientists need to do so in the future.

Given the massive cultural fixation on the spiritual-paranormal outlook, perhaps the most that skeptical inquirers can hope for is that we can lessen the excessive follies of its proponents. Perhaps our most effective course is to moderate untested overbeliefs and encourage critical thinking as far as we can. In my view, all human beings need to use some degree of cognition in ordinary life if they are to cope and function in the world. Our agenda should be to encourage the extension of critical thinking to all areas of life—including religion, politics, ethics, and society.

Looking ahead, I think that we can expect, unfortunately, that spiritual-paranormal beliefs will continue to lure large sectors of humanity. Although the content of their beliefs may change in the light of criticism, some forms of paranormal belief will most likely persist in the future. Skeptical inquirers thus will have an ongoing role to play in civilization. Our mission is to light candles in the dark, as Carl Sagan so eloquently stated, and to become Socratic gadflies questioning the sacred cows of society and cultivating an appreciation for reason.

NOTES

1. Budd Hopkins, *Intruders: The Incredible Visitations at Copley Woods* (New York: Random House, 1987).

2. David Jacobs, *Secret Life: Firsthand Accounts of UFO Abductions* (New York: Simon & Schuster, 1992).

3. John Mack, *Abduction: Human Encounters with Aliens* (New York: Scribner's, 1994).

4. Allan Hendry, *The UFO Handbook: A Guide to Investigating, Evaluating and Reporting UFO Sightings* (Garden City, NY: Doubleday, 1979).

5. Reuters Newsweek poll, conducted in April 2000.

6. Michael J. Behe, *Darwin's Black Box: The Biochemical Challenge to Evolution* (New York: Simon & Schuster, 1996).

7. Paul Kurtz, *The Transcendental Temptation: A Critique of Religion and the Paranormal* (Amherst, NY: Prometheus Books, 1986).

Chapter 16

SCIENCE AND THE PUBLIC
Summing Up Thirty Years of the *Skeptical Inquirer*

The September/October 2006 issue of the *Skeptical Inquirer* marked the thirtieth year of publication of the official magazine of the Committee for the Scientific Investigation of Claims of the Paranormal, which was founded six months before the first issue was published in Fall/Winter 1976 as the *Zetetic* (meaning "skeptical seeker"), under the editorship of Marcello Truzzi. The name was changed to the *Skeptical Inquirer* the following year and Kendrick Frazier was appointed the new editor; he has served with brilliant virtuosity and distinction ever since. Ken had been the editor of *Science News*, and during his tenure at the *Skeptical Inquirer* he also worked full time at Sandia National Laboratories for twenty-three years until his retirement from there in April 2006. He has kept abreast of the many breakthroughs on the frontiers of the sciences and is eminently qualified to interpret the sciences for the general public; hence he continues to be a perfect fit for the *Skeptical Inquirer*.

In preparation for this overview, I reviewed the entire corpus published in the past thirty years, which is available on CD-ROM. What impressed me greatly was the wide range of topics and the distinguished

[*Skeptical Inquirer* 30, no. 5 (September/October 2006): 13–19]

authors Ken has attracted to its pages. I can highlight only some of these in this chapter. I wish to use this occasion to focus on what I believe we have accomplished in the past three decades and to speculate as to what directions our magazine might take in future decades. Today, many threats to science come from disparate quarters—as Ken points out in his editorial, "In Defense of the Higher Values," in the July/August 2006 issue of the *Skeptical Inquirer*. These include efforts to undermine the integrity of science and freedom of research, and we are continually confronted by irrational antiscientific forces rooted in fundamentalist religion and ideology. Given these challenges, no doubt skeptical inquiry will continue to be necessary in the future.

The original name of CSICOP was the Committee for the Scientific Investigation of Claims of the Paranormal *and Other Phenomena*, but this mouthful was deemed too long—and the acronym would have been *CSICOPOP*—so we shortened it! It is clear that the *Skeptical Inquirer* was never intended to confine itself solely to paranormal issues, and the topics it has dealt with have been truly wide-ranging. The subtitle that was eventually developed and now appears on every issue is "The Magazine for Science and Reason," which states succinctly what it is all about. It has encouraged "the critical investigation of paranormal and fringe-science claims," but "it also promotes science and scientific inquiry, critical thinking, science education, and the use of reason."

I

The enduring contribution of the *Skeptical Inquirer* in its first three decades, I submit, has been its persistent efforts to raise the level of the public understanding of science. No nation or region can cope with the challenges of the global marketplace and compete effectively unless it provides a steady stream of highly educated scientific practitioners. This is true of the developing world, which wishes to catch up with the advanced industrial and informational economies, but it is true of those latter nations as well. Today, China and India have embarked upon massive efforts to increase the number of scientists in their countries—China graduates anywhere from 350,000 to 600,000 engineers annually, compared to 70,000 to 120,000 in the United States, of which some 30,000 are foreign born. Alas, we still have a tremendous task, for US students rank only twenty-fourth in scientific knowledge out of the twenty-nine industrialized countries. Only 40 percent of twelfth graders tested had any comprehension of the basic concepts and methods of science. Presumably, even fewer political figures in Washington have the requisite comprehension!

The long-standing policy of CSICOP has been fourfold: (1) to criticize claims of the paranormal and pseudoscience, (2) to explicate the methods of scientific inquiry and the nature of the scientific outlook, (3) to seek a balanced view of science in the mass media, and (4) to teach critical thinking in the schools. Unfortunately, the constant attacks on science, the rejection of evolution by creationists and intelligent design advocates (some thirty-seven states have proposed programs to teach ID and creationism in the schools), the limiting of stem-cell research by the federal government, and the refusal to accept scientific findings about global warming vividly demonstrate the uphill battle that the United States faces unless it improves the public appreciation of scientific research.

Clearly, the major focus of the *Skeptical Inquirer*, especially in its first two decades, was on the paranormal; there was tremendous public fascination with this area of human interest, which was heavily promoted and sensationalized by an often irresponsible media. Our interest was not simply in the paranormal curiosity shop but to increase an understanding among the general public of how science works.

The term *paranormal* referred to phenomena that allegedly went "beyond normal science." Many topics were lumped under this rubric. And many credulous people believed that there was a paranormal-spiritual dimension that leaked into our universe and caused strange entities and events. Included in this mysterious realm was a wide range of phenomena, which the *Skeptical Inquirer* examined within its pages over the years: psychic claims and predictions; parapsychology (psi, ESP, clairvoyance, telepathy, precognition, psychokinesis); UFO visitations and abductions by extraterrestrials (Roswell, cattle mutilations, crop circles); monsters of the deep (the Loch Ness monster) and of the forests and mountains (Sasquatch, or Bigfoot); mysteries of the oceans (the Bermuda Triangle, Atlantis); cryptozoology (the search for unknown species); ghosts, apparitions, and haunted houses (*The Amityville Horror*); astrology and horoscopes (Jeane Dixon, the "Mars effect," the "Jupiter effect"); spoon bending (Uri Geller); remote viewing (Targ and Puthoff); cult anthropology; von

Däniken and the Nazca plains of Peru; biorhythms; spontaneous human combustion; psychic surgery and faith healing; the full moon and moon madness; fire walking; psychic detectives; Ganzfeld experiments; poltergeists; near-death and out-of-body experiences; reincarnation; Immanuel Velikovsky and catastrophes in the past; doomsday forecasts; and much, much more!

The term *paranormal* was first used by parapsychologists, but it was stretched uncritically by advocates of the New Age, the Age of Aquarius, and harmonic convergence to include bizarre phenomena largely unexamined by mainstream science. Murray Gell-Mann, Nobel laureate and Fellow of CSICOP, at our conference at the University of Colorado in 1986—I can remember it vividly—observed that we skeptics do not really believe in the "paranormal," because it deals with things beyond science, and as skeptical inquirers, he reiterated that we were dealing with investigations amenable to scientific methods of explanation. We would refuse to stop at any point and attribute phenomena to occult or hidden causes; we would keep looking for causal explanations and never declare that they were beyond the realm of natural causation by invoking the paranormal; and if we found new explanations, we would extend science to incorporate them. Incidentally, he also denied the feeling of some New Agers "that quantum mechanics is so weird, that anything goes" (*Skeptical Inquirer*, Fall 1986).

Sociologist Marcello Truzzi, who studied satanic cults, pointed out in our very first issue that we intended to examine esoteric anomalous claims, the "damned facts," as Charles Fort called them (hail in July, a rainfall of frogs, etc.), to see what we could make of them. The public was intrigued by such mysteries, and we tried to encourage scientific investigators to explain them and to find out if they ever even existed or occurred.

Almost every issue of the *Skeptical Inquirer* attempted to fathom what was really happening in one or another alleged paranormal area. Thus, Ray Hyman described the technique of "cold reading" to show how guesswork and cues were used by psychics to deceive people who thought that they were having a bona fide paranormal reading. Philip Klass, head of CSICOP's UFO subcommittee, tried to unravel unusual cases of alleged UFO visitations and abductions in answer to astronomer J. Allen Hynek or Bruce Maccabee or other UFO buffs, and offered alternative prosaic explanations to account for apparent misperceptions. Conjurer James Randi and *Scientific American* columnist Martin Gardner looked for fraud or deceit.

This was graphically illustrated in the case of a young psychic named Suzie Cottrell, who had bamboozled Johnny Carson by card reading. Put to the test under controlled conditions, Gardner said that she used Matt Schulein's forced-card trick, and Randi caught her red-handed peeking at the bottom card (see the Spring 1979 issue).

The *Skeptical Inquirer* published what appeared to be solutions to previously unexplained mysteries. We became exasperated with the media—such as NBC's *Unsolved Mysteries*—because they would present persons as having "real" paranormal abilities in spite of the fact that those persons were fraudulent, as in the case of Columbus, Ohio, youngster Tina Resch. Poltergeists supposedly manifested themselves when she came on the scene: lamps shattered, lights or faucets turned off and on. She was exposed by a TV camera that the crew left on while she thought that she was alone in a room: She was seen knocking down a lamp herself and screaming, "Poltergeist!"

I must say that these early years were exciting and exhilarating. We loved working with James Randi, Penn and Teller, Jamy Ian Swiss, Henry Gordon, Bob Steiner, and other magicians, who could usually duplicate a supposedly paranormal feat using sleight of hand or other forms of chicanery.

Deception is unfortunately widespread in human history, and it is revealing to point it out when it is encountered, especially where loose protocol makes it easy to hoodwink a gullible experimenter. Harry Houdini performed yeoman's service earlier in the twentieth century by exposing the blatant fraud perpetuated by Marjery Crandon and other spiritualists and mediums. I surely do not wish to suggest that conscious deception is the primary explanation for all or even most paranormal beliefs. Rather, it is *self-deception* that accounts for so much credulity. There is a powerful willingness in all too many people to believe in the unbelievable in spite of a lack of evidence or even evidence to the contrary. This propensity is due in part to what I have called the "transcendental temptation," the tendency to resort to magical thinking, the attribution of occult causes for natural phenomena. The best antidote for this, I submit, is critical thinking and the search for natural causes of such phenomena.

Some paranormalists complained that we were poking fun at them and that ridicule is no substitute for objective inquiry. Martin Gardner observed that one horse-laugh might be worth a thousand syllogisms, if it dethrones a phony or nincompoop. Editor Kendrick Frazier, in my judgment, has always attempted to be fair-minded, and if an article criticized a proponent of a paranormal claim, he would invariably give that person an opportunity to respond. We attempted to make it clear that we were interested in fair and impartial inquiry, that we were not dogmatic or closed minded, and that skepticism did not imply a priori rejection of any reasonable claim. Indeed, I insisted that our skepticism was not totalistic or nihilistic about paranormal claims, but that we proposed to examine a claim by means of scientific inquiry. I called this "the new skepticism" (see the *Skeptical Inquirer* Winter 1994), to distance it from classical Greco-Roman skepticism, which rejected virtually anything and everything, for no kind of knowledge was considered reliable. But this was before the emergence of modern science, in which hypotheses and theories are based upon rigorous methods of empirical investigation, experimental confirmation, and replication, and also by whether a paranormal claim contradicts the body of tested theories or is consistent with them. One must be prepared to overthrow an entire theoretical framework—and this has happened often in the history of science—but there has to be strong countervailing evidence that requires it. It is clear that skeptical doubt is an integral part of the method of science, and scientists should be prepared to question received scientific doctrines and reject them in the light of new evidence.

II

Looking back to the early years of the *Skeptical Inquirer* and CSICOP, it is evident that the salient achievement was that we called for new investigations—and researchers in our network of collaborators responded by engaging in them.

A good illustration of this is the determined efforts by skeptics to evaluate astrology experimentally. Although not paranormal in a strict sense—it was surely on the fringe of science—nevertheless, the claim that there were astrobiological influences present at the moment of birth could be tested. The "Mars effect" was a good illustration of this. French psychologists Michel and Françoise Gauquelin maintained that the positions of planets at the time and place of birth—in this case Mars (in the first and fourth sectors of the heavens)—was correlated with whether a person would become a sports champion. Egged on by Truzzi and British psychologist Hans Eysenck, we attempted several tests of this claim, and scientists tested the birthdates of sports champions born in the United States and France (and similar tests were made for other planets and professions). The results were negative, but it took twenty years of patient investigation to ascertain that. The most likely explanation for the "Mars effect" is biased data selection by the Gauquelins. CSICOP encouraged other researchers (such as Shawn Carlson[1] and Geoffrey Dean) to test classical astrological claims. The results, published in the pages of the *Skeptical Inquirer*, again were invariably negative. Astrology provided no coherent theory or mechanism for the influence of planetary bodies at the time and place of a person's birth.

Similar efforts were applied to parapsychology. Ray Hyman, James Alcock, Barry Beyerstein, and others were able by serious meta-analyses to evaluate the results of experimental research. Working with Charles Honorton, Robert Morris, and other parapsychologists, they questioned the findings of parapsychological investigations, and they found badly designed protocols, data leakage, experimenter biases, and insufficient replication by independent researchers.

The significant achievement of the *Skeptical Inquirer* was that it helped crystallize an appreciation by the scientific community of the need to investigate such claims. After the establishment of CSICOP, many scientific researchers were willing to devote the time to carefully examine the data. These results were published in the *Skeptical Inquirer*, so there was an independent record of explanation. And anyone who was puzzled by the phenomena could consult this new literature to deflate the paranormal balloon. This applied to a wide range of other phenomena.

Near-death experiences provided insufficient evidence for the conjecture that a conscious self or soul left the body and viewed it from afar—this is better explained by reference to physiological and psychological causes, as Susan Blackmore pointed out in the *Skeptical Inquirer* (Fall 1991).

The ability of fire-walking gurus to walk over hot coals was not due to some mind-over-matter spiritual power but rather because hot embers are poor conductors of heat, and it was possible for anyone to attempt this feat without injury.

Another area of importance was the critical evaluation of the use of hypnosis by UFO investigators, who believed they were uncovering repressed memories that depicted alleged abductions. John Mack, a professor of psychiatry at Harvard, used hypnosis to probe the unconscious minds of certain troubled people who thought they had been abducted aboard UFOs by extraterrestrials. There was a similar pattern in such cases, he said, which was repeated time and time again by his patients: a sense of lost time, flashing lights, out-of-body experiences, and the like. Mack thought this provided strong evidence for the claim; skeptics maintained that this evidence was not corroborated by independent testimony. At one point, Carl Sagan wrote to us, urging CSICOP to undertake an investigation of these claims, which by then were proliferating everywhere. We invited Mack to a CSICOP conference in Seattle in June 1994 to hear what he had to say. There was a colorful confrontation between John Mack the believer and Phil Klass the skeptic—who insisted that hypnosis was unreliable as a source of truth. The influence of urban abduction legends popularized by the mass media predisposed many fantasy-prone persons to imbibe this tale, and the suggestibility of hypnotists reinforced the reality of their subjective experiences. Some critics asked Mack whether he accepted the fantasies of his psychotic patients as true—which gave him some pause.

The Amazing Kreskin, who used hypnosis in his act, appeared at one of CSICOP's conferences expressing doubt that hypnosis was a genuine "trance state" or a source of truth—it seemed to work in suggestible patients because they followed the bidding of the hypnotist. (Incidentally, many skeptics were highly critical of Kreskin for suggesting that he possessed ESP.)

Hypnosis was also used in so-called past-life regressions to provide supposed evidence of previous lives. The *Skeptical Inquirer* carried many articles criticizing this technique. Past-life therapists maintained that the hypnotic state provided empirical support for the doctrine of reincarnation, maintaining that the memory of a previous life was lodged deep within the unconscious. More parsimonious explanations of these experiences are available: creative imagination, suggestions implanted by the hypnotherapist, and cryptomnesia (information stored in the unconscious memory without knowledge of the true source). Again, there was no independent factual corroboration, and these methods seem to rely more on a priori belief in reincarnation than reliable empirical evidence.

Many research issues in psychology were critically examined in the *Skeptical Inquirer*. The work of Elizabeth Loftus is especially noteworthy here. In the decade of the 1990s, the mass media focused on charges that young children had been molested by relatives, friends, and teachers. Many reputations were destroyed after lurid accounts of sexual improprieties were made public. The popularity of such confessions spread like wildfire, and thousands of people claimed that they had been likewise molested. This was dramatized by the McMartin trial in California, where teachers in a day-care center were accused of sexual assaults of young children. This was based on testimony extracted from children and extrapolated by overzealous prosecutors. It had been pointed out that there exits a "false-memory syndrome," fed by suggestion, and that testimony based on this is highly questionable. The *Skeptical Inquirer* was among the first publications to point out the fragmentary nature of the evidence and the unreliability of such testimony. This helped to turn the tide against such accusations, many of which had been exaggerated.

It would be useful at this point to sum up the pitfalls that skeptical inquirers encountered in studying paranormal and fringe-science claims and of guidelines that emerged as a consequence:

- Eyewitness subjective testimony uncritically accepted without corroboration is a potential source of deception (in accounts of molestation, reports of apparitions, past-life regression, UFO visitations, etc.).
- Extraordinary claims demand extraordinary evidence.
- The burden of proof rests with the claimant, not the investigators.
- Paranormal reports are like unsinkable rubber ducks: No matter how many times they are submerged, they tend to surface again.
- There is widespread gullibility and will to believe expressed by certain segments of the population who are fascinated by mystery and magical thinking and willing to accept tales of the occult or supernatural.
- In some cases, but surely not all, blatant fraud and chicanery may be observed, even in young children.
- In evaluating evidence, watch out for hidden bias and self-deception, pro and con (including your own), to determine if something is a pseudoscience or not.

There is no easily drawn demarcation line between science and pseudoscience, for one may be dealing with a protoscience. In my view, we need to descend to the concrete data and we cannot always judge a priori on purely philosophical grounds whether something is a pseudoscience or not (although I agree in general with Mario Bunge's views about the characteristics of a pseudoscience; see *Skeptical Inquirer*, Fall 1984 and July/August 2006).

III

In recent years, popular interest in the paranormal has declined markedly, at least in comparison with its heyday. I do not deny that belief in paranormal phenomena is widespread; however, there are fewer manifestations of it in the mass media, and apparently less scientific interest. In previous decades, there were huge bestsellers whose sales figures numbered in the millions: Raymond Moody's *Life after Life*, Charles Berlitz's *The Bermuda Triangle*, Erich von Däniken's *Chariot of the Gods?* and so on.

Today, very few such books make the *New York Times* bestsellers list, and a top-selling paranormal book is likely to sell only two hundred thousand to three hundred thousand copies. (Sylvia Browne is the current bestselling guru, but there are few others besides her.) And there are very few major television programs devoted to the paranormal, though there are smaller-market cable shows.

Attention has turned to other areas. First, alternative medicine has grown by leaps and bounds. Prior to 1996 very few medical schools taught courses or offered programs in alternative medicine—and the medical profession was highly skeptical of the therapeutic value of remedies such as homeopathy, acupuncture, Therapeutic Touch, herbal medicines, iridology, and chiropractic. This magazine published many articles critical of these areas. It may be that such therapies are useful—the criterion we suggested was to conduct random, double-blind tests of their efficacy. Until there is sufficient data to support a therapy, the public should be cautious of its use. The medical profession needs to be open-minded yet suspicious of therapies until they are demonstrated to work—notwithstanding the evidential value of placebos.

Interestingly, the skeptical movement in Europe has concentrated on alternative medicine, though this is not strictly paranormal but is on the borderline of fringe medicine. I must confess that we are dismayed by the rapid growth of alternative and complementary medicine, which has had enormous acceptance virtually overnight. This is helped no doubt by the fact that it is a highly profitable source of income for both practitioners and the companies that market herbal remedies. Homeopathy is very strong in Europe and is now making inroads in the United States, though its remedies have never been adequately tested. Therapeutic Touch is so widespread in the nursing profession that it has gained great acceptance, though the basis of its curative powers has not been adequately demonstrated. The role of intercessory prayer as a healing method has provoked considerable controversy. Some advocates of prayer have claimed positive results; however, skeptics have seriously questioned the methodology of these tests. The most systematic tests were recently conducted by a team of scientists led by Herbert Benson (see the July/August 2006 *Skeptical Inquirer*). Using fairly rigorous protocols, these tests produced negative results.

Many skeptics have likewise been very critical of schools of psychotherapy, notably psychoanalysis, for lacking clinical data about the efficacy of their methods. In this regard, the Center for Inquiry has taken over the journal *Scientific Review of Mental Health Practice*, edited by Scott Lilienfeld, which evaluates the scientific validity of mental-health treatment modalities. Some people say that the change from evidence-based medicine to other forms of medicine spells the emergence of a new paradigm; Marcia Angel has observed that this shift is toward a kind of spiritual medicine, influenced by the growth of religiosity in the culture.

Over the years, the *Skeptical Inquirer* has dealt with many other areas that needed critical scrutiny, including the efficacy of dowsing, graphology, facilitated communication, SETI, animal speech, the Atkins Diet, obesity, the Rorschach test, holistic medicine, and veterinary medicine. In addition, there have been many articles on the philosophy of science, the nature of consciousness, and the evidence for evolution.

IV

Numerous distinguished scientists have contributed to the *Skeptical Inquirer*, including Richard Feynman, Glenn Seaborg, Leon Lederman,

Gerald Holton, Steve Weinberg, Carl Sagan, Richard Dawkins, Jill Tarter, Steven Pinker, Carol Tavris, Neil de Grasse Tyson, and Victor Stenger. Among the topics examined have been quantum mechanics, the brain and consciousness, and cold fusion. Thus, the scope of the *Skeptical Inquirer* under Kendrick Frazier's editorship has been impressively comprehensive. And I should add that his fine editorials in every issue have pinpointed central questions of concern to science.

In a very real sense, the most important controversy in the past decade has been the relationship between religion and the paranormal—and whether and to what extent CSICOP and the *Skeptical Inquirer* should deal with religious claims. As a matter of fact, evangelical and fundamentalist religion have grown to such proportions that religion and the paranormal overlap and one cannot easily deal with one without the other. The *Skeptical Inquirer* has dealt with religious claims from the earliest. First, it was in the vanguard of responding to the attacks on the theory of evolution coming from the creationists. Eugenie Scott, who served on the CSICOP Executive Council for a period of time, has done great service in critically analyzing "creation science," and the *Skeptical Inquirer* was among the first magazines to do so, demonstrating that creationism is not a science, for it does not provide a testable theory. The young-earth view maintains that earth and the species on it are of recent origin, a view so preposterous that it is difficult to take it seriously. Most recently, intelligent design theory (which rejects the young-earth theory) claims that the complexity of biological systems is evidence for design. Numerous articles in the *Skeptical Inquirer* have pointed out that evolution is supported by overwhelming evidence drawn from many sciences. The existence of vestigial organs in many species, including the human species, is hardly evidence for design, for they have no discernible function. And the extinction of millions of species on the planet is perhaps evidence for *un*intelligent design.

Second, the *Skeptical Inquirer* was always willing to deal with religious questions, insofar as there are empirical claims that are amenable to scientific treatment. Thus, the Shroud of Turin has been readily investigated in the *Skeptical Inquirer* (see, for example, November/December 1999), presenting evidence (such as carbon-14 dating) that indicated that it was a thirteenth-century cloth on which an image had been contrived. Joe Nickell (CSICOP's senior research fellow for the past decade) has said for years that the shroud is a forgery—as the bishop of the area of France where it first turned up maintained. Moreover, Nickell has shown how such a shroud could easily have been concocted. Similarly, the so-called Bible code was easily refuted by Dave Thomas (see the *Skeptical Inquirer*, November/December 1997 and March/April 1998).

In recent years, reports of miracles have proliferated, much to the surprise of rationalists, who deplore the apparent reversion of society to the thinking of the Middle Ages. David Hume offered powerful arguments questioning miracles, which he said were due to ignorance of the causes of such phenomena. There is abundant evidence, said Hume, to infer that nature exhibits regularities; hence we should reject any exception to the laws of nature. In the late eighteenth century, showers of meteorites were interpreted by religious believers as signs of God's wrath. A special commission of scientists in France was appointed to investigate whether such reports of objects falling from the sky were authentic, and if so, if they were caused by natural events.

The *Skeptical Inquirer* has dealt with miracles in its pages, given the great public interest in them. The so-called miracle at Medjugorje, Yugoslavia, at a shrine where the Virgin Mary appeared before young children, was critically discussed (November/December 2002). The conclusion was that the children's testimony has not been corroborated by independent testimony and was hence suspect. But as a result of the attention the children received, they became media celebrities. Oddly, the Virgin never warned about the terrible war that was about to engulf Bosnia and Kosovo. The cases were similar for the numerous other sightings of Mary and of Jesus, which have attracted great public fascination. The investigations of Joe Nickell are models to follow; Nickell refuses to declare a priori that any miracle claim is false, instead attempting where he can to conduct an on-site inquest into the facts surrounding the case. If, after investigation, he can show that the alleged miracle was due to misperception or deception, his analysis is far more effective.

The one area of interest in the paranormal that has also had a resurgence in recent years is "communicating with the dead." The form it has taken is reminiscent of the spiritualism of the nineteenth century, which had been thoroughly discredited because of fraud and deceit. The new wave of interest is fed by appearances on radio and television by such people as Sylvia Browne, James Van Praagh, and John Edward. The techniques the most popular psychics use are the crudest form of cold reading—which they seem to get away with easily. In some cases, they even resort to doing hot readings (using information surreptitiously gleaned beforehand). This latter-day revival of spiritualism is no doubt fueled by the resurgence of religiosity in the United States, but it also shows a decline of respect for the rigorous standards of evidence used in the sciences.

The question of the relationship between science and religion intrigues many people today. It is especially encouraged by grants bestowed by the Templeton Foundation. Indeed, three special issues of the *Skeptical Inquirer*, beginning with July/August 1999, were devoted to explorations of the relationship or lack of it between these two perennial areas of human interest.

These issues of the *Skeptical Inquirer* proved to be the most popular that we have ever published. Most skeptics have taken a rather strong view that science and religion are two separate domains and that science needs latitude for freedom of research, without ecclesiastical or moral censorship. This is one of the most burning issues today. Stephen Jay Gould defended a dissenting viewpoint of two magisteria: religion, which included ethics within its domain, and science. The *Skeptical Inquirer* has consistently brought philosophers to its pages to discuss a range of philosophical questions on the borderlines of science, religion, and morality. Susan Haack, Mario Bunge, and I, among others, have argued that the scientific approach is relevant to ethics and therefore ethics should not be left to the exclusive domain of religion (see the September/October 2004 *Skeptical Inquirer*).

V

Skeptics have often felt isolated in a popular culture that is often impervious to or fails to fully appreciate the great discoveries of science on the frontiers of research. They have done arduous work attempting to convince producers, directors, and publishers to present the scientific outlook fairly. When pro-paranormal views are blithely expressed as true, we have urged that scientific critiques also be presented to provide some balance. Our goal is to inform the public about the scientific outlook. We believe that we still have a long way to go to achieve some measure of fairness in the media. Almost the first official act of CSICOP was to challenge NBC for its program *Exploring the Unknown*, narrated by Burt Lancaster, which presented pro-paranormal propaganda on topics such as psychic surgery and astrology, without any scientific dissent at all. Our suit against NBC citing the Fairness Doctrine was turned down by a federal judge, and our subsequent appeal to the First District Court in Washington was also rejected (see the Fall/Winter 1977 *Skeptical Inquirer*). Conversely, the *Skeptical Inquirer* has been the victim of many legal suits or threats of suits over the years. The most notorious was Uri Geller's protracted legal suits against James Randi, CSICOP, and Prometheus Books. The most recent suit has named Elizabeth Loftus and CSICOP for an article she authored (with Melvin J. Guyer) on the case of alleged sexual abuse of "Jane Doe" in the *Skeptical Inquirer* (May/June 2002). So the struggle that we have waged still continues.

On a more positive note, it is a source of great satisfaction that the *Skeptical Inquirer* is read throughout the world and that CSICOP has helped generate new skeptics' groups, magazines, and newsletters almost everywhere—from Australia and China to Argentina, Peru, Mexico, and Nigeria; from India, eastern Europe, and Russia to Germany, France, Spain, Italy, and the United Kingdom, so that the Center for Inquiry/Transnational (including CSICOP) has become truly planetary in scope. Especially gratifying is the fact that CSICOP has convened meetings in places all over the world, including China, England, France, Russia, Australia, India, Germany, Africa, and elsewhere.

Looking ahead, I submit that the *Skeptical Inquirer* and CSICOP should investigate other kinds of intellectually challenging and controversial claims. It is difficult to know beforehand where the greatest needs will emerge. In my view, we cannot limit our agenda to the issues that were dominant thirty, twenty, or even ten years ago, interesting as they have been. I think that we should of course continue to investigate paranormal claims, given our skilled expertise in that area. But we need to widen our net by entering into new arenas we've never touched on before, and we should be ever willing to apply the skeptical eye wherever it is needed. Actually, editor Kendrick Frazier has already embarked in new directions, for recent issues of the *Skeptical Inquirer* have dealt with topics such as cyberterrorism, "A Skeptical Look at September 11," "The Luck Factor," and critical thinking about power plants and the waste of energy in our current distribution systems. But there are many other issues that we have not dealt with that would benefit from skeptical scrutiny—and these include issues in biogenetic engineering, religion, economics, ethics, and politics.

Perhaps we have already become the Committee for Skeptical Investigation (CSI), to denote that we are moving in new directions. This fulfills our general commitment to science and reason that's stated in the masthead of the *Skeptical Inquirer*. But one may say: There are so many intellectually controversial issues at large in society, which do we select? I suggest the following criteria: We should endeavor to enter into an area, first, if there is considerable public interest and controversy; second, where there has not been adequate scientific research nor rigorous peer review; third, where some kind of interdisciplinary cooperative efforts would be useful; and fourth, where we can enlist the help of specialists in a variety of fields who can apply their skills to help resolve the issues.

We originally criticized pseudoscientific and paranormal claims because we thought that they trivialized and distorted the meaning of genuine science. Many of the attacks on the integrity and independence of science today come from powerful political-theological-moral doctrines. For example, one of the key objections to stem cell research is that researchers allegedly destroy innocent human life—even when they deal with the earliest stage of fetal development or when a cell begins to divide in a petri dish. First is the claim that the "soul" is implanted at the moment of conception and that human life begins at the first division of a cell, and second, that it is "immoral" for biogeneticists working in the laboratory to intervene. The first claim is surely an *occult* notion if there ever was one, and it urgently needs to be carefully evaluated by people working in the fields of biology, genetics, and medical ethics; a similar response can be made to the second claim that it is immoral to intervene. There are many other challenges that have emerged in the rapidly expanding field of biogenetic research that might benefit from careful scrutiny: among these are the ethics of organ transplants, the use of mind-enhancing drugs, life-extension technologies, and so on. The "new singularity," says Ray Kurzweil, portends great opportunities for humankind but also perplexing moral issues that need examination.

VI

In closing, permit me to touch on another practical problem that looms larger every day for the *Skeptical Inquirer* and other serious magazines like it. I am here referring to a double whammy: the growth of the Internet on the one hand and the steady decline of magazine readship on the other. No doubt the Internet provides an unparalleled resource for everyone, but at the same time, it has eroded the financial base of the *Skeptical Inquirer*, and we do not see any easy solution to the deficit gap that increasingly imperils our survival.

Recognizing these dangers, we have extended our public outreach, first by offering for the first time an academic program, "Science and the Public," at the graduate level. Second, we have just opened an Office of Public Policy at our new Center for Inquiry in Washington, DC, the purpose of which is to defend the integrity of science in the nation's capital and to try to convince our political leaders of the vital importance of supporting science education and the public understanding of science.

Finally, the most gratifying factor in all of this has been the unfailing support of the readers of the *Skeptical Inquirer*, who have helped to sustain us throughout our first three decades. Your support has been especially encouraging to Kendrick Frazier, who has worked so diligently in editing and publishing an outstanding magazine. It has been a rare privilege, an honor, for me to have worked with him so closely over these valiant years. We look forward to continuing the great legacy of the *Skeptical Inquirer* into its fourth decade and beyond.

NOTE

1. Shawn Carlson first came to CSICOP's attention with the publication of his paper, "A Double-Blind Test of Astrology," in the December 5, 1985, edition of *Nature*. CSICOP then summarized Carlson's paper as the lead News and Comment item in the Spring 1986 issue of *Skeptical Inquirer*. In November of 1988 Carlson was elected a CSICOP scientific and technical consultant.

Chapter 17

THE NEW SKEPTICISM

A Statement of Principles

Skeptical inquiry is essential for the development of human knowledge. It represents historic traditions in science, philosophy, and learning. We may distinguish skeptical inquiry, with emphasis on inquiry, from classical skepticism, which was apt to be totally negative, even nihilistic.

Skeptical inquiry is positive and constructive; its principles are essential for the development of knowledge about nature and human behavior. Moreover, its methods are relevant to the solution of ethical, political, and social problems.

Any democratic society that wishes to be effective needs to develop the capacity for critical thinking and healthy skeptical inquiry in its citizens. An educated public is the best guarantee of basic democratic liberties, rights, and responsibilities.

In the twentieth century the worldwide skeptical movement has sought to apply skeptical inquiry to paranormal claims. However, it is clear that the methods of critical inquiry used so effectively in science need to be extended to all areas of human interest.

[*Skeptical Briefs* 12, no. 1 (March 2002): 3]

What this means is that beliefs should be treated as hypotheses, tested by evidence, logical coherence, and their experimental consequences. All forms of knowledge should be open to revision in the light of inquiry. As a result, there is a progressive growth of knowledge.

With these considerations in mind, I wish to set down a set of principles, which serve as guidelines for skeptical inquiry:

- Skeptical inquirers maintain that skepticism is an essential part of scientific inquiry and that it should be extended to all areas of human endeavor, science, everyday life, law, religion and the paranormal, economics, politics, ethics, and society.
- They affirm that by using the methods of scientific inquiry, it is possible to discover reliable knowledge. They emphasize the positive powers of reflective intelligence. They believe that the methods of scientific inquiry can expand the frontiers of knowledge and that this can be used for the betterment of humankind.
- They believe that critical thinking is inherent in scientific and skeptical inquiry and that it can also be enlisted to solve problems, reduce hatred, neutralize animosities, and negotiate differences.
- Skeptical inquirers seek clarity rather than obfuscation, lucid meaning in the place of confusion, linguistic definitions to overcome vagueness or ambiguity.
- They do not reject any claim to knowledge a priori; however, they insist that the claim be framed in testable form and that the burden of proof rests primarily with the party asserting the claim.
- Skeptical inquirers ask for facts, not suppositions; experimental evidence, not conjecture; logical inference and deduction, not faith or intuition, to justify hypotheses and establish truth claims.
- They do not believe in absolute dogmas or creeds, set in stone, or proclaimed as Official Doctrine.
- They reject mythologies of salvation, whether old or new, whether based in ancient fears or current messianic illusions, unsubstantiated by rational or empirical grounds. They believe in inquiry rather than authority, reason in the place of custom.
- Skeptical inquirers maintain that reason and science can continue to be used to develop new technologies to alleviate suffering and reduce pain, as well as ameliorate and enhance human happiness.

- They submit that rationality can be used to develop and test ethical principles, moral values, and social policies, and thus contribute to goodness and happiness.
- Skeptical inquirers are not negative skeptics, naysayers, debunkers, or nihilists. They simply wish to oppose hypocrisy and cant, deception and illusion; instead they emphasize the tests of evidence and rationality. In short, they believe that intelligence and reason are the best ways of framing our means and fulfilling our ends.

BIBLIOGRAPHY

Clifford, W. K. *Ethics of Belief and Other Essays*. London: Watts, 1947.

Cooke, Bill, ed. *Dictionary of Atheism, Skepticism, and Humanism*. Amherst, NY: Prometheus Books, 2005.

Dewey, John. *The Quest for Certainty*. New York: Minton, Balch, 1929.

Kurtz, Paul. *The Courage to Become: The Virtues of Humanism*. Amherst, NY: Prometheus Books, 1997.

————. *Forbidden Fruit: The Ethics of Humanism*. Amherst, NY: Prometheus Books, 1987.

————. *Living without Religion: Eupraxsophy*. Amherst, NY: Prometheus Books, 1994.

————. *The New Skepticism: Inquiry and Reliable Knowledge*. Amherst, NY: Prometheus Books, 1992.

————. *Skepticism and Humanism: The New Paradigm*. New Brunswick, NJ: Transaction Books, 2001.

————. *The Transcendental Temptation: A Critique of Religion and the Paranormal*. Amherst, NY: Prometheus Books, 1986.

————, ed. *Skeptical Odysseys*. Amherst, NY: Prometheus Books, 2001.

————, ed. *A Skeptic's Handbook of Parapsychology*. Amherst, NY: Prometheus Books, 1985.

Kurtz, Paul, and Tim Madigan, eds. *Challenges to the Enlightenment: In Defense of Reason and Science*. Amherst, NY: Prometheus Books, 1994.

Popkin, Richard H. *The High Road to Pyrrhonism*. Edited by Richard A. Watson and James E. Force. San Diego: Austin Hill, 1980.

———. *The History of Skepticism from Erasmus to Spinoza*. Berkeley and Los Angeles: University of California Press, 1979.

———. *The History of Skepticism from Savanorala to Bayle*. Oxford: Oxford University Press, 2003.

Russell, Bertrand. *Skeptical Essays*. London: Allen and Unwin, 1928.

Sagan, Carl. *The Demon-Haunted World: Science as a Candle in the Dark*. New York: Random House, 1995.

Santayana, George. *Skepticism and Animal Faith*. New York: Scribner's, 1923.

Stenger, Victor. *God—the Failed Hypothesis: How Science Shows That God Does Not Exist*. Amherst, NY: Prometheus Books, 2007.